BY THE EDITORS OF CONSUMER GUIDE®

WHOLE
KITCHEN
CATALOG

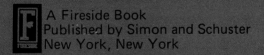
A Fireside Book
Published by Simon and Schuster
New York, New York

CONTENTS

A Fireside Book
Published by Simon and Schuster
A Division of Gulf & Western Corporation
New York, New York 10020

Library of Congress Cataloging in Publication Data
Main entry under title:

Whole kitchen catalog,

(A Fireside book)
Includes index.
1. Kitchens - Remodeling - Catalogs. I. Consumer guide.
TX653.W56   1978   643'.3   78-15468
ISBN 0-671-24145-1 pbk.

Doing Your Own Kitchen 81

Do some of the work yourself to lessen the expense, while gaining pride from a kitchen where you had an input. You'll save money by using a few of these simple tips.

Buyers Guide: Materials 133

A practical guide to your alternatives — from floors to ceilings, countertops to cabinets. What's available, what's best, and what you can expect to pay.

Buyers Guide: Major Appliances 156

Your walls are finished, those new cabinets and countertop installed, and the floor is laid. Now, what about appliances? A selection of the major brands, indicating their features and proper selection criteria.

Directory of Manufacturers 184

Index 189

CREDITS

Introduction — Color Photos

American Olean Tile Co. — pages 5, 8, 9
Florence Perchuk, SVP Kitchens — page 7
Howard Sersen — page 10
John Mathis, Keyline Co., Inc. — page 11
Quaker Maid Kitchens — page 12

Dream Kitchens

Artistic Angles
Designer: Ellen Cheever, C.K.D., Kitchens by Ellen,
Sacramento, CA
Photographer: Don Horton
Owner: Mr. & Mrs. David J. Hammond

Sunny California Contemporary
Designer: Ellen Cheever, C.K.D., Kitchens by Ellen,
Sacramento, CA
Photographer: Don Horton
Owner: Mr. & Mrs. Frank Bouza

Gourmet Collectibles
Designer: Ellen Cheever, C.K.D., Kitchens by Ellen,
Sacramento, CA
Photographer: Don Horton
Owner: Mr. & Mrs. Richard Dirga

Enlivened for Entertaining
Designer: William R. Gedney, C.K.D., Dallas, TX
Photographer: John Alexandrowicz
Owner: Mr. & Mrs. Dix Gedney

Fit for a Bachelor
Designer: Ellen Cheever, C.K.D., Kitchens by Ellen,
Sacramento, CA
Photographer: Steve Marley
Owner: Clint Myers

A Designer's Own Dream
Designer: Howard Sersen, C.K.D., Park Ridge, IL
Photographer: Mark Sersen
Owner: Mr. & Mrs. Howard Sersen

Comfortable Colonial
Designer: Quaker Maid Design Staff, a division of
Tappan Co., Leesport, PA
Owner: Mr. & Mrs. William W. Follett

U-Shape with a Twist
Designer: Howard Sersen, C.K.D., Park Ridge, IL
Photographer: Mark Sersen
Owner: Mr. & Mrs. Robert Wareham

Contemporary Convenience
Designer: Howard Sersen, C.K.D., Park Ridge, IL
Photographer: Mark Sersen
Owner: Mr. & Mrs. John Kirts

Cultivated Farmhouse
Designer: Quaker Maid Design Staff, a division of
Tappan Co., Leesport, PA
Owner: Dr. & Mrs. Frederic B. Thomson

Beauty and the Budget
Designer: KRB Inc., Michael T. Rose, President,
Seabrook, MD

Revolutionary Gourmet
Designer: Roger Wilder, Lee Kimball Kitchens,
Boston, MA
Photographer: David Brown
Owner: Mr. & Mrs. David Crandall

Renovated Rowhouse
Designer: Howard Sersen, C.K.D., Park Ridge, IL
Photographer: Mark Sersen
Owner: Mr. & Mrs. Joseph McNitt

Redesigned Builders Model
Designer: M. A. Petersons Inc., West Hartford, CT
Photographer: Red Beaudin, Inc.
Owner: Mr. & Mrs. Peter S. Youmans

A Habitable High-Rise
Designer: Howard Sersen, C.K.D., Park Ridge, IL
Photographer: Robert Bauer
Owner: Mr. & Mrs. William Hamer

Buyers Guide: Materials — Photo Credits

American Olean Tile Co.
Armstrong Cork Co.
Connor Forest Industries
GAF Corporation
Imperial Wallcoverings
H & R Johnson, Inc.
Kentile Floors
Mannington Mills, Inc.
Marlite Division Masonite Corporation
Masonite Corporation
Maytag Co.
Moen, a division of Stanadyne
The Overton Co.
Supergraphic, Inc.

Cover Design: Frank E. Peiler

Floorplans and Illustrations: Clarence Moberg

Consultants: Joe Kohn and Associates, members of the
American Institute of Kitchen Dealers

Rub a magic coffeepot. Poof! A genie in a chef's hat emerges in a cloud of mocha-java steam. "I grant you the kitchen of your dreams!" he intones. What would your dream kitchen look like? Ultra modern with yards of pristine countertops, enough storage space for your entire present home, and self-cleaning everything? Early American with a fireplace *and* a microwave? A combination greenhouse, family room, cooking center with a spectacular view? Or, how about a professional chef's kitchen with the chef included?

The *Whole Kitchen Catalog* can't produce a professional chef to do your bidding, but it can show you how to make your dream kitchen come true. The photos of real-life kitchens in the next section may inspire you to consider remodeling the entire kitchen. On the other hand, you may spot just one storage idea or simple do-it-yourself project that will bring your kitchen in line with your lifestyle.

Transforming a kitchen from old to new is not a simple task. A practical genie would reveal that the key to success lies in step-by-step planning, rather than trial and error. Even if you only have the time and budget for changing one feature, that change can be part of a larger plan.

Perhaps you just want to replace appliances in an older home. That would update your kitchen, but you would not be remodeling it. If you really want a kitchen that suits your lifestyle, a kitchen that fits your patterns of socializing, of entertaining, of meeting the needs and tastes of your family, then replacing appliances is not enough.

So the first step is not to rush out and buy new appliances to replace the old ones. The first step is to sit down with other members of the household and ask questions. The answers you write down will outline your needs. Once you know your needs, you can evaluate how well your present kitchen meets them. If a sizable discrepancy exists between your needs and your present kitchen's ability to meet those needs, you know that the time has come to consider remodeling your kitchen.

Assessing Your Present Kitchen

The numbers after each question indicate how satisfactory you find the various elements of your kitchen. Circle the number indicating your degree of satisfaction, from number 1 for very poor to number 6 for very good. Then tally up the total of all circled numbers and check the scale below.

Poor 1 2 3 4 5 6 Good

Storage Space. Is there enough and is it easily accessible? Do you need a stepladder or stool to reach shelves? Do you often have to walk across the room for items not stored in the right place?

1 2 3 4 5 6

Work Space. Is there enough counter space for preparing food and for cleanup?

1 2 3 4 5 6

Up-To-Date Appliances. How many more years can you count on your major appliances? If new ones are in the budget and schedule, be sure to find the most energy-efficient appliances, otherwise operation cost may exceed the original price. Are you considering adding appliances, like a microwave oven or trash compactor?

1 2 3 4 5 6

Ventilation. Does your range have a hood vented to the outside? If you have a separate wall oven, is it vented to the outside? Is venting powerful enough to prevent grease deposits on walls and cabinets?

1 2 3 4 5 6

Lighting. Do you have both general illumination and task lighting on counters? Can you see easily into drawers? Can you work without being in your own shadow?

1 2 3 4 5 6

Efficiency. Is the work triangle efficient? By work triangle, we mean the distance between the sink, refrigerator and range—the three main features of the kitchen. Many kitchen designers recommend that the total distance from the front center of your sink to your refrigerator then to your cooktop be at least 12 feet but not more than 22 feet.

1 2 3 4 5 6

Nuisances. Does the oven door or the refrigerator door open across the entry door so that traffic is blocked? Does the refrigerator door open away from the action instead of toward it?

1 2 3 4 5 6

Subjective Factors. Are you satisfied with the color in your kitchen? Is the kitchen big enough? Too big? Is the general look dingy or depressing? Is it closed off from the rest of the house? Do you like the cabinet style? Do you have the modern features you would like?

1 2 3 4 5 6

Your Kitchen Score—Add and Total Here_____

8-16: You are working under a severe handicap. Your kitchen is grossly inadequate.

17-24: Your kitchen has many serious shortcomings that could be improved.

25-32: Although you're not in bad shape, you still would benefit from a remodeling of your kitchen.

33-40: Your problems are rather specific. The *Whole Kitchen Catalog* can help you isolate and correct them.

41-48: You are the exception. Give this book to a friend who needs it.

Evaluating Your Kitchen Needs

Nobody, neither you nor a skilled kitchen designer, can design your kitchen properly without knowing the answers to many questions. Here are some of the questions specialists would ask you. The answers should form the basis for planning and designing your new kitchen.

How big is your household? Size of the family relates directly to the amount of storage space you need in cabinets for dishes and foods. Identifying family members, with ages, can help in several ways. If there are toddlers in the family, you may want an open kitchen so you can keep an eye on them in adjacent rooms. Teenage children leaving soon for college or elsewhere make some storage needs only temporary.

Do you like to cook? If a person really likes to cook, he or she may need a more versatile range, more counter space for food preparation, a larger refrigerator, and more storage for utensils and cookware. If there is more than one chef in the family, a peninsula, island or extra food preparation center might be in order.

Do you like to entertain? If so, you might be wise to consider a wet bar, a wine rack, storage for more glassware and other dishes, a punch bowl, etc. Storage problems can be considerable.

What are your grocery shopping habits? Some families do heavy shopping weekly or biweekly. They might need a separate freezer and/or a big pantry cabinet.

Are you super fastidious? Do you like everything off the counters and behind doors? Or are you the more casual, open-shelf type who enjoys an array of collectibles in the kitchen. One persons clutter is another's antique collection. Also, some people do not mind spending time taking care of items like ceramic cooktops that need daily attention. The amount of care required by some kitchen material is considerable, and you should know before you buy.

What is the motif of your other home furnishings? A kitchen should be in keeping with the other rooms in the home. Other furnishings can supply the key to color preferences, use of fabrics, wall coverings, etc. Ask the rest of the family if they really like what they have.

Do husband and wife both work? A working couple often wants to minimize the time spent in the kitchen. Efficient design is most important. Appliances like microwave ovens, a dishwasher, a disposer, and a compactor may be time-savers, too.

How careful are household members? Safety can be built into a kitchen. Household cleaners usually go in the under-sink cabinet, but storage might have to be placed higher or in a locked pantry if small children are around. Range controls and ceramic cooktops can be hazardous to children and should be made inaccessible to small hands.

What are your family seating habits and preferences? This determines how much dining space is needed in the kitchen. Do you want eating space just for the children or for the family, part of a peninsula or island, or a formal area for separate table and chairs?

Budget, available space, work habits, and personal taste were just a few of the factors considered in designing this gleaming contemporary kitchen.

Budget

After you have assessed your present kitchen and evaluated your needs, there is one more important consideration—budget. Your needs may be vast and your budget only able to cover cosmetic changes like wallpaper and paint. Full-scale remodeling is a major investment, as well as a time-consuming project.

If you are going to stay in the house for an indefinite time and have no intention of selling or moving, it may make more sense to go all the way with a super remodeling job than if you plan to move soon.

If you are planning the kitchen improvement to increase the resale value of the house, then you want to make the kitchen look as great as possible without spending too much money on it. Just about any improvement in the kitchen can be considered an investment that will pay off in increasing resale value, but if your house is valued at $40,000 in a neighborhood of $40,000 homes, a $10,000 kitchen will not increase its value to $50,000. In such a case,

This spacious country kitchen features interesting floor and ceiling treatments in addition to decorative cabinetry and the latest appliances.

Ceramic tile is a beautiful and excellent material for the backsplash area, that part of the wall between the counter and the wall cabinets.

Wood paneling or wood planks are popular materials for one or more walls in the kitchen, to add variety in color and texture.

Vertical grade plastic laminates, thinner grades of the material found on most of the nation's countertops are good as wall material. They are extremely easy to clean, can be bought at most home centers in a tremendous variety of colors and patterns, and are good for backsplash or other wall areas. However, they should not be applied on the wall behind the cooktop because the heat will tend to discolor them. Corian, another countertop material is also available as a wall covering. It simulates marble.

Vinyl-surfaced wall fabrics are one of the most popular materials for kitchen walls. The range of colors and patterns is practically limitless, and they are easy to apply and maintain.

Fabrics can be used on walls away from cooking areas with very decorative effects. Sometimes they are used for accent walls, but often a decorator will get pre-glued fabric to match draperies and surface an entire wall and/or ceiling with them.

Brick and stone in their natural forms can pose problems in cleanability and because of their weight. There are, however, plastic-based simulations of these materials that are light, easy to apply, totally realistic in appearance, and more easily cleaned. These could be overpowering if too much were used, but they can be very good for an accent wall.

Kitchen carpeting can be used on walls, coved from the floor all the way to the ceiling or, more often, up to wainscot height, capped by a strip of molding. Kitchen carpeting has a sponge rubber backing, separated from the surface by a waterproof membrane that makes it easy to wash. It is light in weight and easy to apply.

Ceiling Treatments

Here again, the standard treatment is paint, always in a light color because darker colors tend to "bring the ceiling down" in a room that often is small.

One of the best alternatives to paint is acoustical tile. This can be adhered directly to the old ceiling, but it is especially useful when the ceiling is high (more than 96 inches) and it is used in a suspended ceiling system. Ideally, this suspended ceiling system will incorporate fluorescent lighting panels designed for the system. It helps muffle the many noises of the kitchen (disposer, dishwasher, blender, etc.) and is easy to put up, although it takes care.

Wall coverings often are used on the ceiling. They should be fabric-backed and vinyl-surfaced.

it is better to spend $2000 or $3000 on the kitchen to build your house value up to $45,000. And it can do that.

With those considerations in mind, let's make a quick survey of some of the choices you have.

Cosmetic Alterations

Alterations that are done purely for aesthetic reasons are not different, basically, from changing your hair color or selecting and applying nail polish and lipstick. They are not basic changes. They are changes in appearance.

Wall Treatments

Chances are the walls you have are painted. They can be repainted in new, different colors. You can add painted graphics, available in most areas at art, stationery or variety stores. But for kitchen use, be sure you select a high quality paint that is easy to clean.

Ceiling beams are a fairly popular accessory treatment for the kitchen. Beams can be bought ready-made, either of solid wood or hollow, or they are relatively easy to make with 1/4-inch plywood. Easiest, probably, is to buy prefinished plastic beams made of polyurethane. Not only are they fairly realistic, but they are so light that they can be applied easily with adhesive.

Floor Treatments

Your choices for floors include the various resilient materials in combinations of vinyl and asbestos or vinyl alone, in sheets or easy-to-lay squares, cushioned or uncushioned; wood, in finished planks or parquet; carpeting; or ceramic tile.

The standard of past years, linoleum, is no longer made in this country. It has been replaced by the more modern vinyl and vinyl/asbestos materials.

Sheet goods generally cost more and present more of an installation problem. The adhesive-backed place-and-press tiles are easiest to install.

Countertops

Countertops can be very decorative, so a change in the countertops must be considered as one of the possible cosmetic alternatives.

The decorative laminates on countertops provided by builders usually have somewhat muted patterns, appearing slightly greenish or yellowish from a distance of a few feet. Supposedly these colors go with any appliance or cabinet. But you, in your own kitchen, know specifically what appliances and cabinets you have, so you can be bolder in selecting from the hundreds of colors, patterns and woodgrains available from the laminate manufacturers. Countertop inserts, such as tile squares or a wooden butcher block , can improve appearance immensely.

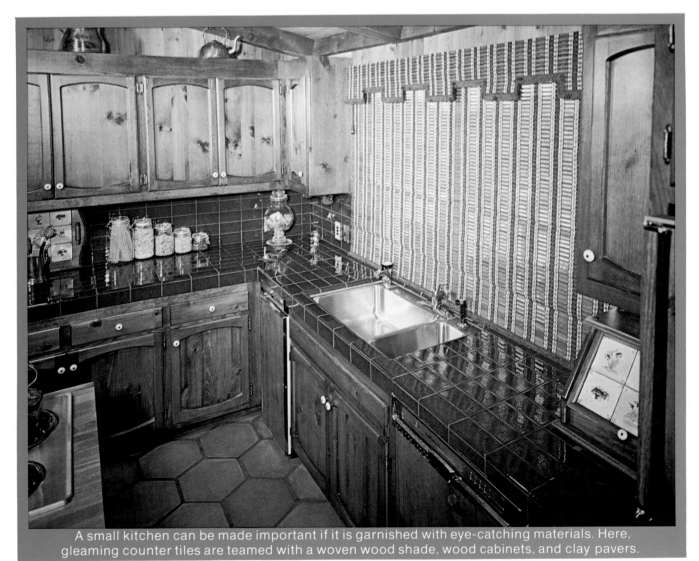

A small kitchen can be made important if it is garnished with eye-catching materials. Here, gleaming counter tiles are teamed with a woven wood shade, wood cabinets, and clay pavers.

Cabinet Refacing

Whether your kitchen cabinets are wood, plastic laminated or steel, you can change their looks without actually replacing them.

If they are painted and the old paint is smooth, you can simply repaint them, after minor sanding, using a gloss enamel. Or you can remove the old finish and apply new stain and lacquer, antiquing if you wish.

If the cabinets are plastic laminate in a dark woodgrain, as was popular through the 1960s, and if the laminate is in good condition, you can buy new laminate and apply it over the old, using the lighter woodgrains that are more fashionable today, or a butcher block pattern or a solid color. Or you can send the doors and drawer fronts out to a local plastic fabricator and have the job done professionally. Then you could paint the exposed face frame and end panels in a matching or somewhat darker color for a new look.

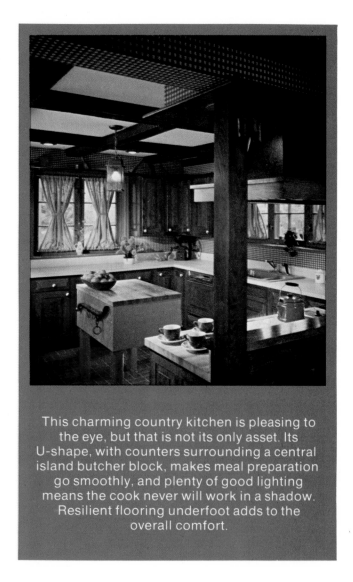

This charming country kitchen is pleasing to the eye, but that is not its only asset. Its U-shape, with counters surrounding a central island butcher block, makes meal preparation go smoothly, and plenty of good lighting means the cook never will work in a shadow. Resilient flooring underfoot adds to the overall comfort.

The older, steel cabinets that were so prevalent in the 1950s can be painted or covered with sheets of plastic laminate. You can buy sheets of laminate and cut them to size.

Another way, especially if the old doors are battered, is to buy new doors and drawer fronts to replace the old. Nearly all cabinets, except those built on-site by carpenters, are built in 3-inch modular widths and in standard heights. So new companies have sprung up in the last several years that specialize in making replacement doors and drawer fronts. Many of these are wood, and many are made of polyurethane and finished to look like wood.

The Functional Alternatives

While cosmetic changes make your kitchen look better, functional changes make it work better. Here we are talking about things you can do short of remodeling, keeping the basic layout. You might need to replace the appliances. You almost surely need new lighting—most kitchens do. Sometimes a simple rearrangement of elements is effective. And sometimes it is possible to add a simple island or peninsula for more storage or work space, or to shorten the work triangle.

Sink Replacement

The sink might be part of your replacement project. Sinks get a lot of use and deteriorate with age. Or you might want to replace a single-bowl model with a double-bowl or triple-bowl. Equally important, you might want to replace old, worn faucets with a handsome new single-lever model, and you might want soap and lotion dispensers or an instant hot water attachment in the ledge. Another worthwhile option is installation of water purification equipment in the sink cabinet. Many of the new faucets have flow restrictors that automatically can cut water use by as much as 50 percent.

Pressed-steel, porcelain-enameled sinks are the lowest-priced. High-quality stainless sinks are the most expensive. Cast iron sinks now come in a wide range of bright colors as well as white. The only other alternative is a Corian sink, a man-made marble, which is formed as an integral part of a Corian countertop. This is quite expensive.

Lighting

When you find yourself working in your own shadow, when you find it difficult to read recipes or to see into kitchen drawers, you have a lighting problem. A poorly lighted kitchen is worse than an inconvenient kitchen. It is an unsafe kitchen.

You need three kinds of lighting in your kitchen.

1. General lighting, for overall illumination,

creates a pleasant environment and lets you see into cabinets and opened drawers.

2. Task lighting beams more intense light directly on jobs at the range and sink, and the countertop work surfaces.
3. Decorative lighting is for special purposes, such as separating a dining nook or eating peninsula from the rest of the kitchen, or to accent a decorative wall.

The two light sources you can choose are incandescent bulbs or fluorescent tubes. Incandescence gives a warmer light and is better if your kitchen colors are in the red-yellow-brown ranges. Fluorescent lighting gives a cold light that favors blues and greens; it tends to flatten out the rich appearance of wood cabinets.

Natural daylight, of course, is a third source, and it can come from windows or from a skylight. But it doesn't lessen the need for other lights, for the obvious reason that you can't turn it on at night.

Remodeling

The average full-scale remodeling job in a kitchen today, with replacement of cabinets and appliances and a changed layout, is more than $6000. On a do-it-yourself basis, you might cut up to 30 percent off that.

Why remodel, when it is so expensive? One reason is that your kitchen is wasteful and/or unsuitable for your needs. Another reason is that you want to, either because you are tired of the old kitchen, or you want to increase the value of the house for resale.

When should you remodel? When there is a change in your lifestyle, because of marriage, divorce, additions to the family, loss of family members, new social habits, increase in income, and because if you delay it will only become more expensive.

You can cut the price, of course, by choosing to remodel only partially. A combination of the cosmetic and functional changes we discussed can amount to a partial remodeling, but that kind of updating and replacing may fall short of creating a kitchen that's yours and yours alone.

Partial remodeling can be the first step in a long-range remodeling plan. A long-range plan would call for a total redesign job on your present kitchen, with a floor plan drawing and elevation drawings showing its entirety. You could figure out a timetable for step-by-step completion over a period of a year or two. This stretches out the payments. First you change the elements most needed. Then each new element gradually would complete the new design.

Partial remodeling might include rearranging appliances, adding new countertops, replacing appliances or adding a peninsula or island. With a peninsula or island you may gain a new location for a

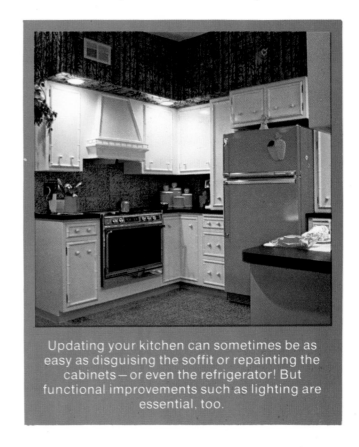

Updating your kitchen can sometimes be as easy as disguising the soffit or repainting the cabinets — or even the refrigerator! But functional improvements such as lighting are essential, too.

sink or range. Or you may gain needed work space or eating area.

How Do You Estimate The Costs?

As a very general rule of thumb, in a total remodeling of a kitchen, the cabinets, countertops and flooring will account for about 50 percent of the cost, the appliances about 20 percent, and the labor about 30 percent.

A fully-remodeled kitchen usually takes 12 to 14 cabinets. The stock cabinets you see in local home centers probably average about $75 per 18-inch base cabinet. But if you want custom cabinets (which offer more specialized sizes and shapes), they average about $150 per 18-inch base cabinet.

Many remodeling contractors estimate kitchen remodeling on a per-foot basis. It is all right to try for a "ballpark" figure on that basis, but don't ever buy that way and use the formula only as a guess. The formula is $275 per lineal foot, on the average across the U.S.A.

That figure combines base and wall cabinets, includes taking out the old cabinets, new wood or plastic-laminated cabinets, countertops, minimum electrical and plumbing hookups and cleanup. It does not include appliances. As an example, if you have 14 feet of base cabinets and 12 feet of wall cabinets, add the two for a total of 26, divide by two and you get 13, and multiply 13 by $275 for a total of

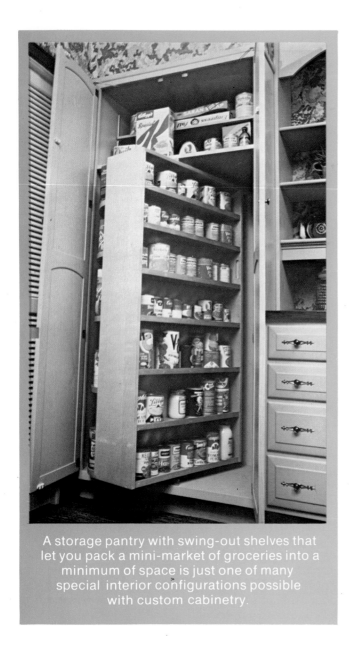

A storage pantry with swing-out shelves that let you pack a mini-market of groceries into a minimum of space is just one of many special interior configurations possible with custom cabinetry.

Professional Help

If you want a professional to do the job, the specialists in kitchen and bathroom remodeling are members of the American Institute of Kitchen Dealers, an association of over 1200 professionals across the country who must quality for membership. The cream of the crop of kitchen specialists will be Certified Kitchen Designers, with the initials "CKD" after their names, corresponding roughly to the "ASID" of the qualified interior decorator.

Other groups include the National Home Improvement Contractors and the National Remodelers Association. While many of the members of these organizations are skilled in kitchen remodeling, their emphasis — for the most part — is on roofing, siding insulation, dormers and the like; many do kitchen remodeling only as a sideline.

Get references from the firm before you sign anything. Firms that are proud of their work will be glad to refer you to their customers. Be sure they have a showroom and are not selling from a catalog. If the showroom does not have kitchen displays, you are taking a chance. And, preferably, the displays should show you both stock and custom cabinets, and built-in appliances as well as free-standing ones.

What you are looking for in a contractor is a solid business person who has an investment in the community, who pays taxes in the community and has a stake in it. When he or she has put thousands of dollars into a showroom it adds to their credibility. As a last step, check the firm with the Better Business Bureau.

Dream Kitchens

Daydreaming about your ideal kitchen is not a waste of time, it's an important part of planning. At the same time as you begin to evaluate exactly what you want changed in your kitchen, you should be collecting kitchen ideas and daydreaming about how they fit into your plans. As you look at the photos of kitchens in the next section, you may be inspired to solve a design problem that has been bothering you. Or, you may come across a feature you never knew existed. All of the kitchens shown are actual ones, used with great satisfaction by people with a wide range of lifestyles — a bachelor, a family with youngsters, a working couple, a family that collects antiques. Over and over again, you will read how their old kitchens did not suit the way they wanted to live and how they achieved dream kitchens that matched their lifestyles. Each family had special problems and requirements that called for imaginative solutions. Remodeling and redesigning a kitchen is a highly personalized adventure; you'll probably pick and choose among the features in these kitchens to make your own dream kitchen a reality.

$3575. For a more common-sized kitchen, say 10 by 8 feet, you would come up with a total of $2475.

But don't trust those blanket figures, and be very wary of buying from any contractor who prices the job that way. The only value of any such formula is to give you a very rough estimate, in your own mind, for what you want to do if you are doing it in a very ordinary way. Any small variation will cost extra. Any part of the job you decide to do yourself will subtract from the formula.

Another way to estimate is to go out and price the cabinets you like, price the appliances you like, and then figure it will cost you about $10 per lineal foot for countertops. Add 50 percent for labor for a total estimated price. Double the countertop estimate if it will include sink cutouts, angles, circular shapes or anything else unusual.

The angled cooktop and artistic shelving are visible from the family room.

Artistic Angles

Sometimes it seems that there is just no way to alter an existing kitchen plan. If the room is tucked inside the home, possibilities for change can be hampered by the surrounding spaces or mechanical or structural roadblocks. Even when the kitchen lies at one end of a house, exterior considerations may limit a remodeling.

All those restrictions seemed to conspire to prevent the owners of this Spanish-style West Coast home from having the gourmet kitchen their cooking skills demanded. Arranged at one end of the half-century-old house were a little family room, a little kitchen, a little breakfast nook, and a little utility room. The owners decided their ten years of mulling over the "little" space problem had gotten them nowhere, so they called in a professional

kitchen designer. "The house was beautiful," commented the designer. "But like so many houses of that style, the kitchen/utility/eating spaces were unworkable by contemporary standards."

While in another house it might have been an easy matter just to move dividing walls, in this one the rooms were arranged around a large, hidden chimney. The exact size and shape of the chimney were concealed and therefore unknown. In addition to opening the rooms that encircled this chimney, the owners wanted more of a view of the backyard from the eating area, plenty of counter space, a planning desk, and a kitchen that was functional but open and decorative as well. The problem frankly stumped them.

As a final specification, the owners were anxious

The family room side of the kitchen counter extension (left) includes a snack bar and bookshelf of the same walnut-stained white oak. From here, the view includes the greenhouse window over the sink, open corner shelves, and the cooktop, positioned at an angle to surround an immovable chimney. The newly opened dining area lies past the wall ovens and angled range (right); new, large windows give a feeling of dining outdoors.

to play a large part in the actual construction of the new rooms. The woman, an artist, wanted no traditional upper cabinets in the kitchen, preferring a creative combination of glass-doored shelving and open corner units that could display her collections and artwork. The man, a school district administrator with free time in the summer, wanted to participate actively in the demolition, plumbing, Sheetrock installation, and painting. While seeking the intangible rewards of pride of accomplishment, the couple also hoped to save substantially on the cost of the work by making at least part of the project do-it-yourself.

The owners, parents of two teenage boys, made it clear that opening the rooms was their first priority. The layout of the utility, kitchen, and breakfast areas at that point was nothing so much as a lesson in how to waste space. The utility room, which held the washer and dryer, had three doors opening into it, eating up wall space that could have gone for storage. The kitchen, also with three doors leading through it, was arranged corridor-fashion, did not

contain a dishwasher, and featured a desk next to the range, resulting in grease splatters on paperwork. In the breakfast room, small windows did not do justice to the possible panoramic view. In short, the three areas were merely utilitarian in design and function.

While many ideas were committed to paper, the undertaking could be planned definitely only after demolition. Only when the chimney was exposed could the exact space available be determined. Once the chimney was visible, it became apparent that nothing would be solved by lining cabinets at right angles to it and to each other; traffic would flow better and counter space could be increased if the units at the center of the room, around the chimney, were askew.

"Waiting until a house is torn apart of course is the least desirable way to work," remarked the designer. "But we could not figure anything mathematically ahead of time. In the end, we took a full-sized template of the chimney walls and cut both the surrounding cabinets and counter from that. All the angles were determined by clearances to counters along other walls, not by any conventional 'rules' of kitchen design."

For the makeover, the sink was replaced without changing its location under a window, and the window was rebuilt into a greenhouse that by itself would have up-dated the room. A dishwasher was installed to the right of the sink. While the amount of counter space stayed the same on either side of the sink, a leg was added at the left to form an L that now runs past what had been a doorway to an adjoining family room. Access to that room now lies at the end of this new counter, and on the family room side, there now is room for a bookcase and breakfast bar.

By moving the refrigerator to an area near the end of the L, space was freed to house two ovens, one of them a microwave. With the ovens, sink, and refrigerator in place, the designer and the owners turned their attention to the angled cooktop counter.

"Because of the way the chimney sat," the designer recalled, "we couldn't just come out 24 inches and run a counter. We would have run into a clearance problem in the table area, and squaring it off also would have been awkward and limiting as far as countertop space. Angling the cabinets here brought the cooktop closer to the oven and sink, made better use of the floorspace in the center of the room, and resulted in additional counter space. A desk and bookcase for cookbooks were incorporated around the corner at the end of this

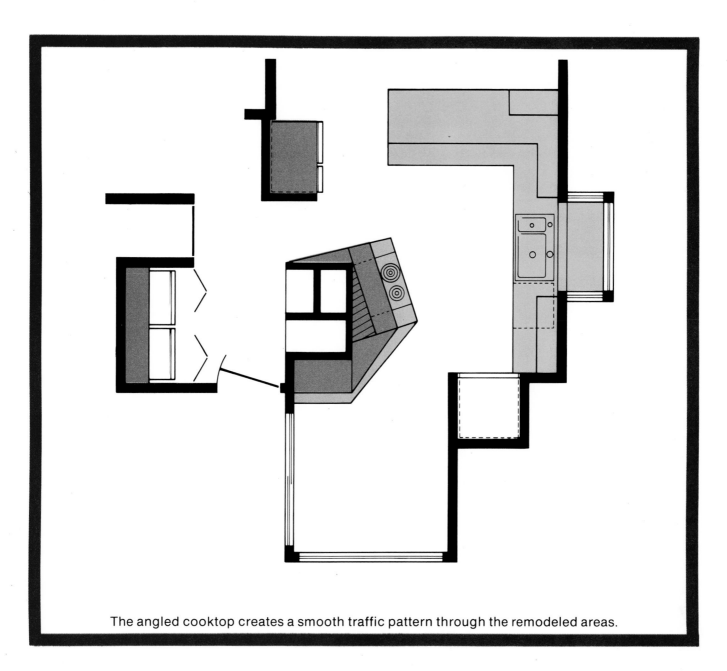

The angled cooktop creates a smooth traffic pattern through the remodeled areas.

counter in the eating area, and the new angle guides people into the breakfast room more naturally now. The view in the room was vastly improved with new windows."

With plans finalized, the owners completed demolition and then worked on the plumbing as professional electricians rewired the rooms. With new recessed lighting and other electrical connections in place, the owners themselves installed the Sheetrock walls, which were taped, sanded, and finally painted in preparation for cabinet installation. The designer reports that by doing the back-breaking part of the project, the owners saved nearly one-third of what the job would have cost; in addition, by leaving the intricate, visible finish work to professionals, they were still able to have the finest of products installed correctly.

After saving money with do-it-yourself labor, the owners also could afford to have exactly the materials they wanted in their new gourmet kitchen. Definitely not a wallpaper or pattern family, they utilized the natural beauty of materials as design elements. Consequently, cabinets are white oak finished in a medium walnut shade; flooring is a hexagonal Mexican dirt-style tile; the countertops are butcher block at the cooktop and a neutral multicolor tile edged in wood elsewhere; and appliances have stainless, black glass, or wood panels so no color is featured.

In keeping with the natural theme, foodstuffs are on display; flour, noodles, cereals, popcorn and other dry, boxed foods are transferred to glass jars in which they are easily and handily stored—and attractive as well. Storage elsewhere in the kitchen takes advantage of every cranny. A bank of drawers holds linens and cutlery, while pots and pans nestle on roll-out shelves under the cooktop. The angled end of the cooktop's wall cabinet is outfitted for spices. There are vertical dividers above and around the refrigerator, and even the backs of cabinet doors are constructed to hold small items.

Meanwhile, storage in the utility room has been greatly increased, too. Instead of the former wall against the back of the chimney, there now are a pantry and a broom closet built around it. The washer and dryer remain in their previous locations, but cabinets were added above for soaps and other laundry aids.

Now that the kitchen/utility/eating areas finally have been modernized, the family truly can enjoy their entire home. In spaces they once merely endured, the couple now enthusiastically retreat with satisfaction in the food, the surroundings, and the magnificent, newly exposed view.

As the cooktop counter continues around the hidden chimney (left), it turns into a planning desk with bookshelves above. In the kitchen itself (right), the wall ovens occupy a niche that once housed the refrigerator; the sink remained where it was, but the window above it was expanded with a greenhouse. The focal point of the room—the range, hood, and cooktop cabinetry—forces a natural work flow and makes a major contribution to the room's decorative interest.

A cooking island with an attached dining counter is the hub of this breezy family room/kitchen.

Sunny California Contemporary

A kitchen can be quite adequate by many standards and still not "feel" right. That is a fact learned firsthand by the owners of this now-remodeled kitchen. Part of a California house that is not yet 15 years old, the kitchen offered relatively new appliances, a fairly up-to-date layout, newer counters, and convenient storage, yet it seemed all wrong for the lifestyle of the family that used it. A kitchen designer was called in to figure out why.

"The family didn't really need a larger kitchen, though that's what they finally opted for," recalled the designer. "They did need one that was arranged differently to coordinate better with an adjoining family room. The people who live here—a contemporary couple who enjoy their house, and their college-age son and teenage daughter—have simple meals at home but like to have friends join them.

"Since they do a great deal of entertaining, they needed a kitchen and family room that would work together to allow people to move about freely. The family room opens onto a patio that surrounds a backyard pool, so this whole side of the house needed to be more open."

The original kitchen had its major work space arranged in an L, with sink and dishwasher under a window along one leg, and the stove and refrigerator along the other. Across the room, tall storage cabinets afforded ample space for keeping brooms and cleaning supplies, but the location of these cabinets meant there was no room for a dining table in the kitchen.

Putting the eating area just at the end of the kitchen in the family room, however, ruined the possibilities for a decoratively pleasing furniture arrangement there. It seemed that no matter how

17

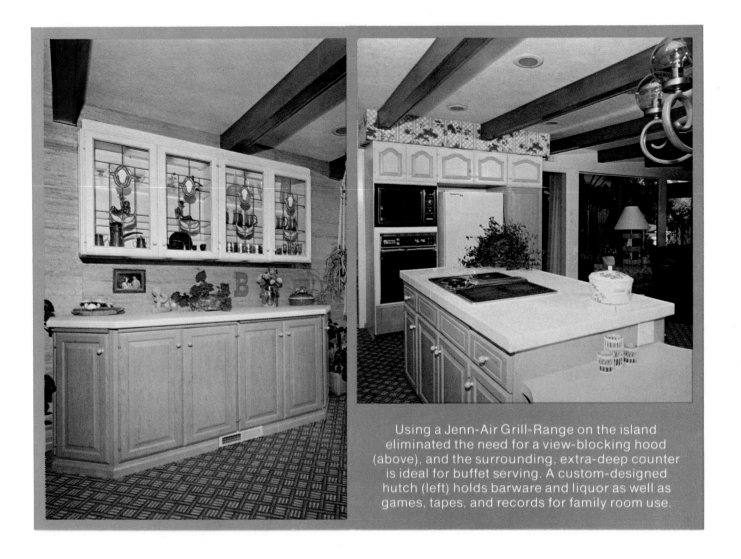

Using a Jenn-Air Grill-Range on the island eliminated the need for a view-blocking hood (above), and the surrounding, extra-deep counter is ideal for buffet serving. A custom-designed hutch (left) holds barware and liquor as well as games, tapes, and records for family room use.

furniture was placed, the entire family room/ kitchen area was full of bottlenecks whenever more than the four family members used the rooms. In spite of plenty of square footage, the entire layout clearly had to be enlarged further if this particular family were to be happy and comfortable as party hosts, a role in which they took delight.

Studying the architecture of the house, the designer noted that there was no reason that the kitchen could not contain a table. With two of the kitchen walls being exterior and a third having been omitted so the kitchen and family room opened into each other, the kitchen could be redesigned quite easily. If it had been a room central to the house, the family might have had to just live with it.

To create a more open overall space, the 10-foot-long stove/refrigerator wall, which was exterior, was pushed back 10 feet; this added 100 square feet to the kitchen and made an overall kitchen/family room area that measured 17 by 31 feet. Of course, extensive roof work and other outside construction—matching wood siding and re-

landscaping, for example—were then necessary. But when the new space was roughed in, the result was a lovely, large room with endless possibilities.

Within this spacious shell, the kitchen window and the sink and dishwasher beneath it remained where they were. A matching window was designed into the extension of this wall, and a new counter running the length of this extended wall now ends in a planning desk, an amenity the previous kitchen did not have.

After the stove/refrigerator counter was eliminated, the range was placed at an island and the refrigerator and ovens along the wall where brooms once were stored. The dining table that had caused so much trouble in the old layout was positioned at one end of the island.

"The owners did not want any kind of bar or counter effect with the island since that reminded them of their apartments during college days," the designer related. "The table therefore had to look like a table, and a hanging fixture over it helps identify it as such; still, by attaching it to the island, the table and cooktop form a single unit visually."

For the cooktop, a Jenn-Air Grill-Range was chosen so an overhead hood and exhaust, which would block the view from the sink counter to the family room, would not be necessary. The range is set into a countertop that is extra deep, reducing the chances of someone knocking a pot from the family room side and also eliminating the possibility of grease splattering beyond the counter. In addition, the extra depth allows storage underneath on both sides. With the eating area in place at the island, the rest of the room was freed so the furniture arrangement could be designed specifically with entertaining in mind.

Once the appliances and other kitchen elements were in place, attention was given to auxiliary areas, such as barware and liquor storage and cabinetry for housing a stereo, television, tapes, games, and records. These were grouped in a large, custom-designed hutch that was positioned for convenient access against the wall near the eating area but out of the way of the main traffic flow. The built-in upper part of this unit has stained glass panels with a tulip motif that reinforces the overall outdoor-greenhouse-plant feeling of the yellow, white, and green interior.

Because the rest of this house is decorated in subdued earth tones, the family wanted something splashy and colorful here that would unite the indoors and outdoors. The green repeats the feeling of the plants that are in an atrium off to one side of the family room, and the yellow gives the room a youthful look. While it is smashing, it also is casual enough for the low-key type of entertaining that the owners enjoy.

Though the kitchen and family room are all one big room now, the designer subtly suggests a separation of function and space with different materials. The counter surfaces are an example: in the kitchen, the counter around the sink and range is a speckled yellow and white tile with white grout; the planning desk and dining table feature a yellow plastic laminate; and the storage hutch counter is white plastic laminate. The areas are united underfoot, though, with a yellow and brown carpet that the designer said was selected to tone down the otherwise bright room. Carpet was chosen over a vinyl flooring for its warmth and comfort, a feature especially appreciated in the family room portion. To further warm the room visually, wood beams were installed overhead; these in turn make it esthetically logical for wood-tone furniture to be used.

All in all, the new arrangement and bright colors make this a natural party room. Now, rain or shine, the space offers a vibrant yet easy-going atmosphere, a cheerful surrounding in which guests can circulate with ease or in which the family can dine alone in comfort.

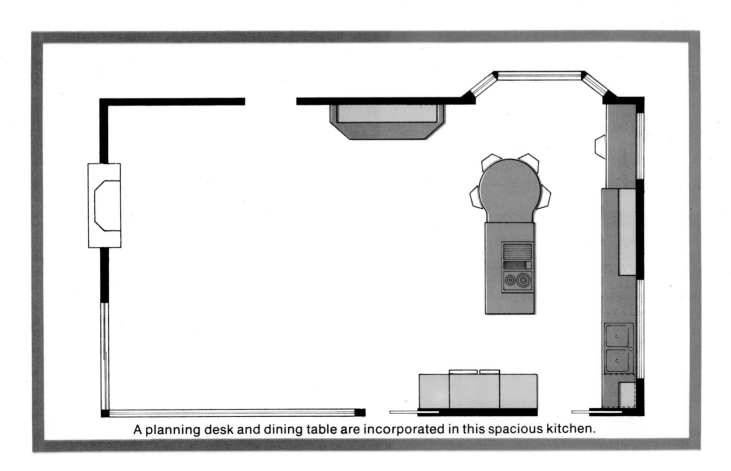

A planning desk and dining table are incorporated in this spacious kitchen.

Serious gourmet cooking takes place in this casual and inviting kitchen, sprinkled with antiques.

Gourmet Collectibles

If it were not for a few giveaways such as the trash compactor and microwave oven, visitors in this antique-filled kitchen might be hard pressed to date its origin. The cabinetry seems crafted in another era, and the placement of the doors, windows and walls is consistent with the remainder of the 60-year-old house.

This delightful combination of old and new reveals the possibilities for a kitchen renovation that is sensitive to the architectural integrity of a house. The family of two adults and two young children that creates gourmet feasts in this space had no interest in a modernization that would look out of place, no matter how beautiful it could be. They were unwilling to sacrifice their home's basic structure for the sake of a newer kitchen design.

When the kitchen designer accepted the challenge posed by this West Coast home, she had to cope with other requirements, too. The owners specified that much of their basic equipment — cutlery, specialized utensils, copper pots — should be out in the open, ready to use. They also wanted to incorporate an antique Hoosier cabinet and a pot belly stove in the final design. And, not least, they wanted the kitchen to be the showplace for their collections of baskets, pottery, cookbooks, woodenware, and other accessories assembled over a 20-year period.

Before its transformation, the kitchen had a rounded peninsula separating the main food preparation area from a dining area. Cabinets above the peninsula jutted out to prevent a view of two win-

20

dows in the dining area, with the result that the kitchen seemed divided into two small spaces, neither very attractive.

The designer began by removing the peninsula, a deletion that did little to harm the room's heritage and which opened up layout possibilities and increased the visual space. With the peninsula removed, the two windows offered light and a view to the entire kitchen, not just the dining corner.

The basic size and shape of the resulting room dictated the placement of the work areas. For architectural and financial reasons, the sink, though updated, remained where it was, just under a large window that provided natural light for that end of the room. Similarly, the refrigerator was replaced in its own original alcove. With the peninsula gone, however, the new cooking appliances could be moved from the old awkward location in a reverse L corner of the kitchen to the expanded cabinet/counter run that extended well into the former eating area. A Jenn-Air Grill-Range was built in with the base cabinets, and the microwave oven was given its own niche above the counter, leaving the countertop free for food preparation.

With the location of the sink, refrigerator and range determined, other appliances could be selected. A dishwasher and trash compactor were items the previous kitchen did not contain; they were placed logically near the sink.

The configuration of the cabinets followed. The owners, whom the kitchen designer describes as "detail-oriented people," wanted cabinets that matched as closely as possible the existing ones, so the designer had the door style copied and constructed to duplicate the originals. The interiors of the cabinets, however, were totally redesigned to receive this family's particular cookware and staple foodstuffs. There are many vertical dividers to separate trays, baking sheets and paper bags. Drawers are compartmented, and there is built-in knife storage. Instead of the usual two levels within base cabinets, most have three—two shallow and one higher to hold cans and boxes of different heights with the least possible wasted space; most of these shelves roll out for easy access, too.

The base cabinet occupying the space where the range once stood is typical of the planning that characterizes this remodeling. It has seven shallow roll-out drawers that hold linens and place mats.

Across the room, an interesting base cabinet with rounded corners was retained and its shape duplicated for an open bookshelf housing a portion of the family's vast cookbook library. In the corner with two newly exposed windows, a desk unit was installed that allows the family to utilize that space without spoiling the windows or the view. A tall, narrow bookcase takes advantage of a few extra inches between the windows and the Hoosier cabinet that means so much to the family. The dining table, once sandwiched in behind the peninsula, now occupies center stage.

The corner featuring a beloved pot belly stove (above) is more than just charming. Utensils on the wall are used daily and the cabinet stores linens. A greenhouse window (below) is the focal point of the sink area and provides additional light.

With the former peninsula removed, the corner windows now give both light and a view for cooking and dining in this area.

custom-made wood unit that was an overrun for their budget. To eliminate future problems with standing water that might rot the wood, the bottom ledge of the greenhouse was tiled and slanted slightly toward the sink for water runoff.

Also for the sake of design, the family opted for a more expensive tile countertop treatment in keeping with the age of the house. They selected an off-white, four-inch square ceramic tile to be installed on the diagonal and grouted with white compound. Part of the extra cost was recouped by having unfinished cabinets installed; the owners painted in the designer's selection of colors—a soft rust for base cabinets and an off-white for the wall units.

These colors were chosen to form a quiet background for the busy display of collectibles and utensils. Interesting utensils and everyday standbys such as knives and whisks are hung at the cook's fingertips along dark-stained ash strips affixed just above the backsplash. The wall behind the pot belly stove was faced with used brick to form an old-time backdrop for copper pans, as well as for wrought iron strips from which small pans, wooden spoons and whisks are hung. Baskets hang from the dark-stained ash beams, and additional collectibles are visible behind the plate rail near the ceiling.

A hardwood floor would have been included in the natural materials used in remodeling, but in this instance, practicality overruled aesthetics. Because the whole family gets into the act in this kitchen, the extra maintenance of a wood floor was rejected in favor of an off-white, easy-care sheet vinyl. "Sometimes, you simply have to compromise," commented the designer.

Because aesthetics was on a par with functionality in this household, the desire for a greenhouse window above the sink created a complex problem. The owners rejected the idea of an aluminum prefabricated unit, not only because of the material but because it would mean altering the existing window opening slightly. The solution was a costly

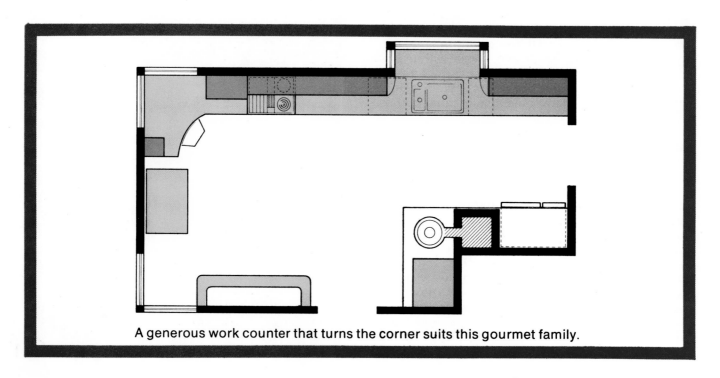

A generous work counter that turns the corner suits this gourmet family.

A cooktop island with butcher block top is the hub of this busy, entertaining kitchen.

Enlivened for Entertaining

When your business demands a great deal of at-home entertaining and your active family of three youngsters necessitates a kitchen that can withstand almost constant use, your kitchen requirements are varied but easily determined. You need plenty of counter space for food preparation and buffets, amenities such as a microwave oven and perhaps a warming drawer, a bar, a planning desk, a family eating area, and the convenience of a dishwasher. The cabinets, of course, must provide storage for the myriad platters, bowls, baking dishes, utensils and foodstuffs that a variety of menus demands.

When a family in Pittsburgh, Pennsylvania, presented these requests, the kitchen designer they approached produced an artful solution. The 12-1/2 by 15-1/2 foot kitchen, coupled to an adjoining 8-1/2 by 15-1/2 foot eating area that contains a table, chairs and planning desk, is just what the family had in mind.

A warming drawer and cutlery drawer fill this side of the island unit. Beyond is the eating area, sized for a gregarious family and their frequent entertaining.

Under the cooktop, the island holds cutlery drawers and sliding shelves for pot and pan storage. The 6½-foot-long counter beyond sees use as a buffet.

Since the designer is the brother of the man of the house and the man's father is a retired architect, the owners had plenty of expertise to draw upon during the planning stages. The home's contractor and an interior decorator were also involved in the design, providing an example of where an abundance of talented cooks serve to enhance rather than spoil the broth.

Since the brother lives in Dallas, the original design thinking was a collaboration of the owners and the local building contractor. Yet, while the kitchen displays many of the creative ideas of those early sessions, the final configuration reveals a good deal of the kitchen designer's expertise.

The original kitchen plan called for the same oak cabinetry, appliances, and island—all located where they are now. The straight wall of pantry storage, however, was redesigned to consist of base cabinets, a counter, and wall cabinets like those in the L-shaped portion of the kitchen. This change was prompted by the couple's frequent, large-scale entertaining. Concluding that the kitchen offered enough cabinets to hold frequently used foods, the designer predicted that the pantry would be used more as backup or bulk storage. In view of that, he suggested moving such storage to a nearby laundry room and substituting adequate counter tops for holding and serving prepared foods during the couple's parties, which run to a dozen or more couples at a time.

The unit that replaces what would have been the pantry is described as a hutch. Its base cabinets contain slide-out shelving and shallow drawers for linens, while the overhead cabinets—which have custom-made leaded glass panels in the doors—hold dishes. Between the base and overhead cabinets is the white plastic laminate counter, extending a generous 6-1/2 feet long.

The original plan called for an L-shaped counter with an island in the working portion of the kitchen, and this basic arrangement was retained. The designer enlarged the overall size of the island, however, so that he could pack more functions into the space beneath the cooktop positioned on it. Specifically, he wanted enough room to add a warming drawer that keeps cooked foods between 140 and 160 degrees; this feature, he said, "will pay handsome dividends for the kind of entertaining my brother and his wife do." To enhance the kitchen decoratively, the designer specified a butcher block countertop for the island.

He also decided to place a microwave oven next to the refrigerator/freezer rather than near the conventional ovens "because of its frequent use for defrosting and warming leftovers." The microwave unit rests on an off-the-counter shelf for a built-in appearance, but the shelf could easily be used for cookbooks by a family lacking such a supplementary cooking facility.

With the double sink positioned under a window, the dishwasher and double ovens to the left, and the refrigerator located at the end of the L's other leg, the designer began to fill the cabinets with inventive space-saving interiors. Instead of the obvious lazy susan for the corner units, for example, he selected swing-shelf modules that have half-circle shelves attached to the door; when the door is opened, the items on the shelves become easily accessible. Elsewhere, cabinets are partitioned to hold trays, cutlery, boxed foods and bread, and many feature slide-out shelving for canned goods and pots and pans. Overhead, he opted for diagonal, adjustable shelving.

Finally, the designer made certain that the kitchen included a desk for menu planning or message taking. "If there's anything overlooked in designing a kitchen," he said, "it's a home planning center." By its very inclusion, the center shows the thoroughness and care with which this kitchen was formed.

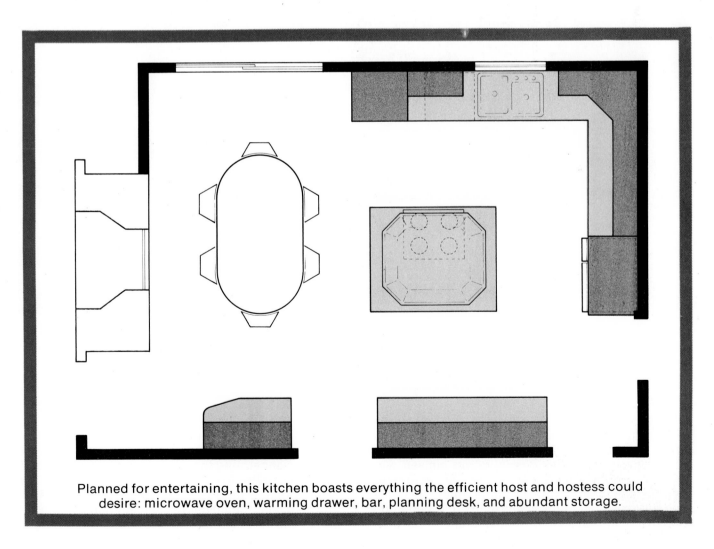

Planned for entertaining, this kitchen boasts everything the efficient host and hostess could desire: microwave oven, warming drawer, bar, planning desk, and abundant storage.

A cooktop/island with plenty of elbow room is tailored to a tall man's needs.

Fit for a Bachelor

When the man of this California house retained it after his divorce, he suddenly found himself with the chance to tailor its space to his particular needs—and stature. A tall, large man, this new bachelor welcomed the opportunity and began his home's remake at its heart, in the kitchen.

The original layout was a typical U-shape with one arm separating the work triangle of range, sink and refrigerator from an adjoining dinette area. The small U made food preparation uncomfortable for the man; also, since he was serving himself, the U's peninsula was just an obstruction to walk around when it came time to enjoy the fruits of his labors.

"Though the kitchen could have been considered adequate for most families, for this client, it was a physically and psychologically difficult space in which to work," explained the kitchen designer.

The man's new single lifestyle affected the design changes, too. "A bachelor does not need a kitchen and the more traditional dinette area," the designer pointed out. "This house has a formal dining room for that sort of entertaining, so though we did keep the resale value of the house in mind, the kitchen could be redesigned pretty much just for the single person."

Redesigning for the single person meant arriving at a layout that unified the cooking and serving motions to minimize time-wasting steps. In addition, since this particular bachelor wanted a party center where he could comfortably entertain both large groups of people at buffets and just a few friends for cards and snacks, those requirements had to be satisfied.

The first step was to eliminate the seldom-used dinette area and its window, joining this space to the kitchen to form a single room measuring 11-1/2 by 20 feet.

The width of the room was sliced with an island that provided space for a new range to replace the old free-standing model. The designer opted for a Jenn-Air Grill-Range because of its built-in ventilation system, which did away with the need for a space-grabbing overhead hood that would have intruded on the new visually open plan.

To the center range island, a custom table was attached to provide room for four or five people or buffet space for parties. This table affords the feeling and function of more than just a bar counter with stools. By attaching it to the island and finishing both in the same plastic laminate (a butcher block pattern that gives the effect of real maple but the advantage of lower maintenance), the table becomes an integral part of the room.

The sink and refrigerator were replaced, but left

A dining table extends the island and is perfect for buffets — or even a poker game.

in the same location. With the new range now moved closer, the sink/refrigerator/range triangle is more compact, freeing the rest of the kitchen for working and serving areas and storage.

The kitchen designer extended the working counter to the left of the sink past the location of the former peninsula into the area previously meant for dining. By eliminating the window here, there was room along the wall for tall pantry storage and a built-in double oven, as well as additional counter space. A Nutone food center installed in this area further updates the kitchen, as does a dishwasher located to the right of the sink. By placing the dishwasher at the right (instead of the left), its door can be left down for loading while the table is cleared, making clearing, scraping and loading a single, smooth, continuous operation.

Once the main kitchen elements were located, the layout of the cabinets fell into place. With so much room in the base cabinets, it was possible to keep upper storage minimal to preserve the open feeling of the room. Indeed, while the actual square footage has not been increased in the new arrangement, the kitchen is distinguished by its open, airy feeling.

The effect is increased by the clear view into an adjoining family room. The family room and kitchen now combine to make this entire section of the house perfect for parties. Summer weekends now see 20 or more people gathered for barbecue parties that start at the grill on a patio, move through the kitchen for side dishes set out buffet style on the table, continue to the bar in the family room for drinks, and end at the pool area for the feast.

The kitchen and family room work together decoratively, too. Lighting was planned in the kitchen to consist primarily of fluorescent strips hidden in a cove and recessed spots strategically located over the island and sink, but the single hanging fixture over the table is repeated in the family room. The sheet vinyl flooring in tones of gold provides easy maintenance for both rooms and coordinates with the warm wood-colored tones of the island counter and the gold ceramic tiles on the sink counter and backsplash. For a dressy touch, companion foil wallcoverings in yellow, orange, green and white were chosen; one pattern covers the walls and soffits, the other lines the ceiling.

All in all, this modernized kitchen now invites visitors to participate in the kitchen festivities while delicately holding them out of the way of the main food preparation triangle. While the lone chef works efficiently on his side of the island, guests can keep him company or even assist without getting underfoot. And, on the days when the bachelor cook feels no need for companionship in the kitchen, he still is encouraged in his culinary efforts by the comfortable workspace.

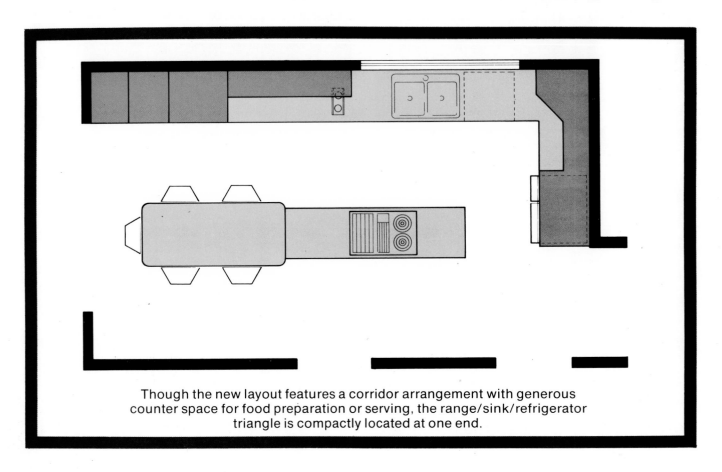

Though the new layout features a corridor arrangement with generous counter space for food preparation or serving, the range/sink/refrigerator triangle is compactly located at one end.

This attractive, well-planned kitchen is a designer's gift to his own family.

A Designer's Own Dream

If you have ever dreamed of creating your own kitchen, you'll envy the designer who worked out the plans for the one shown here. This is the culinary heart of his own home, a Dutch Colonial he shares with his wife and four children. As might be expected of a professional kitchen designer, he considered scores of arrangements for well over a year before deciding on the final layout for the 11-by-12-foot room.

After having lived for two years with the kitchen inherited from the previous owners of the 50-year-old Illinois house, the designer and his family were well acquainted with the problems it posed for their particular lifestyle and tastes. Major functional difficulties included a lack of conveniently located counter space and unimaginative partitioning of the interiors of the old, white metal cabinets; aesthetically, the room was spoiled by an outdated porcelain sink, a clumsy portable dishwasher, and, of course, the cabinets.

Also bothersome were the counter layout and the location of various doorways that seemed to en-

A separate 6½-foot-long counter is outfitted especially for use as a baking center. The ample space is perfect for rolling out doughs, while slide-out trays below hold an array of baking utensils. This space also doubles as a bar for the nearby dining room.

courage a constant parade of children and other guests. Visitors not only had a clear view from the front hall into the L-shaped work space (the range being especially prominent), but since the door to the basement was positioned next to this hall doorway, anyone going to the basement couldn't help but interfere with an already unhappy cook. To further compound the traffic situation, access from the kitchen to the dinette and dining room was in a corner diagonal to the basement and front hall

passages. When the designer's children and their active friends were in the house, the room resembled Grand Central Station.

The designer's wife preferred a U-shaped kitchen, which she believed would keep the children out of her way unless they were actually helping her. An avid baker, she also asked her husband for a large counter area offering plenty of handy storage for her baking supplies and utensils.

The designer realized that if he were going to

The range, sink, and dishwasher (above) are incorporated in the new U-shape the designer's wife requested, partly so she would have a compact work space and partly to isolate her from their four active children. Throughout the efficiently planned kitchen, cabinets are outfitted to take advantage of every inch of interior space. A spice rack (left) in a wall cabinet has shelves that turn like pages in a book, while base cabinets feature such space-utilizing ideas as semicircular, swing-out shelving.

increase the amount of counter space substantially and give his wife her U, he would have to move the doorways. Yet he wanted to retain front hall access to the kitchen, and he obviously couldn't eliminate the door to the basement.

The solution was first to reposition the basement doorway from the kitchen wall to a foyer wall. Turning the door at a right angle to its former location meant shifting the basement stairs about 2-1/2 feet away from the kitchen wall and con-

structing a landing; the stairs themselves could still be utilized. Then, the hall doorway along the same kitchen wall was moved about three feet, allowing the counter space gained in the kitchen to be extended even further to complete the U. These changes yielded 8 more linear feet of counter and cabinet space over the old arrangement, while concealing the kitchen from visitors entering the front door.

With the kitchen shape and space determined,

the designer proceeded to plan the cabinetry "from the inside out. I always start a kitchen design by considering what people's storage needs are, and I considered our own kitchen the same way. I thought about where the small appliances should be stored for easy access and where the foods most used by the children—breakfast cereals, snack foods, sandwich breads—could be located so that the kids could get at them without interfering with their mother. And I knew I wanted to include slide-out shelves, corner units, and other interior features that made the most of the space available."

After shuffling these pieces of his puzzle for months and discussing various possibilities with his wife, the designer eventually devised the present arrangement. The triangle formed by the range, sink and refrigerator is confined to the U portion of the room, while the fervently desired baking center occupies its own 6-1/2 foot long counter on the fourth wall of the room. The only

holdover from the previous kitchen is the range.

Inside the cabinets is a wealth of storage that dwarfs the area available in the previous kitchen. The baking center wall is a good example. Base cabinets conceal a bread box and built-in slicing board, as well as ample slide-out shelves for mixers and bowls. Perhaps the most ingenious use of storage space, though, is a canned-goods pantry that nestles against a concealed laundry chute; the pantry stands 7 feet high but only one can deep.

Elsewhere, there is a spice rack consisting of shelves that, in addition to being exposed on both sides, turn like pages in a book. A corner base cabinet has a semicircular turn-out shelf attached to the door. When the cabinet door under the sink is opened, the waste container slides out. In short, the new kitchen—with its maximum utilization of space, raised-panel cabinetry of rich oak, and its abundant lighting (center chandelier, recessed down lights in the corners, and under-cabinet fixtures)—reflects a talented kitchen designer.

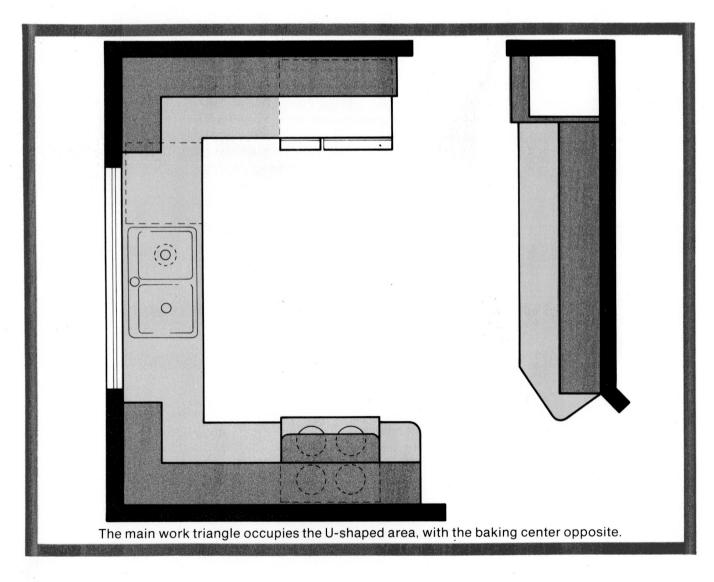

The main work triangle occupies the U-shaped area, with the baking center opposite.

Colonial-style cabinetry goes luxurious in this modern, fully-equipped kitchen.

Comfortable Colonial

Aficionados of Colonial design often have trouble planning a modern kitchen, but the Pennsylvania couple that uses this handsome family kitchen has found a way to combine Colonial flavor with modern convenience. By specifying dark pine cabinetry of Early American styling that incorporates the latest in interior configurations—lazy susans, appli-

ance "garages," tray storage, slide-out drawers for pots and pans—they obtained the best of both worlds. Their kitchen serves as the heart of the new, single-story, Colonial-design house that the couple has filled with a lifetime's collection of antiques.

After having lived in more than a dozen homes

during their marriage, the owners were kitchen design experts themselves by the time they sat down to draw up this kitchen for their custom home. They knew precisely what they did not want, and they strove to correct the shortcomings they had encountered in past kitchens. With their children grown and out of the house, they could afford both economically and aesthetically to have a kitchen as luxurious as they desired for entertaining large groups of friends and/or family.

Part of this luxury meant being able to display cherished "conversation pieces," as the man calls their crockery and dinnerware. While some people might think of display shelves as dust catchers, this couple wanted plenty of open spaces in which to showcase their antiques.

Working with a kitchen design firm for this portion of their to-be-built home, the couple designated a space measuring 10 by 13 feet for the working portion of the kitchen and an adjoining area of the same dimensions for eating and a bar. The two areas are separated by a peninsula that adds counter and storage space convenient for both the kitchen and the dinette; both sides permit access to the base and overhead cabinets, and the counter is a natural buffet or pass-through for serving. In conjunction with the nearby bar, the counter also facilitates handling the large cocktail parties they give frequently.

All three areas—kitchen, eating, and bar—are coordinated visually with the same Colonial-style cabinetry. Such care was taken to maintain a consistent style with the furnishings in the rest of the house that the base cabinets even feature hutch-like contours; their depths diminish as they approach the ends of the counters, giving each section a bow-front shape. Since the wall cabinets above also cut across corners, there are few

The built-in bar/hutch nestles into its own niche at one end of the dining area (above), adding to the comfortable country theme. It can be seen from the kitchen, past the peninsula (above, left). This 10-by-13-foot kitchen features two, L-shaped work counters, one of which (left) contains the sink, dishwasher, and refrigerator. The range, double ovens and microwave oven are tucked into the second L (pictured on page 33).

right-angled junctions in this kitchen.

The appliances and food preparation areas are arranged in the kitchen area in two L-shaped sections; these sections face each other across a traffic path that cuts diagonally through the room. One of the L's contains the appliances—including a smoothtop range, double oven, and microwave oven—and workspace necessary for cooking. The other L, designed for food preparation and cleanup, is laid out with the side-by-side refrigerator/freezer at one end, then the dishwasher and double-bowl sink under a window, and, finally, the peninsula. Placing the dishwasher to the left of the sink allows cleanup chores to proceed from the eating area to the sink without interference from the open dishwasher door. Panels that match the wooden cabinets help modify the bright colors and stark lines of all the appliances.

The bar area is strategically placed between the kitchen and the dining room that lies past the kitchen eating area. Organized like an antique hutch, the bar cabinets are recessed into a wall with exposed brick above and between the cabinets and counter. Four wall cabinets flank a three-tiered wine rack, while some of the family's prized Early American plates line the arch overhead. The bottom section of the bar contains a great deal of storage, and the additional bar sink relieves the cooking area of frequent interruptions during the cocktail hour.

To keep the kitchen as cozy as a true Colonial cookery, the owners decorated the room with a predominantly yellow small-print wallcovering, a yellow and white brick-patterned flooring, and beams that carry the woodsy look to the ceiling. Although theirs is a totally new kitchen, the impression it creates is one of comfort that has lasted and will last for many years.

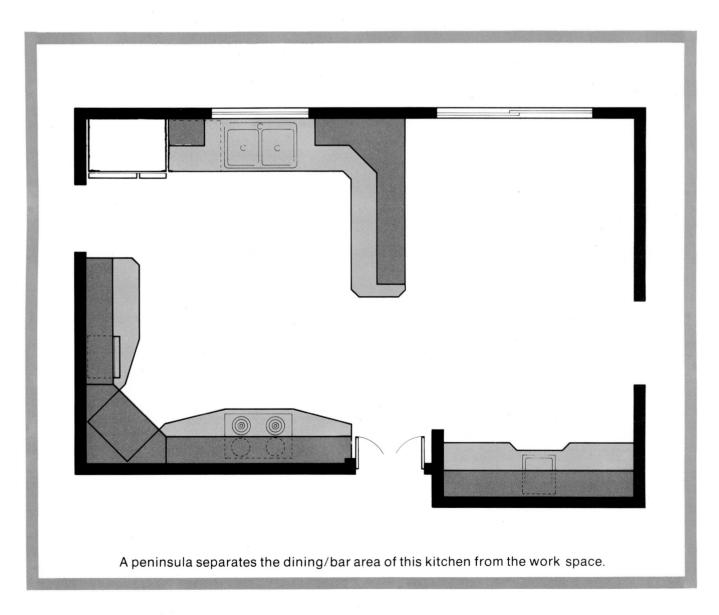

A peninsula separates the dining/bar area of this kitchen from the work space.

Updated lighting and added counterspace characterize this improved, U-shaped kitchen.

U~Shape with a Twist

Standard kitchen plans of yesteryear were so predictable that without looking you would know that the sink was under the window and that the eating area consisted of a table and a few chairs. This kitchen in a 55-year-old, two-story, Colonial-style house in Illinois was no exception; it offered an unimaginative arrangement of appliances and cabinetry and random locations of doorways to the dining room, rear yard, and a bathroom. The 9-by-13-foot room contained the essentials, but they were laid out with no particular thought to maximizing storage capacity or minimizing inter-

ruptive traffic. When the current owners bought the house about eight years ago, they called in a kitchen designer to change all that.

"The couple had four children in elementary school at the time," remembers the designer. "So they asked me for a kitchen plan that would keep the children out of the main work area. Also, being a family of six, they needed plenty of storage for foods and dishes and adequate counter space for preparing large meals."

The designer found little that was technically incorrect with the old range/sink/refrigerator tri-

An unusual, rounded peninsula, an extension of the counter, occupies the space where the dining room door once was. The shallow pantry is on the far wall.

Moving the sink to the corner allows a generous counter to the left (instead of one, merely adequate in size, on either side). Roll-out shelves increase storage utility.

angle, but he suggested that the sink be moved into a corner. The result of this alteration was a U-shape with one generous counter and another that offered suitable room, instead of two equal counters of merely adequate length. He did not change the location of the refrigerator and range.

Though the earlier kitchen had also formed a U, the range lay at the end of one counter and met the door frame to the dining room. An exposed range is a safety hazard in any house, but especially so in a home full of active youngsters. In this case, the designer decided that the doorway was what

should be moved, not the range. By blocking up the opening and shifting the new doorway to the end of this same wall, he developed a corridor pattern to keep traffic from the three doorways at one end of the kitchen. As a by-product, the designer acquired a perfect spot for eating — in front of the wall where the old dining room doorway had been. The present kitchen's rounded eating bar is an extension of the counter between wall and base cabinets in this newly created area.

"The family wanted a place in the kitchen where two or three people could eat breakfast or lunch," the designer explained. "Everyone eats dinner together in the dining room, but their schedules seldom mesh at other times." When not being used for informal dining, this counter acts as another work center or as a surface for serving or clearing the dining room. Bar stools slide out of the way under the counter when not in use.

The oak cabinetry in English Manor style was equipped with a variety of interiors to meet the owners' many needs: slide-out trays for pots and pans in base cabinets to the left of the range; a spice rack on a wall cabinet door to the right of the range; divided drawers for cutlery and corner turn-out shelves in base cabinets; slide-out towel rods beneath the sink; and—next to the refrigerator—a sandwich bar base cabinet that contains a slicing board, cutlery drawer, a second drawer for napkins or more utensils, a deep bread box drawer with steel liner, and a slide-out shelf tray with a wire rack dividing the space to hold bottles upright.

For extra storage, the owners opted for wall cabinets 33 inches high instead of the usual 30 inches. To facilitate reaching the shelves easily, they gleaned the extra 3 inches from the standard 18-inch clearance between counter and wall cabi-nets; in this kitchen the clearance measures just 15 inches. A matching cabinet panel was fabricated to dress up the dishwasher, retained from the old kitchen but installed where the sink used to be.

A surprise storage area was uncovered when an ironing board was removed from a niche along the same wall as the bathroom entry. About 20 inches wide, the niche was just deep enough to accommodate shelves one can deep.

In addition to the cabinetry and a leather-look vinyl wall covering, the room was improved both decoratively and functionally by installing all new lighting. The old kitchen had a center ceiling fixture and a recessed light at the sink; yet even with both turned on, "the kitchen would have had better lighting with candles," according to the designer. The new Tiffany-type ceiling fixture provides general overhead lighting, while the several recessed downlights at the sink area and abundant under-cabinet fixtures supply task lighting.

If anyone ever needed proof that an unimaginative arrangement of appliances and cabinetry could be transformed into a highly functional and visually appealing kitchen, this one should cancel any doubts or questions.

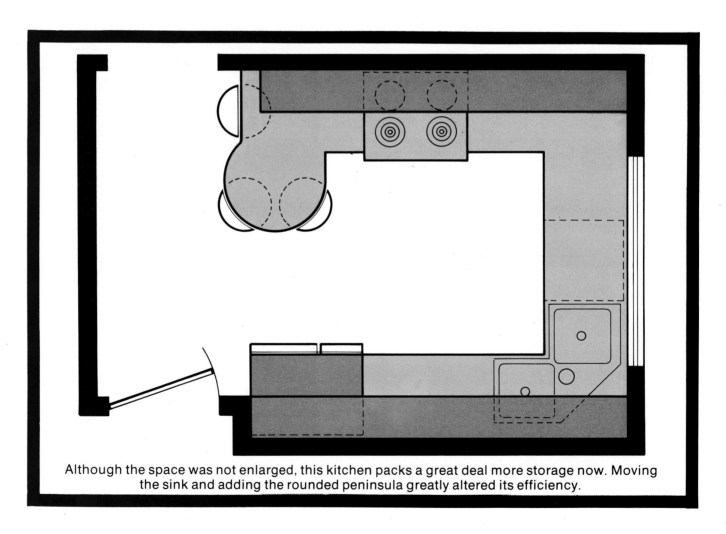

Although the space was not enlarged, this kitchen packs a great deal more storage now. Moving the sink and adding the rounded peninsula greatly altered its efficiency.

Contemporary Convenience

This unusual peninsula stands where a wall once blocked the view from the kitchen.

Plaster flew for weeks when the owners of an awkward, closed-in kitchen in a 40-year-old house decided to transform it into this fun-to-use, open space. The job was barely finished in time to serve Christmas dinner, but the young couple with two preschool-age children never doubted their new, youthful kitchen would be well worth the effort.

And it was an effort. Relying on a kitchen designer, the owners decided to retain only the appliances; the floor plan itself started completely from scratch. As it worked out, the new kitchen design involved blocking up a window and moving a wall,

leading to a general rearrangement of rooms throughout the first floor of the two-story, Georgian-style house.

When the couple first conferred with the designer, they outlined three requirements for their new kitchen. First, the mother wanted the room to be open enough so that she could watch her youngsters at play in an adjoining room. The children had been playing in a basement family room, but she found she couldn't supervise them adequately at such a distance. Second, the new kitchen clearly had to provide more usable counter space and

The sink (above) turns a corner to allow more cabinets and counter space; before, it was directly under the window and the counter dead-ended into the wall. The other end of this counter run (right), which used to house the stove, now is open work space with cleverly conceived storage below. Blocking a window made room for the refrigerator and vast pantry storage.

The view from the new family room/dinette is equally appealing. By making the peninsula extra deep, the designer gained storage on this side for games and linens.

increased storage. The previous layout offered so little storage that the family was forced to keep some food and other kitchen items in the basement. And third, the couple wanted a buffet serving space to be used for informal get-togethers.

When the designer saw the kitchen, he understood their requests. While accessible from the living room, dining room, rear yard and basement, the 9-by-14-foot kitchen was visually isolated; the only things the four entries succeeded in doing were to create constant, interruptive traffic and to diminish the possibilities for cabinet and counter layout. The designer noted that the sink, range and refrigerator were located along two parallel walls to form a nice working triangle, but he also realized

that the components were so close to each other that they crowded out sorely needed counter space. Instead of forming convenient work centers separating the major appliances, the largest counters were off to the side—next to the refrigerator and along a third wall.

After studying the rest of the house, the designer determined that the living room was large enough to accommodate a dining area at the end nearest the kitchen. This freed the formal dining room to be made into a family room with dinette. When the couple agreed to these changes, the designer created a view from the kitchen to the dinette/family room by removing the wall and doorway that had separated the rooms. In their place, he suggested a peninsula. Traffic patterns have been shifted so that people can pass from the family room to the dining/living room and even to the basement by rounding the peninsula and cutting through a corner of the kitchen, never entering the work area.

Once the traffic patterns were improved, the designer could position the appliances and cabinetry. It made little sense to move the plumbing to an entirely different spot, but the sink corner was improved significantly by placing the bowls at an angle and continuing both base and wall cabinets around to the dining room doorway. Previously, the sink had been directly beneath the window shown, and the counter had ended just to the right of the sink. The dishwasher was retained to the left of the sink, but next to it—where the range once stood—there are now cabinets and a counter. At last, the kitchen offered a full-scale preparation space.

The old range was incorporated into the peninsula but with a new hood vented outside through the soffit. Next to the range, the peninsula was made to surround a new floor-to-ceiling partition that was made necessary by heat ducts and other mechanical considerations. This wall turned out to be an excellent backdrop for more wall cabinets and a microwave oven for which the previous kitchen had no room.

Along a third wall that before held only a counter, the designer created a neat, uninterrupted space by blocking up a window. Here he placed the refrigerator and a pantry 24 inches deep with room for storing canned goods as well as cleaning tools and supplies. The family no longer has to trek to the basement for a can of soup.

Similarly, the family need no longer have guests pass through the kitchen for a buffet supper. The designer made the peninsula extra deep so that even with the range there, sufficient counter space is still available. Below is carefully planned storage that is accessible from all three sides.

Base cabinet storage on the family room/dinette side holds games and dining accessories, while end units and kitchen base cabinets are outfitted with various space-saving devices—including corner swing-out shelves—to fully utilize all the storage capacity throughout the kitchen. A tray storage unit makes the most of a slim space next to the sink, while cabinets elsewhere feature divided drawers and slide-out shelves. With the installation of all new lighting (a hanging Tiffany-type fixture, recessed downlights, and under-cabinet lighting) and a decorative blue and white geometric print wallcovering, the room became a comfortable and happy work space for a growing family.

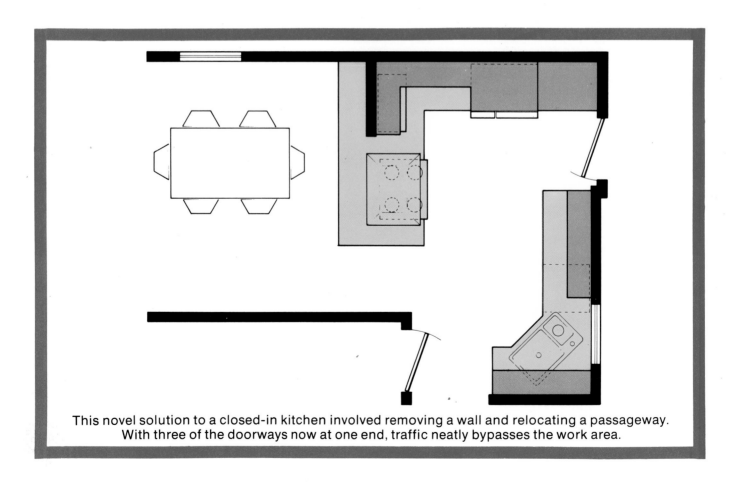

This novel solution to a closed-in kitchen involved removing a wall and relocating a passageway. With three of the doorways now at one end, traffic neatly bypasses the work area.

A bounty of cabinet storage and generous work space surround this cooktop island.

Cultivated Farmhouse

The family that enjoys this generously equipped kitchen bought the Pennsylvania farmhouse of which it is a part in 1952. At the time, they thought the kitchen addition to the 240-year-old structure represented the latest word in design. Then just four years old, the kitchen featured white metal cabinets and stainless steel sinks and counters, with a thoughtfully planned layout that was perfect for their family. A large U contained the range/sink/refrigerator triangle, while the other end of the 12-1/2 by 17-1/2 foot area was crammed with additional storage cabinets and a table where the kids could eat or do their homework without being underfoot. As if all that were not enough, an

8-by-13 foot butler's pantry with a large freezer and second sink contained additional storage in cabinets and closets.

As the years passed, the family redid the flooring four times and replaced appliances in eight stages; finally, though, they admitted it was time to end the piecemeal renovations.

For advice, the owners enlisted the aid of their own son, who by this time (1975) had grown up and decided to be a kitchen designer. No one could have been more aware of the need for a face-lift or as sensitive to what was worth retaining of the existing appliances and cabinetry.

"My parents wanted to keep the basic layout," said the designer. "After all, they had lived with it for nearly 25 years and were used to it. But besides that, it was a good, efficient kitchen that had stood the test of actual use. The cabinets and appliances

A wealth of garden vegetables can be prepared on the peninsula table, which also serves for dining or work space for the owner/veterinarian, whose home office is this corner.

needed updating, though, especially since the rest of the house had been improved."

Accordingly, windows and doors were not altered, since no major structural changes were necessary. Existing appliances were upgraded but kept in the same locations—the double wall ovens and refrigerator at either ends of the U, with the new triple-bowl sink in the center. In addition to replacing appliances, the owners added a trash compactor to the right of the sink and a dishwasher to the left, a microwave oven next to the double wall ovens, and a freezer next to the refrigerator. They replaced the table in the center of the U with an island that incorporates a smoothtop range. They substituted rich pecan cabinets for the old white metal units. The pantry cabinets were simply freshened with robin's egg blue paint to match the new plastic laminate counter and table tops.

The heart of this updated farmstead now has room for a television (above), double wall ovens (below), and cabinets with myriad special interior features (right), such as Lazy Susans for corner cabinets and appliance "garages" at the backs of counters to help minimize clutter.

These were only the most visible aspects of the kitchen's transformation, however, other changes took place behind the scenes. The interiors of the new cabinets, for example, are crammed with space- and labor-saving devices. Every corner cabinet has a Lazy Susan in it to better utilize formerly dead storage space, and the portion of the butler's pantry that used to house the giant freezer now contains a storage pantry unit designed to hold an abundance of grocery items. The pantry has shallow shelves lining double doors, with interior storage space for cleaning tools and supplies. In addition, closed-door compartments along the walls at the backs of the counters conceal small appliances that would otherwise consume valuable work or shelf space.

In the eating area, the designer substituted a table-height, rounded peninsula for the old family table in front of the window. A TV sits on one counter, while the other cabinet unit is equipped with desk, phone, and bookshelves. Since the man—a veterinarian—receives calls at any hour (including mealtimes), this area serves as a convenient home office.

At least insofar as the flow of cooking chores is concerned, this new kitchen is very much like the old one. The main cooking center is still to the left of the sink, while food preparation and cleanup continue to take place to the right. The doctor enjoys a convenient location for his home office, and the family can still take informal meals in the kitchen. But the new kitchen offers a level of aesthetic and practical appeal that the old one could not approach. Combining the latest in modern appliances with contemporary cabinetry and space-saving devices, this remodeled kitchen shows just how far the art of kitchen design has progressed since 1948.

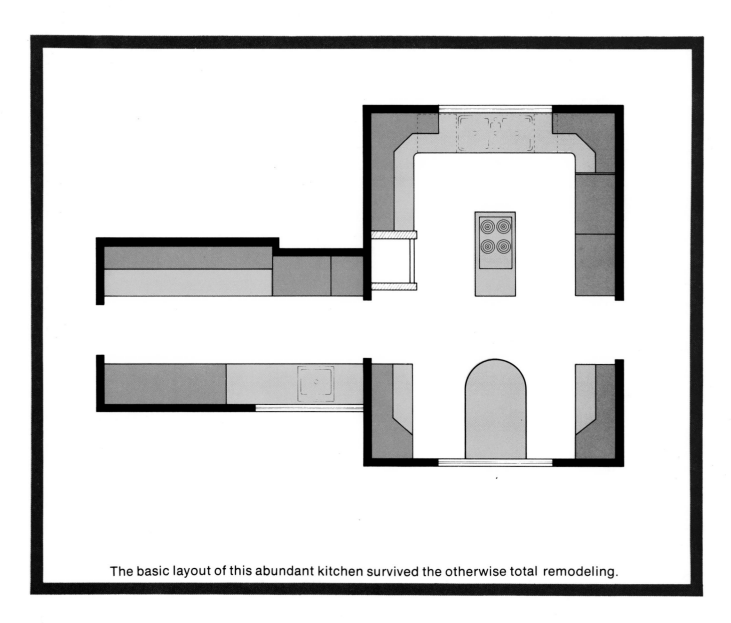

The basic layout of this abundant kitchen survived the otherwise total remodeling.

Kitchen cabinetry wraps a corner and continues into the family room for extra storage.

Beauty and the Budget

A budget of $3,200 for a totally new kitchen, including appliances, might sound skimpy to anyone who has priced kitchen essentials recently, but a builder of suburban townhomes in Maryland shows us that the result need not look cheap. In fact, the 7-by-12-foot kitchen is efficiently equipped with a continuous-clean, double oven and range; self-defrosting, 15.6-cubic-foot refrigerator-freezer; dishwasher; disposal; plastic laminate counters with integrated chopping block; extra-tall, walnut-trimmed cabinets; pantry; and sheet-vinyl flooring. And these are arranged in a corridor layout that could be duplicated by any homeowner considering a remodeling.

"The galley arrangement, with cabinets and appliances lined up along two facing walls, allows a compact sink/refrigerator/range triangle," said the designer who planned the kitchen. "It's almost possible to prepare a meal without moving, yet there still is plenty of elbow room."

The $3,200 cost of this kitchen, when built in early 1977, comprised a $400 gas stove, a $250 refrigerator, a $150 dishwasher, a $50 disposer, $200 countertops, a $100 sink and $700 of cabinetry; the remaining $1,350 was the labor cost for installation. For a slightly higher price, a similar corridor kitchen/family room could have had more cabinets along the wall next to the refrigerator or wall cabinets above the family room extension of the stove countertop. Other changes could have been made in the number of drawers and shelves inside the cabinets or pantry. Some of the families that bought this model chose to upgrade to appliances with additional convenience features.

In the townhome model shown here, the kitchen cabinetry extends into an adjoining family room in a reverse L. Base cabinets in the family room form added storage either for kitchen items or for games, barware and liquor, or paperwork and telephone books. Through a doorway at the other end of the kitchen lies the formal dining room.

One of the families that bought a home with this floor plan is a couple with three daughters, aged 1 to 7 years; the mother said that after living with the dining room/kitchen/family room layout for two years, there is little she would change. She has a

This charming kitchen belies the constraints of a budget. It's fully equipped with double ovens, dishwasher, and disposal, compactly located for efficiency, and there is liberal storage in the cabinets and in a pantry between the refrigerator and the dining room.

dining table in the 10-by-12-foot family room where she and her husband entertain another couple frequently for dinner and bridge and where the family generally dines for all its meals. The formal dining room is reserved for entertaining larger groups and for special occasions.

The food for all meals, though, is prepared with ease in the compact kitchen. The woman works comfortably, making family fare that usually runs to simple items such as steaks, spaghetti, stews, soups, and chicken "prepared all kinds of ways." Yet, even when friends gather for a cooperative dinner, the double ovens and various work areas allow for multiple cooks.

The counter to the right of the refrigerator forms the main preparation area, especially since the family added a microwave oven in this space. Some

washing and chopping of vegetables is done on the butcher block to the right of the sink, above the dishwasher; this area doubles as a cleanup space after a meal when the dishwasher is being loaded.

Whether she is making a meal or cleaning up afterward, this homemaker notes that everything is within easy reach. Canned goods and dry foods are stored along with fine china in the pantry to the left of the refrigerator, a location convenient to both the kitchen and to the dining room. The 42-inch-high cabinets, a foot taller than standard, make good use of vertical space elsewhere in the kitchen, and drawers at the left of the range and at the top of each base cabinet offer ample space for silverware, pot holders, and assorted cooking utensils. "I don't have to walk far for anything," said the woman. "It's all at my fingertips."

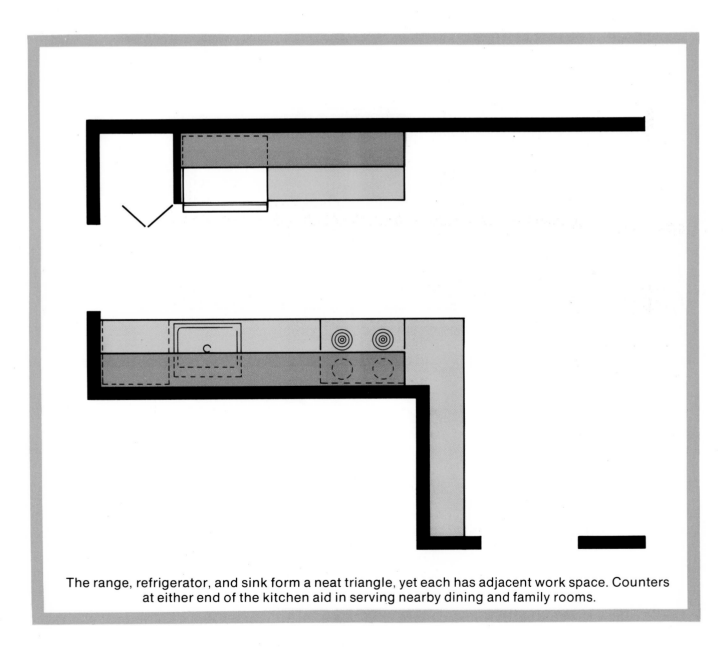

The range, refrigerator, and sink form a neat triangle, yet each has adjacent work space. Counters at either end of the kitchen aid in serving nearby dining and family rooms.

Lit by a dramatic skylight, the culinary heart of this Colonial home has been revolutionized.

Revolutionary Gourmet

Time might stand still in the rest of this pre-Revolutionary house, but the exciting culinary center of the 11-room home now functions as no Colonial inhabitant would have dared dream. While the family that occupies the Massachusetts home are lovingly restoring the traditional features the two-story home originally boasted, their desire for a faithful restoration stopped at the kitchen door. The woman, who unhesitatingly labels herself "an excellent cook," had no interest in baking bread in a brick oven. Instead, she wanted the ultimate in convenience and efficiency for preparing repasts of French, Chinese and Italian cuisine for her husband and two young sons.

"I love old homes, but I needed a kitchen in which I could easily move around," she told us. "When we bought the house, the kitchen had been 'remodeled' with a tacky, knotty pine paneling that made the room dark. On top of that, it was a small, core kitchen, central to the house, so it always felt claustrophobic and uncomfortable to me. There wasn't enough room for a dining table, and it was just plain inefficient; anyone coming in the back door passed through the kitchen, and it seemed someone always was in my way."

While she wanted a replacement that was up-to-date in every way, this gourmet cook specified that a new kitchen must not spoil the house's classic, center-chimney design. There were to be no ultra-modern additions that would impair the character of the home, inside or out.

The kitchen designer accepted this design limitation and immediately seized on a dilapidated, unheated rear porch as the site of the new kitchen. Because the space already was a part of the house and was conveniently adjacent to the current kitchen, there would be no change in the exterior appearance of the house.

Simply by relocating the back door that led through this porch, the designer turned the entire area into a tranquil, 10-by-22-foot cul-de-sac where the woman could put her creative talents to work without unnecessary interruption. At the same time, the bulk of the former kitchen is left free to form an airy passageway from the new kitchen to a library, the dining room, and a rear hall. In this open space, the fireplace that once was used for cooking remains as a cozy reminder of days gone by.

The kitchen designer began the remodeling by removing the wall that separated the porch from the kitchen, carefully maintaining two support columns that eventually would frame an island with a butcher block counter. Two banks of windows were cut into an exterior wall, at the sink and breakfast areas, and a skylight above each of these spaces opened the sloping ceiling for additional light. One of the main objectives of the project—flooding the kitchen with sunlight—already had been achieved. The rest of the kitchen started taking shape after the exterior walls were insulated and mechanical necessities were put in place.

The owners of the house had fallen in love with a German line of cabinets that was available with natural pine doors and easy-care plastic laminate interiors, perfect for blending with the home's wide-plank pine flooring and white walls. After perusing the manufacturer's catalog, they decided on the various interior configurations they desired, including a towel bar, utility shelf, lid holder, cutlery dividers, plastic dry food storage containers, pull-out table, tray divider, roll-out vegetable baskets, and pop-out wastebasket. It was up to the designer to arrange these in a logical sequence for maximum efficiency.

"I first created a working triangle between the sink, range and refrigerator that meant the fewest steps for the woman," the designer recounted. The sink, a double-bowl model that features a waste disposer in the smaller compartment, is at the center of the counter under one set of windows. Behind the sink, at the island, is a Jenn-Air Grill-Range, chosen because it does not require an

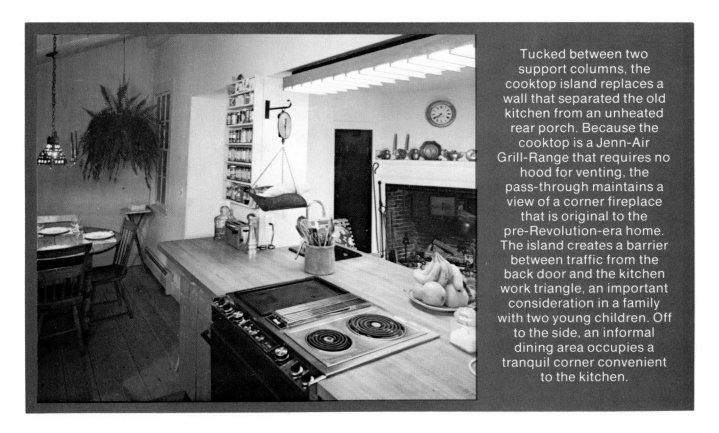

Tucked between two support columns, the cooktop island replaces a wall that separated the old kitchen from an unheated rear porch. Because the cooktop is a Jenn-Air Grill-Range that requires no hood for venting, the pass-through maintains a view of a corner fireplace that is original to the pre-Revolution-era home. The island creates a barrier between traffic from the back door and the kitchen work triangle, an important consideration in a family with two young children. Off to the side, an informal dining area occupies a tranquil corner convenient to the kitchen.

An unheated porch was enclosed to make room for the kitchen and dining area in this pre-Revolution-era house. The first inhabitants cooked on the corner fireplace.

exhaust hood that would have prevented an open, airy feeling at the island. From the refrigerator, positioned along the counter that forms an L with the sink counter, there are only a few steps to both the sink and the stove.

This arrangement left one end of the kitchen free for a greenhouse breakfast area large enough to hold a table and four chairs; it is here that the family takes breakfast or that the parents entertain another couple for an informal dinner. "We enjoy this plant-filled area so much that we use it a lot," said the woman. "In fact, the whole kitchen is an exciting space to be in."

Much of the excitement, especially for the cook, comes from the surprises tucked behind cupboard doors. To the right of the sink, for example, are three roll-out baskets for storage of vegetables, including potatoes and onions. The next base cabinet, directly across the aisle from the range, has cutlery dividers in the drawers and a lid holder on the door. Under the sink, which has an instant hot water dispenser, there is a towel bar and wastebasket with cover that flips up when the cabinet door is opened. Past the dishwasher lies a corner cabinet with a convenient lazy susan.

Rounding the corner, the L continues with anoth-

er base cabinet with more roll-out baskets for other staples and boxed food storage. Above the counter, seven plastic canister drawers are mounted on the underside of the wall cabinets; these hold herbs, dried peas and beans, and dry cereals. While the main kitchen portion of this L ends with the refrigerator, at the opposite side of the refrigerator there is a tall storage cabinet for items not needed on an everyday basis.

While the counters for the L-shaped portion of the kitchen are champagne-colored plastic laminate, the woman opted for maple butcher block on the double-depth island. "I wasn't worried about the added care everyone says it needs," said the woman. "I don't hesitate to cut on it—I think that develops its character. The point is to have it there and use it." On the range/oven side of the island, the right-hand base cabinet features four tray dividers; to the left, there are a two-shelf base cabinet and another that holds a bottle basket with handle and a pull-out shelf for spices. On the wall above, additional spices are on display in a seven-shelf, shallow, open cupboard.

The reverse side of this island, in what was the former kitchen, houses base cabinets with drawers, shelves, and a pull-out table. A bar sink on this side

52

of the island is appreciated both for pre-dinner conversation (since it keeps guests out of the main work triangle) and for servicing the nearby dining room and library. When needed, the pull-out table acts as extra counter space for mixing drinks, but most of the time it sees use by the children or the woman of the house.

"The table serves for a variety of projects," she related. "It works very well for extra serving for the dining room or as extra counter space when we clear the table after a meal. The kids use it for drawing and its location keeps them out of the way and off the breakfast table. And I use it for my desk work, too."

Much of the woman's desk work stems from a door-to-door fish delivery business she has, so naturally, much of the cooking that goes on here

features fresh fish.

For a lot of her cooking she depends heavily on a microwave oven that is built into a wall cabinet at the end of the sink counter-run nearest the breakfast area. This location makes the microwave handy for rapid warming and for reheating leftovers.

The family's reaction to the new kitchen has been dramatic. "The boys can help out more easily now," reports the woman, "and my husband is starting to enjoy being in the kitchen, too, because it is so open. I thoroughly enjoy spending hours there. It functions extremely well and overall has a very special feeling when you walk in. It feels comfortable, and the beautiful corner fireplace gives it authenticity. Still, the new kitchen is not jarring. It's simply a refreshing note, a contemporary space that blends extremely well with our early house."

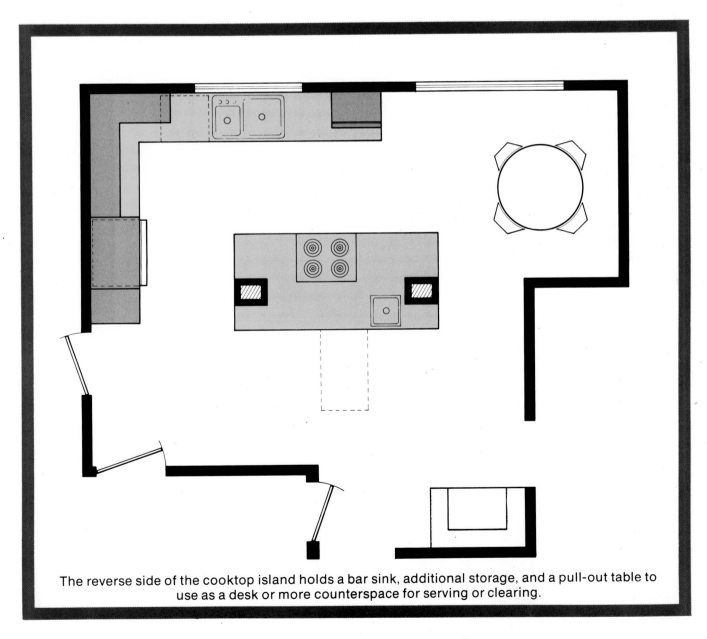

The reverse side of the cooktop island holds a bar sink, additional storage, and a pull-out table to use as a desk or more counterspace for serving or clearing.

Renovated Rowhouse

Rich wood cabinetry and modern appliances transformed the antiquated kitchen that for years occupied this long, narrow space in a Victorian townhouse on Chicago's North Side.

A small corridor kitchen, jam-packed with storage space and every amenity the home cook could desire, is the cooking center of a century-old rowhouse in an elegantly restored Chicago neighborhood. The 8-1/2 by 14-foot space housed nothing more than an antiquated sink, stove and refrigerator when the owners, a working couple, bought the worn-out home in 1968. After a months-long renovation of the entire two-story structure, however, the kitchen emerged along with the rest of the house as a fine example of vivacious contemporary life in a Victorian shell.

The architect who planned the renovation included in his design a rough layout for the kitchen, which was to occupy the same space it had previously. But when the couple went to select cabinets and decided to take advantage of the kitchen planning service that was included in the cabinet price, they learned the early plan could be vastly improved.

"At the time, I was on a gourmet binge," laughed the woman. She was trained as a home economist, though she now works in a different field."I was enjoying entertaining and shopping for the equipment necessary to make a specific dish, so all the paraphernalia posed an interesting puzzle of how to get the most into the limited space available."

In addition to the gourmet cookware the woman had collected, the kitchen also had to house a rapidly expanding cookbook library and include a counter or table at which the couple could have breakfast or coffee and plan menus. Since they love fresh fruits and vegetables "for maximum nutrition," they also requested that counters incorporate a maple butcher block insert where these could be prepared; similarly, bread baking necessitated a smooth surface for kneading dough, so a ceramic counter-saver was a requirement.

When the kitchen designer began to work with the couple, he noted their general suggestions for placement of the various appliances and decided that the most cabinet space could be gained by reversing the locations of a back door and a window that overlooked the back yard. With doorways to the dining room and a hall already consuming valuable wall space, repositioning the back door so it would not create an additional break in counter runs was almost mandatory. With this accomplished, the designer set to work outfitting the cabinets so every square inch would be utilized.

"The sequence of food preparation and storage determines the placement of kitchen equipment and cabinetry," explained the designer. "The logical placement of the sink was near the window, and by making it a double-bowl corner model, there was more counter space left between the sink and the range."

To the left of the sink, between it and the back door, is bar storage, including glassware and liquor bottles on roll-out shelves. This location is handy for mixing drinks, as well as for serving them in the

One side of the remodeled corridor kitchen contains the sink, dishwasher, and double-oven gas stove. Thoughtfully planned counters allow chopping on a maple insert and dough kneading on a ceramic counter-saver.

dining room that lies through a doorway at this end of the kitchen. Since dinner guests frequently congregate in the kitchen for pre-dinner cocktails and conversation, having the bar at one end of the room leaves the other end relatively free for unhampered dinner preparation.

To the right of the sink, knives hang on magnetic strips above the 30-inch-wide butcher block insert, which the woman says "is terrific because I can chop and just sweep the debris right into the disposer." The dishwasher below can be loaded easily from the sink and unloaded into the cabinets above "without having to move a foot," reports the wom-

A growing cookbook collection is housed above a cozy snack bar (left) next to the refrigerator, making the most of a tiny nook. Underneath the counter, curved to extend the surface area without creating a traffic hazard, is additional cabinet storage for note pads, telephone books, and myriad recipes. The microwave oven (right) was a later addition that completes the now ten-year-old appliance lineup; the working couple who uses this small kitchen finds it vital for quick and nutritious food preparation. Ovenware is stored on slide-out shelving below.

an. The designer took advantage of the fact that both she and her husband are tall; instead of soffits, he installed a 25-inch-high row of cabinets above the regular 33-inch-tall wall cabinets. The extra cabinets above keep all the most frequently used dinnerware close to the dishwasher.

On the sink side of the gas, double-oven range, the doors of the upper cabinet are designed to hold small spice jars and tins. Bins in drawers below are compartmented for sugar, flour, bread, and cookies. On the other side of the range, another work center with the ceramic counter-saver can be used as a resting place for hot pans or as additional space for chopping and slicing. Cooking utensils and pots and pans are stored in this area in cabinets that feature adjustable height roll-out drawers, vertical tray dividers, and carousels in corner

units. One shallow drawer here was designed especially for lids.

Facing the U-shape made by the sink/range counter run is a wall with additional cabinetry for foodstuffs and serving dishes, a side-by-side refrigerator, and the eating area the couple wanted. Instead of simply installing a 24-inch-deep straight counter for a snack bar, though, a rounded shelf that protrudes slightly into the room allows enough space underneath for both knee room and 12-inch-deep storage. Part of this undercounter storage is accessible from the edge of the counter; there are even drawers for storing desk items — note pads, pencils, and the telephone book, since the phone hangs on the wall above the table. The rest of this undercounter space can be reached by opening a door that faces the dishwasher. It is here the home economist "keeps my hopes and dreams—the recipes I've wanted to try and haven't." Also down here are cookbooks that have been weeded from the vast collection displayed on open shelves above the table."I cannot get rid of cookbooks," the woman admits. "I adore them."

Though this efficient kitchen was designed with just the couple in mind, their 8-year-old son has usurped his mother's place at the snack bar and breakfasts with his father while she packs the day's lunches. He eagerly joins in for meal preparations and holiday baking. "He does roll-up cookies, makes a mean scrambled egg dish, and can stuff a turkey," said his mother. A favorite dish is pie made from pumpkins the family picks on a Wisconsin farm. "We cook the pumpkin in the microwave and then blend it in the blender and we're through."

The microwave oven was added to the kitchen nearly five years ago after the woman worked with a major manufacturer and "learned firsthand what it did." Indeed, the microwave is a vital appliance for this family, not only because both parents work outside the home but because of the types of foods they prefer. For themselves, the family puts the microwave to work for quick defrosting and for cooking the fresh vegetables they love. And when there's company for dinner, usually six to eight people, the hostess shoos everyone from the kitchen about ten minutes before the first course is served and makes last minute preparations that "couldn't be done without a microwave."

With the microwave, the family feels their kitchen renaissance is as complete as anyone would want. In fact, recently they began renovating another, larger Victorian home, and one of the first persons they turned to for design assistance was their former kitchen designer. "We told him we want the same kitchen all over again," say the owners.

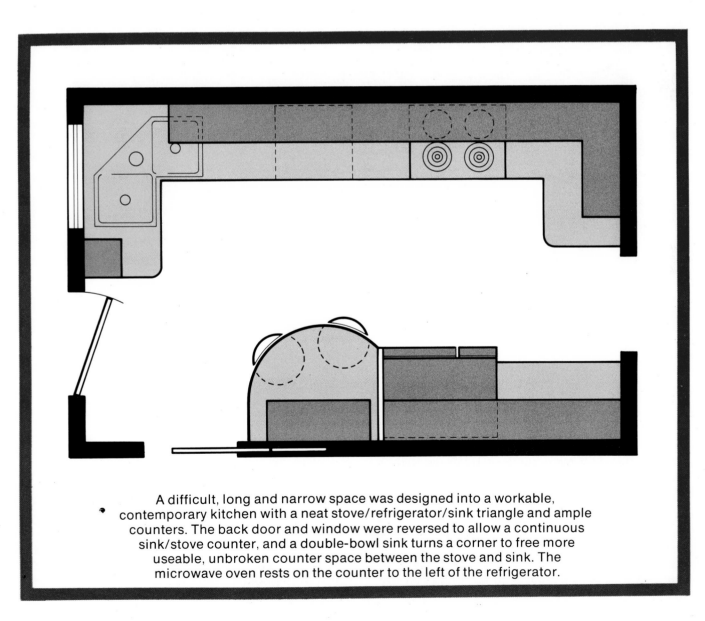

A difficult, long and narrow space was designed into a workable, contemporary kitchen with a neat stove/refrigerator/sink triangle and ample counters. The back door and window were reversed to allow a continuous sink/stove counter, and a double-bowl sink turns a corner to free more useable, unbroken counter space between the stove and sink. The microwave oven rests on the counter to the left of the refrigerator.

A novel cooking/snack bar peninsula opens this previously hemmed-in kitchen.

Redesigned Builder's Model

This kitchen had everything—a trash compactor, instant hot water, dishwasher, waste disposer, and plenty of cabinet space—*before* it was remodeled. It occupied the same space it does now in a 14-room, contemporary ranch-style home in Connecticut, and it was used by the same family. An on-the-go couple in their mid-30s with three children, they had bought the expensive home six years ago when it was brand new. What was wrong?

"The major objection was the closed-in feeling of the space," explained the kitchen designer who was called in to completely remake the kitchen. "The kitchen had dark pine cupboards and was a separate room with no view of the family room. The children, who were pre-schoolers when the family moved in, had grown and were more active and also more frequently underfoot as they went from the back door through the kitchen to the rest of the house. Their mother wanted a new kitchen de-

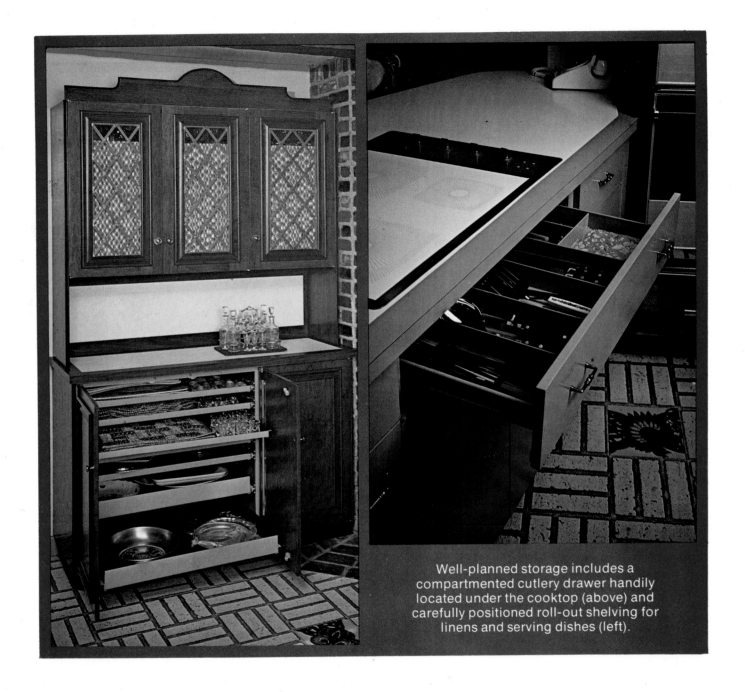

Well-planned storage includes a compartmented cutlery drawer handily located under the cooktop (above) and carefully positioned roll-out shelving for linens and serving dishes (left).

signed so she could watch them playing in the family room or talk to them when they came in without actually having them *in* the kitchen. She wanted to be insulated from all the traffic here.''

In addition to having the kitchen layout redesigned, the woman wanted to upgrade many of the appliances, replace some of them with larger models, and add a microwave oven and warming drawers; she also felt she needed more specialized cabinets with more interior features such as vegetable bins, tray dividers and linen drawers. "This woman is a young, fashionable 'neatnik' who wants everything up-to-date, spotless, and in its place,'' the designer commented. "After six years of using this kitchen, which really was nothing more than a

standard builder's model, she knew exactly how she wanted to change it to suit herself.''

In conjunction with the kitchen remodeling, other rooms in this area of the house were to be revamped. The arrangement of closets in an adjacent "mud room" was totally inadequate and the path from the garage to the kitchen was so circuitous that people had to go through the laundry room when they came in carrying groceries. In short, the whole kitchen wing of the home no longer suited the family's needs.

The first step was to make the working triangle—from sink to range to refrigerator—more compact than before. In the previous kitchen, there was a major appliance or work center on each of the four walls. When the wall between the kitchen and family room was removed and a snack bar peninsula added closer to the remaining U, the kitchen was opened visually but the number of steps needed to move from one area to another was substantially reduced.

In deciding where the sink, range and refrigerator should be positioned, the designer divided the kitchen into three major areas: the preparation area, clean-up area, and cooking and serving area.

In the portion of the kitchen planned for food preparation is the new refrigerator, a 48-inch-wide Sub-Zero. Base cabinets just to the left provide storage for root vegetables, and there is a section of vertical dividers for paper bags and trays. Built-in above is the new microwave oven, placed in this area for quick defrosting or other preliminary cooking. Other cabinets are outfitted with cutlery drawers; bread box drawers for bread, crackers and cookies; and shelves for storage of everyday groceries, to be replenished from a larger storage pantry in the nearby "mud room." Another important addition was under-cabinet lighting.

Turning the corner to the sink wall, which overlooks the landscaped front yard, the preparation area blends into the cleanup area. The corner base cabinet swings out for easy access to salad and mixing bowls, while a cutting board just under the counter slides out, and, overhead there is a swing-out spice unit. Because the cook is unpackaging goods in this portion of the room, the old trash compactor is located here. A can-opener is installed in its own niche in the wall just above the counter. Not only is it convenient for opening canned goods while fixing a meal, but the placement above the counter allows room for tall juice and coffee cans.

At the new sink, which has a new, larger-capacity disposer, the designer reused the instant hot water dispenser and gave the woman two soap dispensers, one of which she uses for soap, the other for hand cream. Cabinets on this wall hold everyday china, making it convenient to unload the new dishwasher or to find a plate when making a sandwich in the preparation area. Paper towels hang from a wall cabinet to the left of the sink, and underneath the sink are a door-mounted basket and a roll-out shelf for cleaning supplies. "There's no fishing around or under sink pipes in this household," the designer observed.

Moving into the cooking and serving area, you see cabinets compartmented for casseroles, cake

A mix of new and reused appliances allows this newly rearranged kitchen to function better.

dishes, and serving platters. Also in keeping with the woman's desire for neatness, an appliance "garage" with sliding doors was built to fit at the rear of the counter and hide the numerous small appliances and canisters that normally clutter a countertop.

Above the new, self-cleaning electric wall ovens there is deep storage for large items such as roasting pans, and below is the warming drawer unit with five stainless steel pans that the previous kitchen did not have. "The owner finds these necessary since her active family has varied schedules," the designer said.

Though the family dines in the family room or dining room when it is time for dinner, they did want an eating area in the kitchen for breakfasts, quick lunches, or coffee. By creating a snack peninsula, rather than using a separate table, they gained additional counter space for a cooktop and more cabinet space below. The base of the angled peninsula conceals four roll-out shelves for pots and pans; one large drawer with cutlery dividers and even a separate section for pot holders; another drawer for silverware, located here to be directly across from the dishwasher and for easy access from the snack bar.

"From this peninsula, the cook is in a command position," the designer noted. "The woman is doing the final tasks at the stove area, and when standing there she can converse with the family already seated at the table. She also can serve right there; in fact, for entertaining this makes an excellent buffet area.

Throughout the blue and green kitchen, base cabinets are Capri blue, textured steel, which hides fingerprints, and wall cabinets are dark-stained pecan wood with a Capri blue molding. Their interior designer carried the blue onto the white, plastic laminate counter with a 2-1/2 inch wide custom border and finished the floor in a white, brick-patterned vinyl tile with inserts that echo the pattern of the window shade.

Is the family happy with its shiny new kitchen? The kitchen designer reports that breaking down the regimentation of four walls in this part of the house has made them realize the limitations of the home elsewhere, and now they are rethinking the design of the entire structure. "Where before they had a room, room, room," he said, "they now want area, area, area." Indeed, the kitchen has become an open, airy space that prompts the lady of the house to rhapsodize, "Now I smile when I cook."

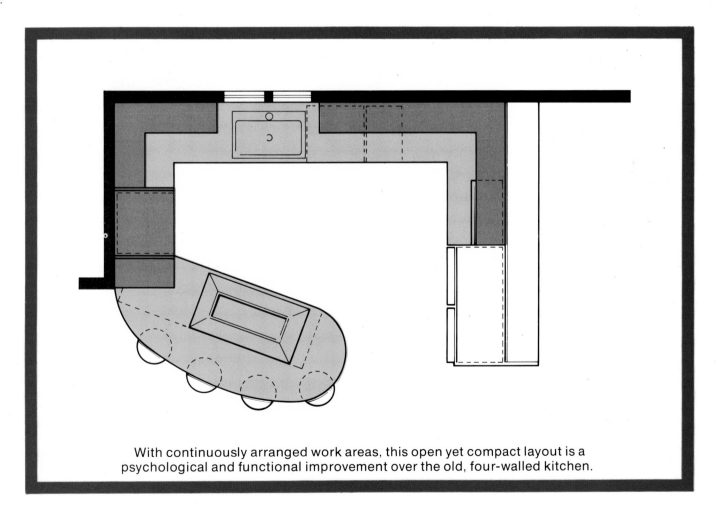

With continuously arranged work areas, this open yet compact layout is a psychological and functional improvement over the old, four-walled kitchen.

This highly imaginative arrangement of a kitchen's essentials bears no relation to the previous layout.

A Habitable High~Rise

Since kitchens in high-rise condominium buildings are designed to appeal to a wide range of potential buyers, seldom does one find an existing condominium kitchen that has real character or fits unique needs. The kitchen shown here belongs to a couple who bought their Chicago unit for reasons other than the kitchen that this one replaced. As soon as they closed the deal, they phoned the designer who had created a dream kitchen in their suburban house years earlier. "They wanted that same design in half the space," the designer recalled.

Though all he could do was give them half their suburban kitchen, the result still represented a vast improvement over the thoughtless arrangement that had existed in the condominium previously. The best that could be said for the windowless, 9-1/2 by 11 foot kitchen was that everything in it was new. Therefore, the designer decided to retain all the appliances except the refrigerator, which the owners wanted upgraded to a side-by-side model with a drink dispenser in one door. In addition to the existing appliances, though, the couple also wanted a warming drawer, an amenity they had found useful in their previous home for keeping foods warm for a late dinner. The cabinetry, a style the designer termed "junk," was scrapped.

The owners were seeking a more open feeling between an adjoining dinette and the kitchen, and they also wanted a better sink/range/refrigerator triangle. As it stood, the refrigerator was off by itself at one end of the room in a niche created by concealed heat ducts.

The designer began by removing the upper portion of part of the wall that separated the dinette and kitchen. By matching the wall height with that of the kitchen counters, he immediately created a sense that the two rooms were intimately related. Tearing out this wall, however, meant that the range had to be moved. Its new location, directly across the length of the room, puts the range next to a doorway that is not only a safety hazard but also visually unattractive when viewed from the front door. The designer points out, however, that most traffic goes through the dinette entrance and that there are no young children to worry about. To conceal most of the range from the front hall, he is planning to fabricate a side panel that matches the kitchen's raised-panel oak cabinetry.

To accentuate the view out the kitchen into the dinette, he moved the sink from its previous spot at the middle of a long counter to the end of the counter nearest the new opening. Anyone working at the sink now has to turn only slightly to face away from a wall and out the kitchen.

When determining a place for the sink, the designer decided to turn it on the diagonal to cut the corner formed where the old sink counter and new half-wall counter meet. Doing so achieved a landing and serving space to the left of the sink for dishes and foods passed between the kitchen and dinette, and keeping the sink turned from the long counter allowed the designer to maximize that counter's length. In addition, placing the sink at the end of the room not only created a long counter for food preparation, but it also brought the sink closer to the refrigerator, which had found a new home at the opposite end of the same wall against which it had started. Part of the previous doorway to the dinette had to be rebuilt to hide the side of the refrigerator facing the dining room.

The niche previously occupied by the refrigerator now contains a storage pantry that has rows of shelves on its doors as well as inside, a truly indispensable unit in a small kitchen with little storage space. Other interior cabinet features include slide-out shelves, corner swing-out units, a built-in spice rack, lazy susans, a bread drawer, and compartments for trays and cutlery.

To enhance the feeling of openness, the sense that this kitchen is just a part of a much larger space, the designer selected the same clay paving tiles found in the front entry hall for the kitchen and dining area, too. The earth tones in the tile are echoed in the kitchen's butcher block plastic lami-

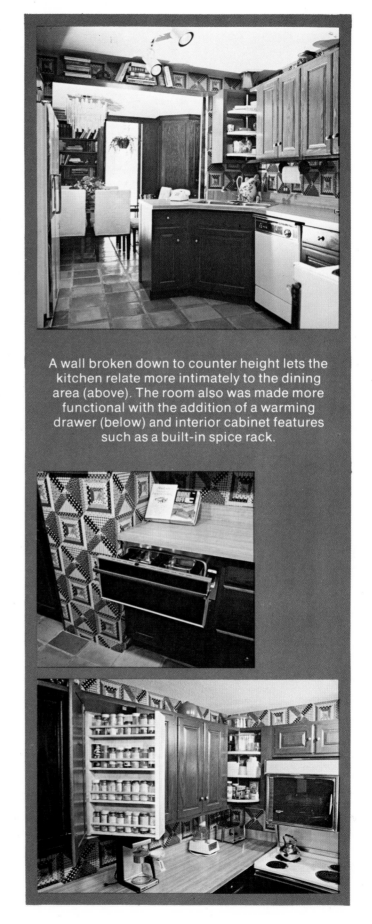

A wall broken down to counter height lets the kitchen relate more intimately to the dining area (above). The room also was made more functional with the addition of a warming drawer (below) and interior cabinet features such as a built-in spice rack.

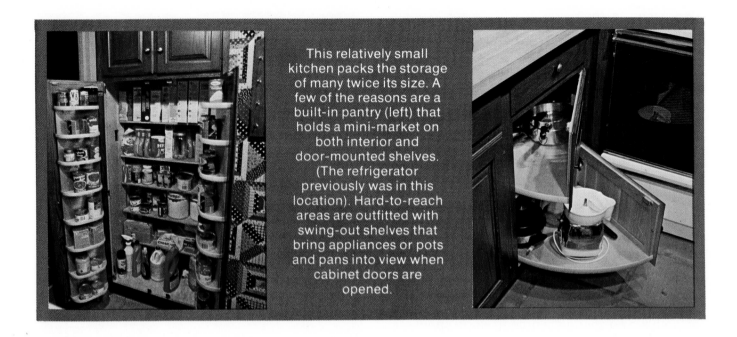

This relatively small kitchen packs the storage of many twice its size. A few of the reasons are a built-in pantry (left) that holds a mini-market on both interior and door-mounted shelves. (The refrigerator previously was in this location). Hard-to-reach areas are outfitted with swing-out shelves that bring appliances or pots and pans into view when cabinet doors are opened.

nate counter tops and in the patchwork-design wallcovering. A touch of modern in this country-style kitchen is achieved via the track lighting mounted on the ceiling. The earlier kitchen had one center ceiling fixture, "no different than kitchens had 50 years ago," the designer commented, "proving that buying a new home doesn't mean you'll get a modern kitchen."

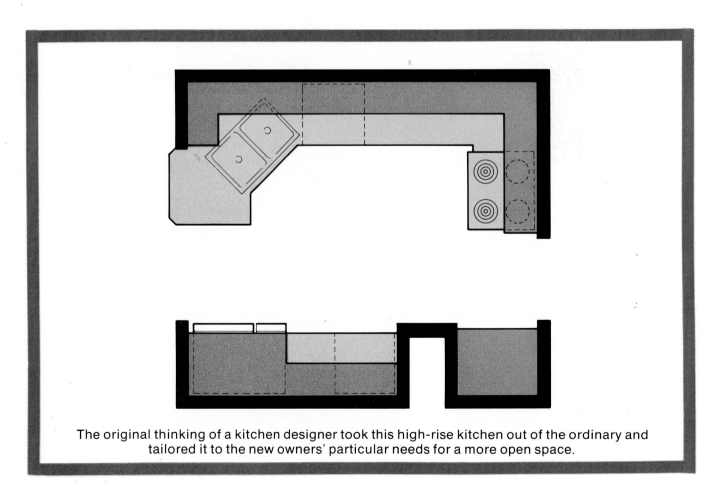

The original thinking of a kitchen designer took this high-rise kitchen out of the ordinary and tailored it to the new owners' particular needs for a more open space.

Planning And Designing Your Own Kitchen

Designing your own kitchen is a game of inches. You will be buying and installing a good number of cabinets and appliances—all of which have specific sizes—and there is no room for error. The first step in planning and designing a kitchen, therefore, is to measure completely and accurately the space available and to record your measurements on paper.

Use a 6-foot folding carpenter's rule for maximum accuracy when measuring. Never use a household yardstick, and avoid retractable steel tape measures. The yardstick is too short, and the tape can sag or slip.

Measure all room dimensions to within 1/16 inch, and record each measurement as accurately as possible. Remember, even a very slight error can spell major difficulties later on. If the space you think can accommodate 120 inches of cabinets and appliances turns out to be no more than 119-1/2 inches, for example, your original plan may prove unfeasible.

Before you actually start taking measurements, make a rough outline of the entire room on a grid sheet. Then start at one corner and measure the distance from the corner to the window trim at a height of 36 inches above the floor (the height of the countertop). Proceed by measuring from the outside of the window trim on one side of the window to the outside of the window trim on the other, from that trim to the door trim, and so forth, recording each measurement accurately on the grid. Write each measurement down as you go along, without trying to add them up. Adding them up as you go along diverts your attention and leads to errors. Be sure to note all obstacles—e.g., chimney offsets, radiators, etc.—on the grid sheet. Also indicate on your sketch the location of all existing electrical outlets, light switches, and lighting fixtures.

As you finish a wall, add up all the measurements. Then make another overall measurement to check your addition. If you discover any discrepancy, start all over again.

Now indicate on the sketch where all doors lead, the door and windowsill heights, and the height from the windowsill to the top of window trim. Also measure and indicate the height of the ceilings, from floor to ceiling, and the height and depth of the existing soffit (the extended wall above the upper cabinets); soffit

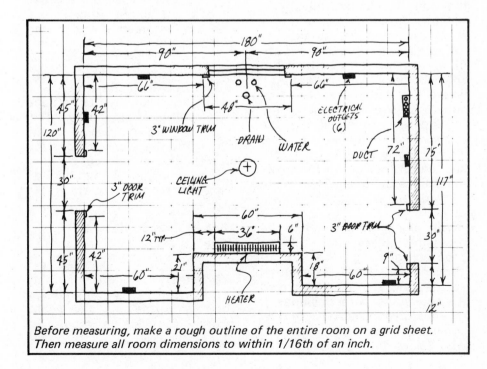

Before measuring, make a rough outline of the entire room on a grid sheet. Then measure all room dimensions to within 1/16th of an inch.

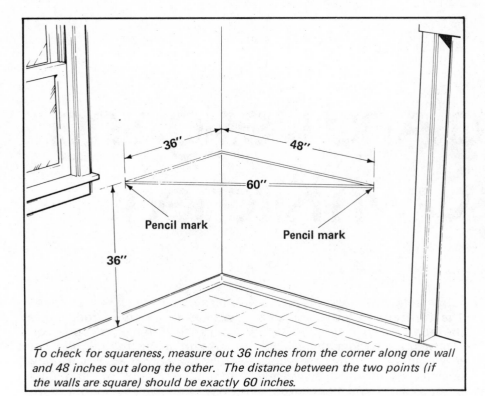

To check for squareness, measure out 36 inches from the corner along one wall and 48 inches out along the other. The distance between the two points (if the walls are square) should be exactly 60 inches.

height should be measured from the floor to the soffit.

Mark the grid sketch for the drain location and the incoming water lines, but keep in mind that you can move the sink location one way or the other; all you have to do is turn and extend the drain trap (it need not go straight into the wall) and then extend the incoming water lines to the faucet.

It is essential that you check the squareness of the room's corners. Corners are seldom perfectly square, and discrepancies in squareness must be allowed for when designing the layout of the kitchen. At a height of 36 inches above the floor, measure precisely 3 feet out from the corner along one wall and 4 feet out from the corner along the other. Make a pencil mark at each point, and then measure the direct distance between the two points (the hypotenuse of what is supposed to be a right triangle). The distance should be exactly 5 feet. If it is less than 5 feet, then the angle between the two walls is less than 90 degrees. If the distance is greater than 5 feet,

then the angle is more than 90 degrees. Make a note of any lack of squareness so that your countertop can be ordered or cut to match the actual shape of the corner.

Be sure to draw the entire room on your grid sheet, not just the walls you think will be involved in your kitchen installation. As you get into designing your kitchen, the distances to other walls or parts of the room will become quite important. And where you find corners out of square, be sure to note both the distance along the wall and the distance 24 inches out from the wall; you will have to plan your kitchen for the shorter measurement since the cabinets won't fit if sized for the longer measurement.

With an accurate sketch of the room in front of you, you can proceed to design the kind of kitchen you want. Remember, you need not replace the old with the new in the same positions. If that old kitchen was designed by someone who never met you, who knew nothing about your

family or your social habits and needs, it is quite likely a bad design for your family. You don't want to perpetuate a bad design. Analyze your needs, and let those needs be your guide for the new kitchen.

Start At The Window

You have to start somewhere, and the best place is usually the window. Since most home-owners want the sink under the window, that is where the plumbing lines generally are located. Thus, one element is in place already. If you want to reserve the window for an eating area, you can move the plumbing lines, but doing so can get expensive and complicated and should be avoided unless you're willing to add several hundred dollars to your costs.

Assuming that the plumbing lines will stay where they are, you should start thinking about storage space and counter work space. You must provide for enough of both, and you must position both in the right places.

The idea behind efficient storage is to store everything at the point of first use. That means, for example, that dinner dishes should be stored as close as possible to the dining area where they are first used. If that is impractical, they should be stored at the point of last use—i.e., near the dishwasher and sink.

When looking at the things you must store, think about basic activity centers of the kitchen. The following list of items to be stored and the best locations for storing them should be of some help when planning a kitchen for maximum storage efficiency.

- Utensils. The tools of the kitchen include pots and pans, cutlery, baking dishes, etc. They are best stored near the range.

- Dinnerware. Store fine china in or near a separate dining room; store the everyday dishes near the eat-in kitchen area.

- Food. Place packaged,

canned and bottled groceries (generally plan on a week's supply) in cabinets, ideally in a tall pantry cabinet with revolving or swing-out shelves. Fresh perishables go in a refrigerator and/or freezer, except for potatoes, onions and the like, which should be stored in bins or drawers. All food storage areas should be as near as possible to the food preparation center.

● Cleaning Supplies. Soaps, detergents, and cleaning implements generally go in an under-the-sink cabinet, while bigger items such as mops and brooms can go in a tall utility cabinet; the utility cabinet need not be located in the kitchen as long as it is fairly handy.

● Kitchen Linens, Paper Goods, Place Mats, etc. It's a good idea to get these items out of the way. A paper caddy with paper towels, aluminum foil and plastic wrap can be recessed into a wall near the food preparation or cleanup center. Linens should be placed in a drawer. All of these items, though, should be stored near the point of first use.

● Small Appliances. As manufacturers produce and promote more highly specialized appliances (to make a hamburger, to make a pizza, to pop corn, to broil, to open cans, to toast, to mix, etc.), storing these devices in the kitchen gets to be more and more of a problem. A severe case of countertop clutter is a common kitchen malaise these days. One answer is to build in as many small appliances as you can. There are toasters and can openers that can be recessed into the wall. There are two brands of mixing centers, Ronson and NuTone, that have a base built into the countertop with separate attachments for food processing, mixing, blending, meat grinding, knife sharpening, can opening, ice crushing, fruit squeezing and other functions. The advantage is that all of these attachments can be stored in one cabinet beneath the counter, leaving nothing but a metal plate occupying precious countertop space.

● Trash. Although trash quickly exits the room, you must plan a storage place for it while you are working in the kitchen. A trash compactor can be particularly valuable for a large family, especially if the unit can be built in where a cabinet would otherwise go. Most compactors take up the space of a 15-inch base cabinet, although one brand—the Waste King—can fit in a 12-inch space.

The Activity Centers

Storage areas, combined with countertop work space and appliances, form the activity centers of the kitchen: the sink, the range or cooktop, the refrigerator/freezer, the food preparation center, and the serving center.

The sink area includes a minimum of 30 inches of counter space to the right of the sink and 24 inches to the left (for right-handed persons), dishwasher adjacent (usually on the left), disposer under the sink, and compactor on the right. A double-bowl sink is very handy—even when the sink area includes a dishwasher—if space permits. This area should contain storage facilities for foods that need washing and for fruits and vegetables that don't go into the refrigerator. Cabinets with roll-out bins or shelves are ideal for such purposes. While most cooking pots and pans belong near the range, sauce pans and the coffeepot go best in the sink center.

The range or cooktop area should include at least 18 inches of counter space on either side; a ventilating hood and fan above; and storage for pots, pans, seasonings, and cooking utensils. In cases where the cooktop and oven are separate, allow 15 inches of countertop space on the working side of the oven.

The refrigerator/freezer area should allow a minimum counter work space on the door-opening side of 18 inches. The popular side-by-side refrigerator/freez-

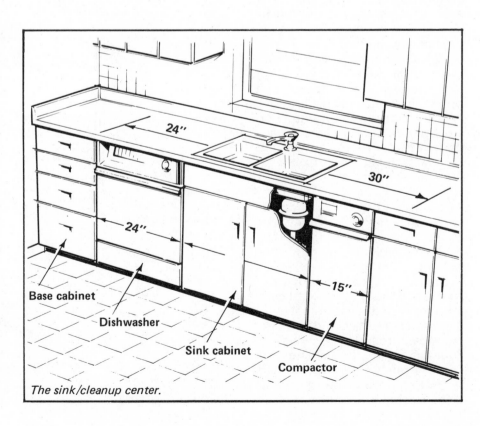

The sink/cleanup center.

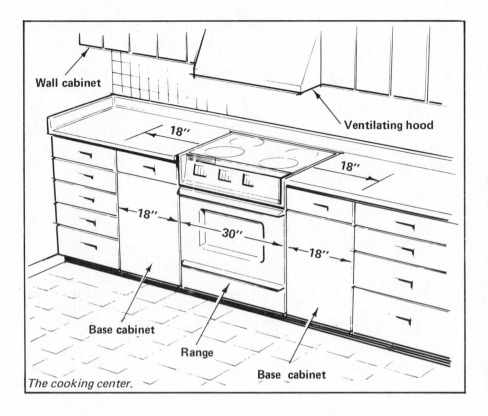

Wall cabinet

Ventilating hood

18"

18"

18"

30"

18"

Base cabinet

Range

Base cabinet

The cooking center.

sink can be part of the 36 inches needed for a food preparation center.

Planning The Kitchen Layout

Once the sink is placed, you know how to go about supplying the storage and counter needs for it. You know that the range goes to the left of the sink and that the refrigerator goes to its right. You also know the storage and counter needs of these two activity centers.

Or do you? Not quite. We have been talking in averages and minimums. In your particular case, you might need more countertop or more storage space. Remember, in your kitchen you have to reach compromises between what you need, what you would like, and the space available. The way you resolve these opposing factors is what makes the kitchen uniquely yours.

You should always keep in mind, though, that you want to end up with a work triangle of not

ers defeat this design principle because the refrigerator side is always on the right, with the freezer side on the left. Since the door-swing is a short arc, however, the side-by-side unit seldom presents any serious interference problems. The refrigerator and freezer doors should open more than 90 degrees so that crispers and shelves can be easily removed. The refrigerator is the hub of the food storage center, so kitchen planners try to incorporate other food storage facilities—e.g., base cabinets or a pantry cabinet—close by.

The food preparation center requires at least 36 inches of counter space, generally between the sink and range or between the sink and refrigerator.

The serving center is usually positioned near the cooking center; ideally, it should be between the cooking center and the eating area. It requires 30 inches of counter space for serving; for keeping ready-to-eat foods; and for storing trays, platters, serving dishes, napkins and the like.

Note that you can combine many counter space requirements. For example, the 30 inches needed to the right of the

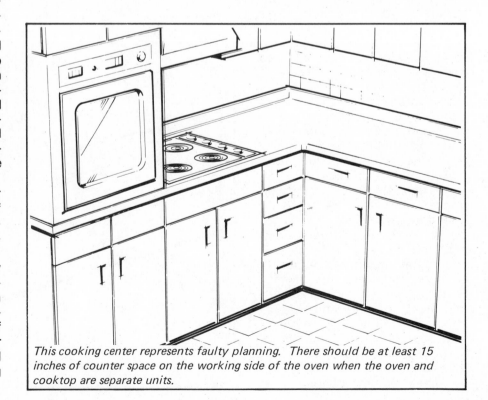

This cooking center represents faulty planning. There should be at least 15 inches of counter space on the working side of the oven when the oven and cooktop are separate units.

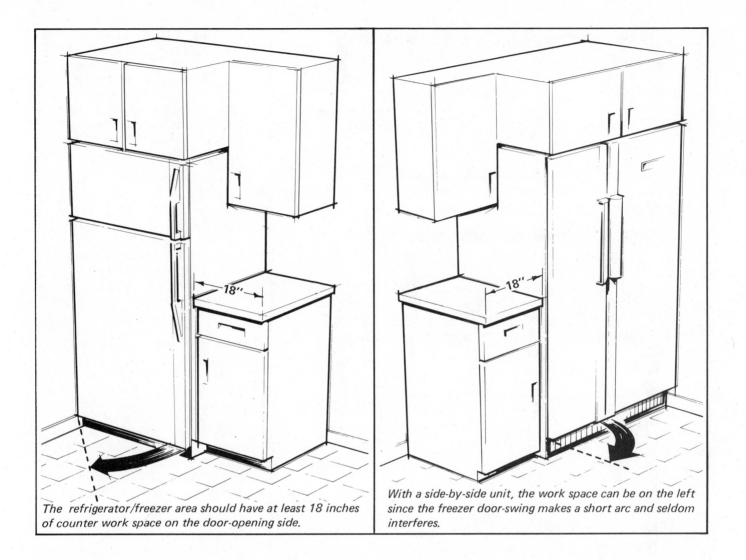

The refrigerator/freezer area should have at least 18 inches of counter work space on the door-opening side.

With a side-by-side unit, the work space can be on the left since the freezer door-swing makes a short arc and seldom interferes.

less than 12 feet and not more than 22 feet. The work triangle is, quite simply, the straight-line distance between the center fronts of the sink and range, range and refrigerator, and refrigerator and sink. No two of the basic activity centers in a kitchen should be less than 4 feet apart nor greater than 9 feet apart. The following distances are considered ideal: sink to range—4 to 6 feet; range to refrigerator—4 to 9 feet; refrigerator to sink—4 to 7 feet. There are several kitchen layouts that will fulfill these requirements.

The one-wall kitchen is the simplest possible kitchen layout. Obviously, there'll be no work triangle when the entire kitchen is along one wall. The one-wall layout can provide ample storage and work space, but in doing so it usually puts too much distance between the work centers on the flanks. A single person or a couple might be able to tolerate a one-wall kitchen. But generally, it is not a good kitchen, and almost never is it a desirable one.

The corridor kitchen that is open on both ends, permitting traffic to cross two legs of the work triangle, is a kitchen layout to be avoided. A closed corridor, on the other hand, can be very

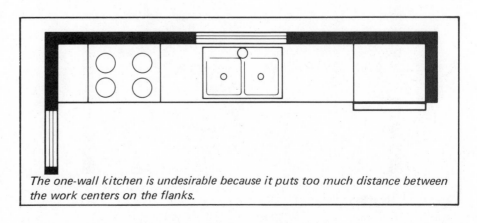

The one-wall kitchen is undesirable because it puts too much distance between the work centers on the flanks.

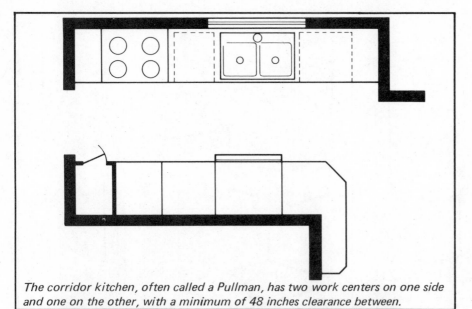

The corridor kitchen, often called a Pullman, has two work centers on one side and one on the other, with a minimum of 48 inches clearance between.

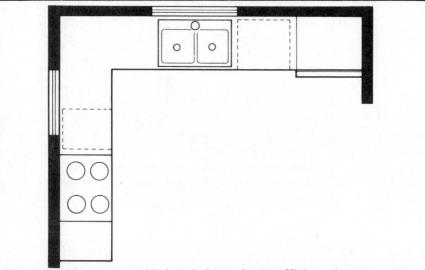

The L-shape is a common kitchen design and quite efficient where space is limited and no doorways intervene.

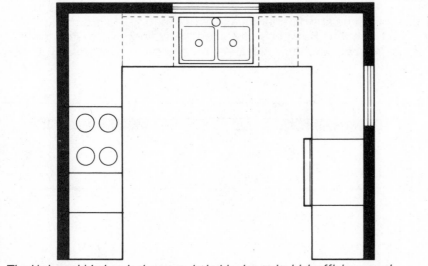

The U-shaped kitchen is the most desirable due to its high efficiency and maximum storage.

efficient. Often called a "Pullman" kitchen, the corridor has two work centers on one side, one on the other, and a minimum of 48 inches clearance in between. Since cabinets and appliances take up 2 feet on either wall, a corridor layout requires a kitchen that is at least 8 feet wide.

The L-shaped kitchen is quite common and makes for a very efficient work triangle open to other activities such as eating and recreation. The two legs of the L are on adjacent walls with no intervening doorways. The layout works well where space is limited; where there is a great deal of space, an island can be added or a peninsula extended inward on either leg to maximize efficiency.

The U-shaped kitchen is the most efficient, provides the most storage, and is the most desirable. The kitchen is arranged on three adjacent walls with a work center on each wall; often, the U can open onto eating or recreation areas or other activities. If an island or peninsula is added to an L-shaped kitchen, the layout can quickly be altered to the preferable U-shaped design.

A door within an L or U layout transforms those kitchens into what is called a broken L or a broken U. Such broken layouts usually suffer a loss of efficiency due to traffic.

Designing Safety Into The Kitchen

A great many potentially hazardous activities take place in the kitchen. In addition to cutting and chopping and grinding and slicing, people in the kitchen are often carrying hot items, probing into drawers and cabinets, and operating appliances.

All this means that the kitchen can be a place where accidents happen. Although most accidents are attributable to human carelessness, the kitchen itself can be designed so as to make the probability of accidents far less likely and to reduce the severity of the accidents when they do occur.

The key to safety in the kitchen is to maximize efficiency and to minimize potential hazards. Here are some guidelines.

1. Make sure that your kitchen offers an efficient and effective work triangle. This means that the total distance from sink to range to refrigerator should not be less than 12 feet nor more than 22 feet. Specifically, the various work areas should not be closer than 4 feet nor farther than 9 feet from one another. Less distance means you are too cramped, more means you must constantly take extra tiring steps.

2. Make sure your kitchen is well lighted, with sufficient general and task lighting.

3. Make sure your kitchen offers ample storage space and that access to the items stored poses no danger. Shelf space higher than 72 inches above the floor can present a hazard because a stool or ladder is generally required to reach things stored there.

4. Make sure you have ample counter space, including the proper amount of work space alongside the range and refrigerator. Otherwise, you will be doing too much transporting of hot pots and cold foods.

5. Minimize the number of sharp corners in your kitchen. Square corners on island or peninsula tops are hazardous to hips and hands, and therefore they should be rounded.

6. Vent hoods should be at least 56 inches above the floor and not protrude more than 18 inches from the wall. A hood that protrudes more than 18 inches should be moved slightly higher. If a vent hood needs to be more than 60 inches above the floor (for instance, if the cook is much taller than 6 feet), a higher powered vent fan will be needed to compensate for the loss in venting efficiency.

7. Avoid the exasperation of a

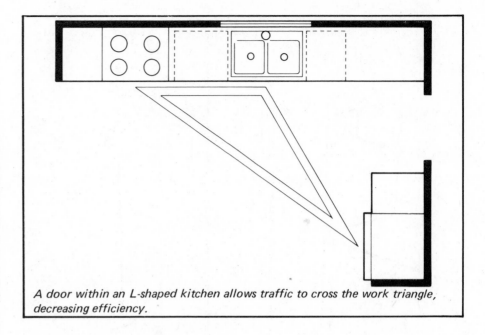
A door within an L-shaped kitchen allows traffic to cross the work triangle, decreasing efficiency.

refrigerator door that does not open into the work triangle; of oven or other appliance doors that block doorways or bump each other when opened; of appliances placed too close together or too close to either a wall or corner so that the action of doors or drawers is inhibited.

8. When selecting a new range and positioning it in the kitchen, consider the fire and burn hazard. You should not be forced to reach over steaming pots to reach the controls, and the burners should be far enough from window curtains and combustible wall coverings.

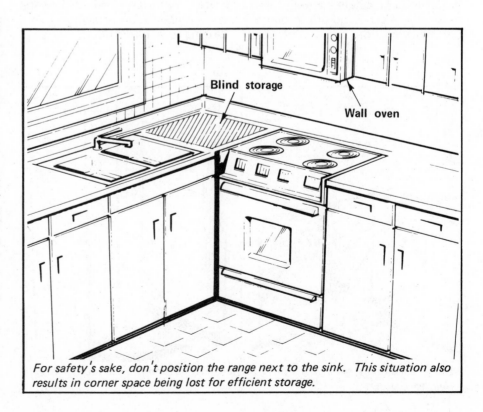
Blind storage

Wall oven

For safety's sake, don't position the range next to the sink. This situation also results in corner space being lost for efficient storage.

Refrigerator and wall oven each need separate counter space and therefore should not be placed next to each other.

8. Garbage disposers must be handled with caution. Although batch-feed models usually require that a cover be put in place before operation can occur, insertion of a hand has been known to activate the batch-feed type. Continuous-feed disposers are activated by a switch. You can have a batch-feed disposer

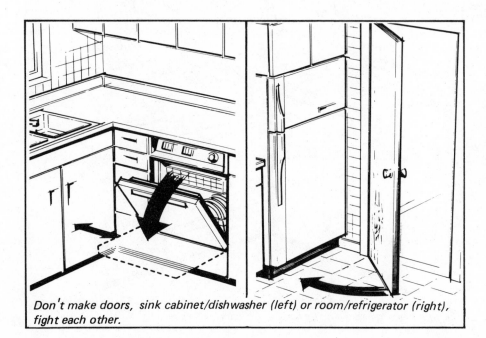

Don't make doors, sink cabinet/dishwasher (left) or room/refrigerator (right), fight each other.

turned into a switch-operated unit for safety; if you do so, be sure to position the switch at least 6 feet from the disposer for maximum safety. Of course, the same distance between switch and disposer applies to continuous-feed units.

How To Plan A One-Wall Kitchen

You don't have many choices regarding appliance placement in a one-wall kitchen, but you can put some flair into the layout.

The room should be a minimum of 14-3/4 feet long and 5 feet wide to conform with basic planning principles on counter space and appliance placement. A kitchen with at least those minimum dimensions allows for a sink area of 33 inches in the center; 36 inches of counter to the right of the sink as a food preparation area; 36 inches to the right of that area for the refrigerator; 24 inches for the dishwasher to the left of the sink; 30 inches for the range to the left of the dishwasher; and then 18 inches of counter space for work space and safety to the left of the range. The counters and appliances will protrude 24 inches from the wall, and you should allow at least another 36 inches (and that is truly a minimum) for movement.

The work triangle in this one-wall kitchen consists of a straight line measuring from the refrigerator at one end to the range at the other. This distance should not be extended any more than necessary even if the kitchen is longer than the one described. Extending the work "triangle" merely adds extra steps, and the amount of counter space provided in the example above is certainly ample.

If the room is smaller than the minimum, design principles go out the window and you must do the best you can. Fortunately, manufacturers of kitchen products offer several items to the person who must plan a one-wall layout in a room of less-

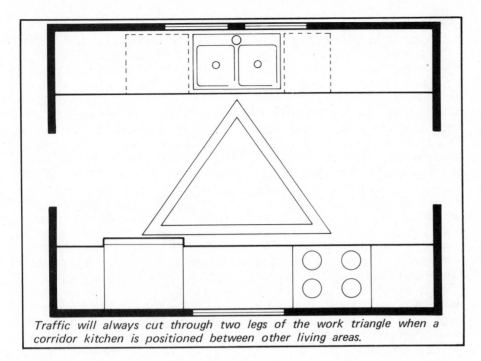

Traffic will always cut through two legs of the work triangle when a corridor kitchen is positioned between other living areas.

can consider several options for increasing counter and storage space. Since wall cabinets are only 12 inches deep compared with 24-inch deep base cabinets, you could install a run of wall cabinets along the opposite wall in a room that is, say, 6 feet wide. Such cabinets can be ordered with the toekick, or they can be set on 2x4's recessed 4 inches and painted black. If additional work space is required, this run of wall cabinets can be topped with a countertop 13 or more inches deep. If you need storage space more than the counter space, you can either stack the standard wall cabinets to reach all the way to the ceiling or put in high (84-inch) utility and pantry cabinets that are no deeper than the wall cabinets.

than-minimum dimensions.

You can buy a compact kitchen—sometimes called a unit kitchen—that comes all in one piece. Compact kitchens are made of steel and are available in various colors. Frequently found in hotels or resort apartments, they combine a small under-counter refrigerator and a small sink with a small cooktop (usually two burners) that has a small oven underneath. They range in size from as little as 2 feet (acceptable only for a vacation home or as an auxiliary kitchen in, say, a recreation room) up to 6 feet and more. The all-in-one compact kitchen is not the only solution, however. There are a good many space-saving products that can help in a conventional kitchen that must be squeezed into a room of limited dimensions.

Modern Maid makes a combination "Cook and Clean Center," which in a 30-inch space includes a cooktop with a dishwasher underneath and an eye-level oven above. General Electric makes a dishwasher that will fit under a shallow (6-inch bowl) sink. Ranges and refrigerators are also available in nar-

rower-than-standard dimensions.

If the room is wider than 5 feet but narrower than the 8 feet required for a corridor kitchen, you

How To Plan
A Corridor Kitchen

The corridor kitchen utilizes the two opposing walls. It is easy to

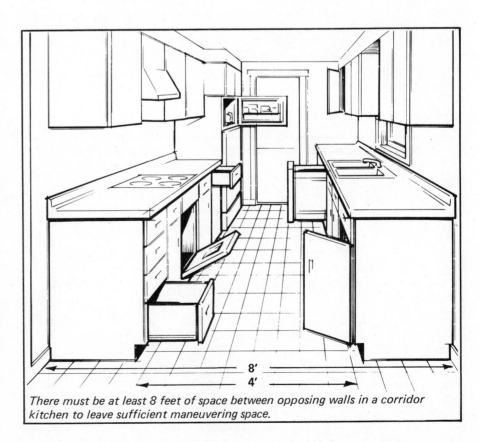

There must be at least 8 feet of space between opposing walls in a corridor kitchen to leave sufficient maneuvering space.

install because there are no corners, and since it results in a maximum of counter space with a minimum of floor space, it is extremely efficient in terms of space utilization. It requires at least 8 feet of space between opposing walls, which leaves 4 feet of maneuvering space after the cabinets and appliances are installed.

If the corridor is positioned between other living areas of the home, a problem will exist with through traffic. Traffic will always cut through two legs of the work triangle, an unavoidable defect in this kitchen design that simply must be tolerated.

If the corridor is a cul-de-sac with only one opening, the traffic problem will be lessened. With an eating or hobby area at the far end, however, the traffic problem will appear once again.

If the corridor is more than 10 feet wide, you can solve any traffic problems by creating an island kitchen. The sink and refrigerator—with their countertop work spaces—would go on one wall, the range would be placed in an island (generally opposite the sink), and approximately 4 feet of maneuvering area would remain in between. With such an arrangement, it would be best to have at least 2 feet of counter

space on either side of the range; assuming that you choose the popular 30-inch range, the island should therefore be 78 inches long and 24 inches deep. Standard base cabinets on either side of the range would provide valuable storage space, and you could use regular wall paneling to cover the back of the range since it would be exposed to traffic. As you might expect, extending utility lines to the range-equipped island could prove quite costly.

In any corridor kitchen, you should try to avoid placing the range and the refrigerator opposite each other. Situations in which it is necessary to have the oven door and the refrigerator door open at the same time could prove annoying.

How To Plan An L-Shape Kitchen

An L-shape kitchen involves turning a corner, and therefore it will normally be a little more expensive than a corridor design. It is a very popular layout, can be very efficient, and gives considerable latitude in appliance placement. Although an L-shape won't necessarily provide any more storage or work space than

a corridor design, it does succeed in protecting the work triangle from cross-traffic.

The actual L-shape can be derived from two adjacent walls, or it can be formed by extending a peninsula out from a wall. A peninsula is often used when the room is large, especially when it can also function as a divider between the kitchen area and an eating or family activity area.

For efficiency and the saving of many thousands of steps, plan the appliances and work spaces so that they run sequentially from refrigerator to sink to range to serving area. The refrigerator usually goes against a wall at one end of the L.

The problem of turning the corner introduces opportunities for different design elements, some of which can waste space. The easy and cheapest way to turn the corner is with a blind base cabinet and a blind wall cabinet. A blind cabinet is one that has an unfinished part that butts against the side of the cabinet already in place. The butted area can vary by several inches—helpful in compensating for measuring mistakes. Unfortunately, there always will be a blind corner walled off from you by the cabinet walls.

In a blind base cabinet, you can get semi-circular shelves that are attached to the cabinet door and come out to you when you open the door. Such shelves are not available in a blind wall cabinet.

A better answer is frequently a Lazy Susan corner cabinet, available for base and wall. Some of these units have a corner door that opens to expose Lazy Susan shelves, while others have a pie-cut in the shelving to which doors are attached to form the corner. A push on the door in either direction spins the entire assembly around.

Another way to turn a corner is to design the sink or, less frequently, one of the appliances into the corner at an angle. Some double-bowl sinks are made in a pie-cut corner configuration,

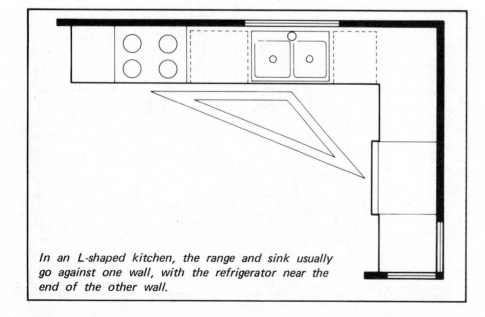

In an L-shaped kitchen, the range and sink usually go against one wall, with the refrigerator near the end of the other wall.

How To Turn A Corner

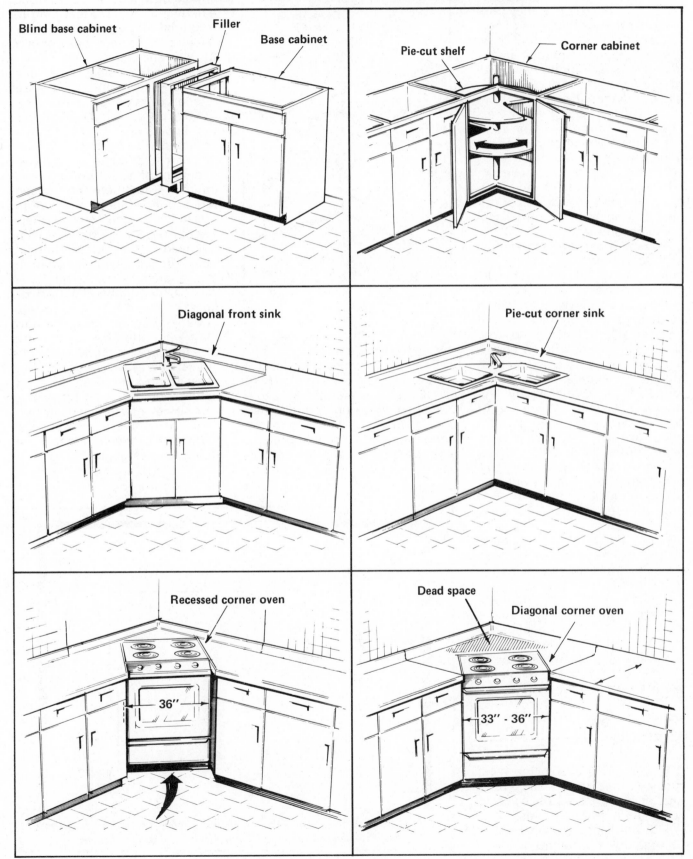

Blind base cabinet · Filler · Base cabinet

Pie-cut shelf · Corner cabinet

Diagonal front sink

Pie-cut corner sink

Recessed corner oven — 36"

Dead space · Diagonal corner oven — 33" - 36"

with one bowl going on either side of the corner.

The main disadvantage to corner installations is that they consume a great deal of wall space. For example, a range that is 30 inches wide requires 45-1/4 inches of space along each wall of the corner. A 33-inch sink, placed diagonally, requires at least 42 inches along either wall. In addition, the space in the cabinet beneath is limited in its usefulness because you can't reach all the way into it. This space can be utilized quite effectively, however, for sacks of potatoes or onions or dog food, or for waste container storage.

Assuming average appliances, a typical L kitchen would require—from left to right—36 inches for the refrigerator; 24 inches for the dishwasher (which automatically means 24 inches of countertop); 33 inches for the sink; 18 inches of counter before turning the corner; another 18 inches of counter before the range; then 30 inches for the range; and a final 18 inches of counter beyond the range. If a built-in oven and cooktop were being used, the cooktop could go in the same place as the complete range but there would be no good place for the wall oven until after the full run were complete. In other words, the wall oven would go at the opposite end from the refrigerator, and thus add another 24 to 30 inches to the layout.

Try to avoid the tendency—very common with L-shape kitchens—to crowd appliances close to the interior corner. Crowding almost always leads to future unhappiness with the newly designed kitchen.

How To Plan A U-Shape Kitchen

A U-shape is the best, the most efficient, and the most popular kitchen design. It adapts easily to large and small rooms, and —with the basic appliances distributed on its base and two legs

Avoid crowding appliances into the L-shaped kitchen's interior corner.

—it shortens the distances between the work centers.

The kitchen must be at least 8 feet wide at the base of the U (10 or 12 feet is preferable to avoid cramped working conditions), and each leg of the U must be long enough to accommodate a major appliance and the associated work space. A leg that will accommodate a refrigerator should be at least 4-1/2 feet long; a minimum of 5-1/2 feet long for a 30-inch range; and no less than 6 feet for the leg that contains the sink and dishwasher.

These dimensions are minimums, and while a U-shape kitchen of minimum dimensions permits unrestricted operation of the appliances, it results in a cramped working area. For an efficient work triangle, try to have a minimum of 4 feet up to a maximum of 8 feet between the centers of the fronts of any two appliances. Since the U-shape works well in large kitchens without making the work triangle too long, kitchen designers often install a diagonal sink, range, or wall oven at the two interior corners.

Many U-shape kitchens have long legs, often flaring out into an eating area and often with one leg serving as a divider from another living area. Frequently, an eating counter is incorporated on one side of a long leg/divider.

When one of the legs serves as a divider between kitchen and dining or living room, the cabi-

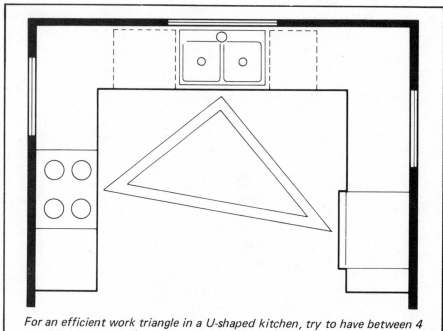
For an efficient work triangle in a U-shaped kitchen, try to have between 4 and 8 feet between the centers of the fronts of any two appliances.

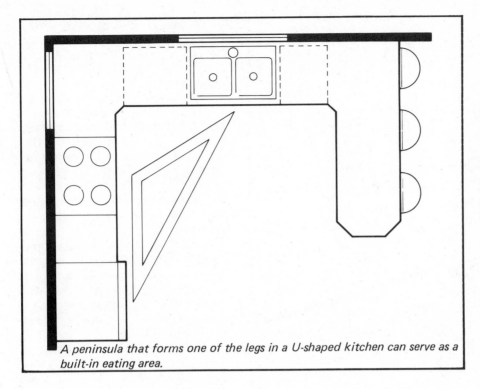

A peninsula that forms one of the legs in a U-shaped kitchen can serve as a built-in eating area.

When the purpose of an island or peninsula is only to increase countertop space, either one need only be 18 inches deep from front to back. To add cabinets under an island or peninsula of this depth, put wall cabinets—the kind that are only 12 inches deep—on a kickrail; base cabinets are 24 inches deep and would not fit.

Normal island countertop depth is 26 inches. When a sink or range is to be installed in an island, though, this depth should be extended to 36 or even 38 inches to allow for spatter and splash.

How To Plan An Eat-In Kitchen

Most people like to have an eating area in the kitchen, ranging from a snack bar to full dining facilities.

For family dining, you must allow about 12 to 15 square feet per person to accommodate a table, chairs, and the people themselves. A family of four, for example, requires at least 48 square feet of floor space to ac-

nets along that leg often open from both sides to give access from both rooms. Double-opening cabinets are available through home centers as well as from custom kitchen specialists. While the home center may not carry these cabinets as in-stock items, they can order them for you.

How To Plan Island And Peninsula Kitchens

Islands can be designed into a kitchen to add countertop work space, to provide a place for sink or range plus work space, to provide an eating area, or to provide something extra like a built-in barbecue or bar with hospitality center. An island can also serve to change a one-wall kitchen into a corridor kitchen.

A peninsula can provide one leg of an L-shape kitchen, one or two legs of a U-shape kitchen, or create added counter space or eating area for any kitchen.

Both islands and peninsulas function well in large kitchens to make the work triangle more compact. The entire kitchen

might be an island, with wall cabinets suspended from the ceiling. Two islands can be used to form a corridor kitchen in a large room, and one island might even form a one-wall kitchen in a large open area.

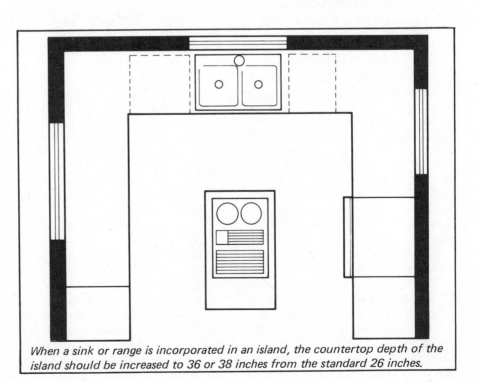

When a sink or range is incorporated in an island, the countertop depth of the island should be increased to 36 or 38 inches from the standard 26 inches.

Allow 21 inches of space along a peninsula counter for each adult who will be eating there.

commodate a table and four chairs. Each adult needs 21 to 24 inches of table space, and you should allow a minimum of 36 inches of clearance between the table and a wall to edge around a seated person. A minimum of 32 inches is needed for a seated person to rise from a table, and serving around a table requires clearance of 44 inches from table to wall.

Snack counters along peninsulas or islands generally have the same clearance requirements for movement behind the chairs, and you still should allow 21 inches of space along the counter for each adult. By multiplying the number of people who will eat at the counter by 21 inches, you will arrive at the counter length you need.

The height of a counter used for eating need not be the same height as the kitchen work surface. A table-height counter will be 28 to 32 inches high; an eating counter the same height as the kitchen work counter will be 36 inches high. For the lower counter, a person will need 20 inches of legroom when sitting on a chair 18 inches high. For the higher counter, a person will require a bar stool with the seat 24 inches from the floor. With this higher stool, required knee space decreases to 14 inches.

A high bar—more common when the eating counter backs up a sink or range center—will be 42 to 45 inches high. The height protects from spatter and splash, and it helps provide an open barrier from an adjacent living area. A standard high bar stool with a footrest will work well with the high bar.

When creating these eating areas, remember that the eating counter doesn't have to match the kitchen counter. It can be a contrasting color and/or pattern (a woodgrain top provides a rich look); at a different level; and it can be flared out, angled, or circular. Designing an eating counter, thus, is a good place to use some imagination.

Lighting And Color In The Kitchen

Lighting in the kitchen must be planned from two points of view—decorative and functional. The decorative aspect depends not so much on the shapes of the fixtures, but rather on the way the light affects color rendition. As for the functional aspect, two types of illumination are needed—general, overall lighting, and localized lighting in work areas.

General daytime illumination is usually provided by windows. Some homes, however, are built with interior kitchens, where little daylight is available. In some cases, a skylight could be added to bring in daylight.

With daylight, window position has much to do with color rendition. North and east windows catch the morning sun, while those on the south or west get most of their light in the afternoon. Morning light tends to favor the cooler colors like blues or greens. Afternoon light is kinder to the warm red or earth-colored tones.

Artificial light can be used to supplement daylight and to provide lighting at night. It can be divided into two categories—incandescent (bulbs) and fluorescent (tubes).

Incandescent light is 'warmer'—i.e., more pleasing to skin tones, natural woods, and the color of food. The light always comes on immediately, can be readily hooked to a dimmer switch to control its strength, and the bulbs or fixtures are less expensive. However, incandescent bulbs do generate more heat and consume more electricity, while putting out less actual light per watt than a comparably sized fluorescent tube. This kind of lighting source is best for the general dining area of the kitchen and for areas where food is prepared.

Fluorescent tubes are 'cooler' in heat output and in color rendition. Compared to incandescent bulbs, they are more energy efficient and produce about 250 percent more light for the current used; service life is about seven times that of the incandescent bulbs. Tubes provide more even illumination with less glare, but there can be a slight flicker or hum (partially alleviated with diffuser panels and proper installation). Color rendition is 'flatter' in the standard bulbs, though this can be eliminated by the use of Deluxe Warm White tubes that are designed to simulate the warmer tones of the incandescents. As a specific lighting source, fluorescents serve well as a general overall light in the kitchen and as specific task lighting over countertops and other areas.

One of the better ways to provide general illumination in the kitchen is to install a full luminous ceiling. This type of ceiling simulates natural daylight because it comes from above and in a broad source. It is important when such ceilings are installed that they are situated along the centerline of the room, with the tubes spaced at least 10 inches apart, and covered by diffusers (these spread the light and correct the flickering problem). Unless installed during new construction, however, luminous ceilings will drop the actual height of the ceiling in older homes. It will defeat the purpose of the illumination if the distance of the light fixtures to the diffusers is less than 15 inches; there will be shadows and the light will not be properly diffused.

There are also available square or rectangular ceiling boxes with either tubes or bulbs that are surface mounted on the ceiling. These boxes come in various sizes and are intended to replace the single fixture that was (and is) often standard general lighting in many homes.

Aside from a good source of general illumination, the well planned kitchen should have directional or task lighting over the general work surfaces. Counter areas can be well-lighted by the use of under-cabinet fluorescent fixtures. Minimum size should be 12 to 18 inches long. Use 15 watt tubes spaced about 30 inches apart.

Sinks that are beneath or close to a window can be adequately lighted by one of two methods. Two 40-watt tubes mounted over a diffuser can be placed in the soffit or a 75 watt incandescent downlight can be centered over the sink.

Lighting requirements over the range are usually covered by the fixture built into the range hood. Typically, such fixtures take a 25-watt incandescent bulb or a 15-watt fluorescent tube; the latter should be the Deluxe Warm White type for the best color rendition. An alternative would be to use a recessed ceiling or soffit downlight with a 75 watt incandescent bulb focused down on the range top.

Designing Extra-Activity Kitchens

A kitchen is very often the focal point of home activities. Therefore, when planning a new kitchen design—assuming, of course, that sufficient space exists—give a good deal of thought to incorporating facilities for the extra activities that could take place there. Here are a few ideas.

● The Family Room Kitchen. Your kitchen need not be a separate room at all. For example, you can create a kitchen quite easily at one end or on one side of a big living room/dining room. One-wall, corridor, L, or U kitchens are all possibilities, though the L and U require a good deal of open space.

The problems with the family room kitchen are few, but they must be considered. Ideally, housekeeping should be impeccable. Many people do not like to see open shelving or pot racks in a family room kitchen. Don't forget, moreover, that a family room kitchen allows more noise and smells in the living area of the home than does a kitchen in a closed room. The dishwasher, disposer, ventilating fan and refrigerator all are sources of noise.

● The Home Office. The kitchen can be a convenient place for a home office, and the facilities for an office can be designed into a kitchen quite easily.

An office in the kitchen calls for a dropped desk area with a counter about 6 inches below the regular 36-inch counter height. The desk should be at least 24 inches wide, with its depth matching the cabinet depth at that point. A single apron (shallow) drawer can be placed beneath the desk top, but it is essential that the drawer not interfere with knee space. A drawer unit or a two-drawer file can be placed beside the open knee space under the desk top.

If the desk area is positioned at the end of a cabinet run, an alternative to the drawer unit would be a narrow tray storage cabinet placed sideways against the wall. Again, it is essential that ample knee space be provided.

● The Communication Center. A complete intercom system—one that includes a two-way communication system between the kitchen and the bedrooms, rec room, and basement; smoke and intruder alarms; radio and tape music facilities; and even a sophisticated closed-circuit TV for supervision of the children's play area can be installed in the kitchen. Such an installation should be out of the work triangle, however.

● The Craft And Hobby Center. The kitchen affords a well-lighted area in the heart of the home for working on crafts and hobbies. Like the home office, the craft and hobby center that is incorporated in the kitchen may require little more than a cabinet or two suited to the activity, but if the hobby is one that requires a kiln or soldering or otherwise produces heat and fumes, an extra ventilating hood over the area should be installed.

● The Hospitality Center. The

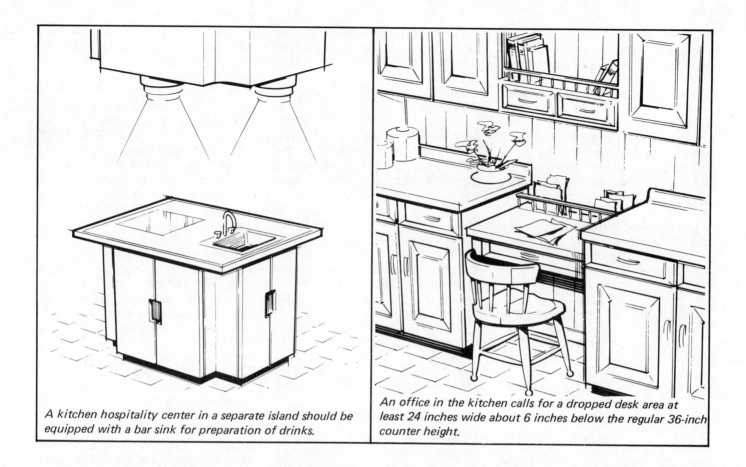

A kitchen hospitality center in a separate island should be equipped with a bar sink for preparation of drinks.

An office in the kitchen calls for a dropped desk area at least 24 inches wide about 6 inches below the regular 36-inch counter height.

kitchen is frequently the place where drinks are prepared, and there's no reason—where space allows, of course—for not installing a bar there. Since the bar should be well removed from the work triangle, the ideal place for it would be a peninsula separating kitchen and living area. On the living area side, the peninsula would be equipped with a separate bar sink, an under-counter refrigerator and ice maker, liquor cabinet, and a wine rack overhead or to the side. It could also contain an indoor barbecue unit but such a unit would have to be vented.

● The Greenhouse Center. There are actual greenhouses made to fit in kitchen windows, and several bulb manufacturers offer grow lights to help plants thrive. The grow lights can provide a very pleasant lighting effect in the kitchen. Since kitchens develop special heat and humidity conditions that differ from

other home areas, it is essential to consult a plant expert on the plants to buy for a kitchen greenhouse. Be sure to tell the expert whether your kitchen appliances are gas or electric; the difference is important when it comes to plant selection and care.

If you are into greenery to any serious extent, you will need a place for potting, seeding and transplanting. You can install a second sink in the kitchen (much like a vanity cabinet), and provide for seating or standing space around it.

The sink should have a gooseneck faucet and a spray attachment, and you will need open shelving or cabinets for pot storage and an extra drawer for utensils. A pull-out or lean-out bin works well for soil storage.

Plants can be displayed in the kitchen window, on each side of the sink, hung from the ceiling, or on an island or peninsula. Be sure, though, that whatever surface is used for plant display is

waterproof. Raw wood shelves deteriorate rapidly and therefore should be avoided in greenhouse installations. Formica-type plastic laminates are good and so are vinyls, especially when wrapped around the edges of the shelves.

● The Laundry Center. The best place for laundry facilities is not in the kitchen itself, but rather in a separate room adjacent to the kitchen. Washer and dryer units require about 5 feet of wall space, and they extend 27 to 33 inches out from the wall, with space allowed for ducts and hoses behind. If possible, the dryer should be positioned against an outside wall for easy venting of the hot, moist air to the outside.

Cabinets for all laundry supplies must be in close proximity. A deep utility sink, plenty of counter space (at least 48 inches), and at least a 5-foot aisle for ironing space must also be designed into the laundry center.

Doing Your Own Kitchen

Once you have designed your kitchen, there still remains one problem: Who's going to do the work? Any kitchen furnishings' dealer will plan your kitchen, order the necessary materials, and arrange for their professional installation. He will usually offer a guarantee and the kitchen will be done in a minimum amount of time with as little disruption as possible of your home routine. But you will pay for these services, and this cost factor can be prohibitive.

An alternative is for you to do some or all of the work yourself. This can result in some substantial savings, in addition to the satisfaction you can have from knowing that you did the work yourself. There are, however, some things you should consider before assuming that you can do the work required. Let's look at some of the problems in self-installation and see if it is right for you.

● **Materials.** You can figure on paying about the same for materials no matter who does the final installation. While some dealers will give you a price break if you buy everything through them, it will not be any great saving. It pays, however, to get the best materials you can afford. In the long run, you will pay about the same for quality materials as you will for inexpensive ones 'on-sale.' Good materials will keep that new look much longer, are easier to work with, and better made. Your new kitchen will be with you for some time.

● **Labor.** In construction, material costs are typically smaller than labor costs. Kitchen remodeling is no different. If you do some of the installation work yourself, you may find great savings. However, before making a do-it-yourself decision purely on a cost basis, you should consider several things.

Do you have the training or experience to do the job you want done? A carpenter may charge upwards of $10 an hour to install a run of cabinets and you would save this if you did it yourself. But he is a professional, will know how to do the job right, and can do it in a minimum of time. Most importantly, he will know how to correct the mistakes that will inevitably be made (true of any construction job). Setting a run of cabinets, for example, is an exacting job that has to be done correctly. If a carpenter does the work and you are not satisfied, you can complain; if you do it, you may have to live with it.

Do you want the long-term clutter and dislocation such a large-scale do-it-yourself project will entail? You will be doing much of the work in your spare time, and this means that you will not be able to complete the whole kitchen for weeks, perhaps months. While you can space out the flow of work to suit your schedule (doing ceilings and walls one weekend, for example, and the floors the next), some jobs will require a much longer span. It will usually take an experienced carpenter at least a day to set a run of cabinets—in new construction. Older homes require more preparation and work. The walls are usually out of plumb, the floors not level, and there may be plumbing or electrical problems. The project will take longer to complete.

● **Tools.** You must be familiar with tools and how to use them. The instructions in this section are based on the premise that you will already know something about the general work at hand. Do not attempt any major plumbing or electrical work unless you have experience in these areas! If you make a mistake and have to call someone in to rectify it, the cost may be more than if you had the job contracted out originally. Check your local code. It may be mandatory for such work to be done by a licensed plumber or electrician, especially if it has to be inspected.

Basically, do-it-yourself labor in the kitchen comes down to time versus money. If you have the time and skill to do the job yourself; then by all means go ahead. You will save money and it will be fun to do something that you can take pride in for years (if you do it right, that is). It may be cheaper, however, to have somebody come in and do the more difficult parts.

With these questions in mind, look over your kitchen again and see what jobs you can do to save the labor costs. Simple cosmetic changes like painting or hanging wall coverings are fairly easy, as are stripping and refinishing old cabinets. But in critical areas like setting cabinets, the task is more difficult and demanding and it has to be done right.

The following do-it-yourself instructions are intended to supplement knowledge that you already have. They are not specific to any one particular kitchen. You can save money by doing-it-yourself, but make sure you know how to go about it first. Have fun.

Doing Your Own Kitchen: Cabinets

In rooms other than the kitchen, style is set by the furnishings, wall coverings and draperies. In the kitchen, it is the cabinets that set the style. They usually dominate the room merely because they cover such a large percentage of the walls. Cabinets, in a sense, are the kitchen's basic furnishings.

Since so much of a kitchen's styling depends on the cabinets, they should be selected prior to the flooring, wall coverings, etc. All the other elements should then be selected to harmonize with the cabinets.

What about the appliances? The most popular appliance color has always been white, and white will go with any cabinets. Green and gold appliances require a bit more thought, but they generally blend in well with almost any cabinet color and woodgrain. One of the latest trends in appliance exterior design is the black glass front. More expensive than a painted surface, the black glass does blend nicely with any cabinet style.

One way to solve a possible (though unlikely) mismatch between appliances and cabinets is to add decorative fronts to the refrigerator, dishwasher, and compactor. These fronts are wood panels made by the cabinet manufacturer in a color and pattern that match the cabinets selected. The decorative fronts truly integrate cabinets and appliances into a single motif.

Most appliance manufacturers offer "front kits" consisting of metal frames that attach to the appliances. The frames are designed to hold a sheet of plastic laminate or other material to match the wood tones of the kitchen.

The four most popular cabinet styles are Contemporary, Traditional, Provincial, and Colonial (also called Early American).

Contemporary cabinet styling is characterized by straight, clean lines. Twenty years ago these cabinets were white enameled steel with flush doors and drawer fronts or flush overlay. Today, most contemporary cabinets have plastic laminate surfaces, many in bright solid colors.

Traditional styling usually features raised or recessed panels on drawer and door fronts. Normally quite conservative, traditional-styled cabinets are frequently made of oak in a wide color range. They can contribute to a look of elegance in the kitchen, especially in the more decorative versions.

Provincial is a fairly common style, characterized by a flat door with moldings applied to the faces of doors and drawers. French Provincial is noted for simple arcs in the moldings at the corners, while Italian Provincial has more complicated arcs and frequently some additional decorative touches as well. Common material for the Provincial styles is birch, although maple is also used as are plastic laminates in any color or woodgrain.

Colonial and Early American are theoretically two

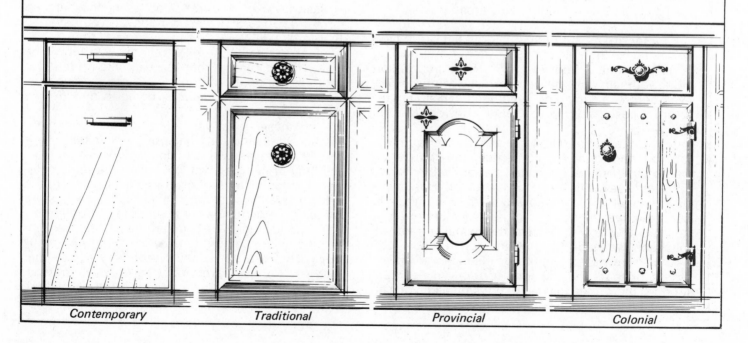

| Contemporary | Traditional | Provincial | Colonial |

different styles, but cabinet manufacturers mix them so much that the two approaches represent variations on a common theme. In theory, a pegged, Early American board and batten door should never be called Colonial, while a raised-panel cherry door should never be called Early American. Colonial is a more rustic style, while Early American is always well-joined and finished. Knotty pine and maple are common materials for these styles. The board and batten look is achieved today by routing V-grooves vertically on the doors and horizontally on drawer fronts—either randomly or with even spacing.

There are also many special styles achieved through the use of colors, graphics, wood carvings, and other decorative techniques. Manufacturers offer cabinets with hand-rubbed tints (light blue, for example) that allow the woodgrain to show through, while paints and decals can create a mod or graphic theme.

Style, of course, is a matter of personal preference, and no particular style is inherently superior. Just remember that cabinets must be chosen either to complement a theme or to remain essentially neutral. For example, an elegant Traditional style cabinet would hardly go well in a kitchen emphasizing a Provincial or Colonial decorative theme.

Cabinet Types And Sizes

Kitchen cabinets come in a variety of types and sizes to suit the various storage needs throughout the kitchen.

Wall cabinets are so named because they are generally mounted on the walls, although they can be hung from the ceiling over a peninsula or island; they can even be put on a toekick and used as base cabinets.

Although wall cabinets are a standard 12 inches in depth (with the doors projecting an extra 3/8 to 3/4 of an inch), they can differ greatly in height. Those 12 to 15 inches high are usually mounted above high refrigerators and high oven ranges, while the ones 18 inches high are used over standard ranges, over the sink (when there is no window, of course), and over smaller refrigerators. The wall cabinets 30 inches high are the basic storage units for dishes, glasses, and foods. Custom manufacturers frequently offer these cabinets in models reaching 32 or 33 inches high.

Diagonal corner cabinets are also 30 inches high, as are the blind corner wall cabinets that are useful in turning corners in an L-shape or U-shape kitchen. Diagonal corner cabinets can be fitted with either regular or revolving shelves.

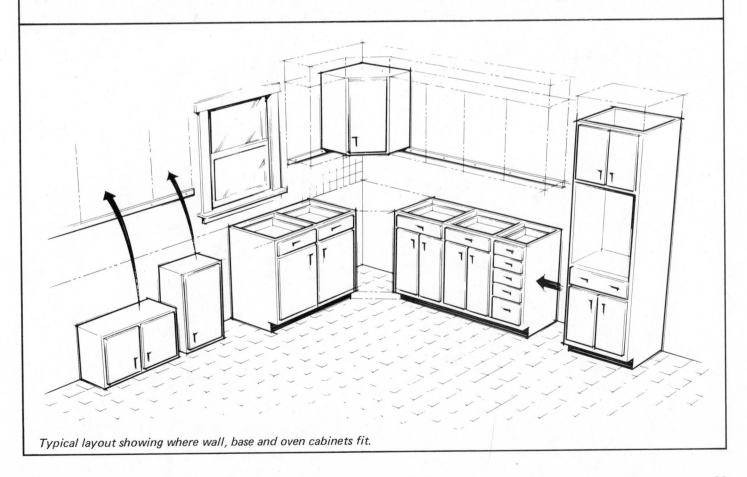

Typical layout showing where wall, base and oven cabinets fit.

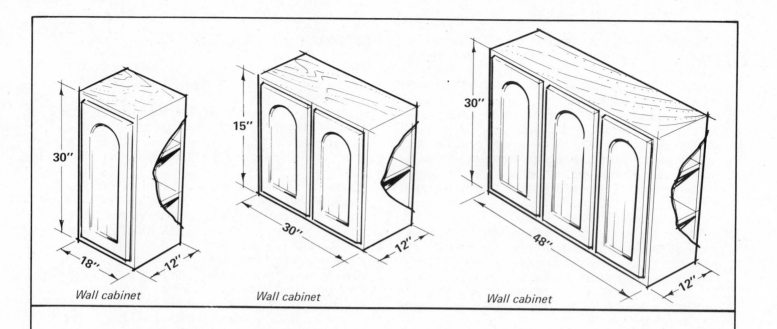

Wall cabinet   Wall cabinet   Wall cabinet

Peninsular wall cabinets for use over the range or sink are generally 18 inches high, while those for storage are 30 inches high and frequently open on both sides for easy access to stored items. They are usually hung from a soffit.

The other basic type of kitchen cabinet is the base cabinet. Base cabinets are 24 inches deep and 34-1/2 inches high, including the toekick which measures 4 inches deep and 4 inches high. Base cabinets are used for storage.

As with wall cabinets, base cabinets are available in diagonal corner, blind corner and Lazy Susan corner units for turning corners in L- and U-shape kitchens. Like their wall counterparts, peninsula base cabinets may have doors opening on both sides for access from either direction.

While the usual base cabinet has one drawer at the top, some base cabinets consist entirely of drawers (called base drawer units); they usually are placed near the sink and range. Under the sink itself is either a sink front or a sink cabinet. The sink cabinet is a complete box with a floor and back, whereas the sink front has no floor or back (although an optional floor can usually be obtained).

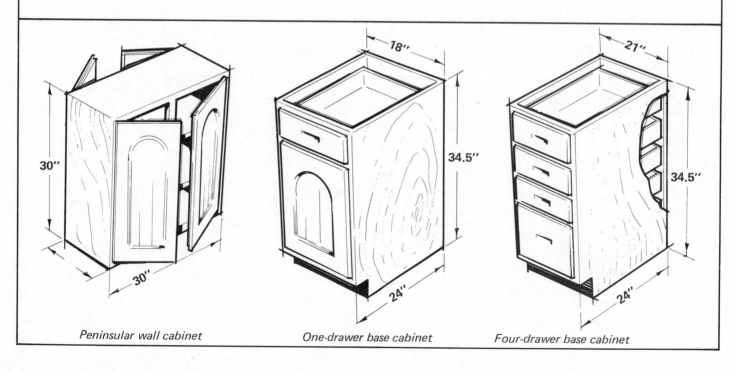

Peninsular wall cabinet   One-drawer base cabinet   Four-drawer base cabinet

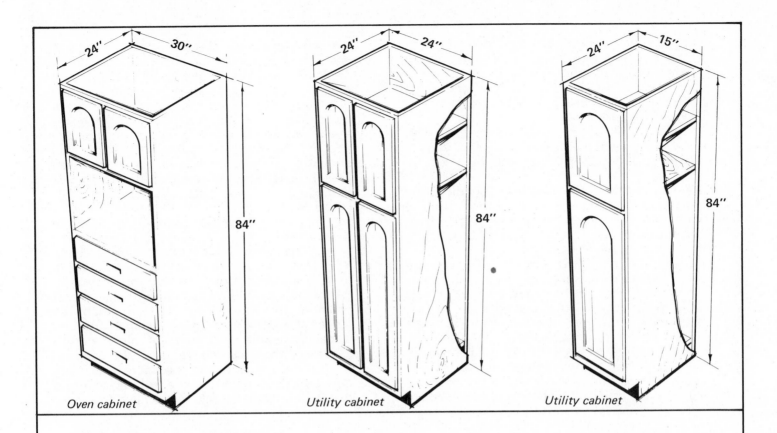

Oven cabinet   *Utility cabinet*   *Utility cabinet*

Oven cabinets are tall cabinets used for installation of wall ovens. Available in stock sizes of 24 or 27 inches wide and 84 inches high, oven cabinets are designed for either a single-cavity oven or a double oven.

Tall utility cabinets reach up to 84 inches high. Usually 18 or 24 inches wide, they can be used for various storage needs (mops, brooms, cleaning supplies, etc.) Fitted with adjustable, revolving or fold-out shelves, these cabinets can also function as pantries for bulk food storage.

What happens when a run of cabinets fails to fill a given space? Manufacturers offer wall and base fillers to fill in the odd dimensions. Fillers can also provide clearance for drawers in a corner, render a decorative termination to a cabinet run, etc. Just how many and what type of fillers are needed depend on the size and style of the kitchen.

How To Install Kitchen Cabinets

Kitchen cabinets must be installed with painstaking care, and that's not easy. The floor must be prepared so it is reasonably level, and the walls where the cabinets will be mounted must be made so that they are as close to perfectly plumb as possible. Any high or unshimmed low spot on the wall or floor can cause racking of the cabinet, and the racking of the cabinet will force the drawers and doors out of line.

The most expensive cabinets cannot compensate for improper installation. If poorly installed, the best cabinets will work no better than the cheapest. In other words, the person who installs cabinets carelessly is throwing his or her money away.

Before you get started, equip yourself with the following items: one or two helpers; a 1x2-inch strip of wood (to use as a cleat to help support wall cabinets); an electric drill with a 1/8-inch bit and a 90-degree drilling adaptor; a 4-foot level; a screw-

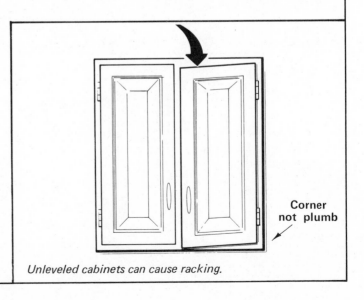

Unleveled cabinets can cause racking.

driver, a T-brace (made from a 54-inch length of 2x4 topped by a 1-foot piece of 2x4 mounted at right angles and covered with carpet); a box of 2-1/2 inch No. 10 wood screws; a couple of C-clamps; wood shingles for shims; and a box of toggle or molly bolts.

When you have everything you need—including, of course, the cabinets, follow these instructions for mounting your new cabinets properly.

1. Before starting, make sure your electrical and plumbing rough-in is complete. Then examine carefully your design drawings, familiarizing yourself with just how the base and wall cabinets are supposed to run.
2. Prepare the room. Shave or sand down all obvious high spots in walls.
3. Locate the wall studs behind where the cabinets will be, and mark the locations of the studs on the wall. Although the distance between studs—center to center—should be 16 inches, you cannot rely on that standard distance, especially in older homes. Therefore, be sure to mark the location of every stud along the run, placing the marks both above and below where

the cabinets will be. You will want to be able to see the marks after the cabinets are in position.

4. Move all the cabinets, still in their boxes, to an adjacent room where they will be handy but will not interfere with your work. Check your drawings once again, and then number the boxes and the appropriate wall locations to make sure you get the cabinets in the right place. You should start installing from a corner, and you should install the wall cabinets first (to avoid damaging the base cabinets). Therefore, arrange the cabinets in the adjacent room in a way that makes for an easy and orderly flow into the kitchen.
5. Attach the 1x2-inch strip to the wall precisely. You want to be able to rest the bottom back of each wall cabinet on it when you move the cabinet into position. For standard 30-inch wall cabinets, the top of the cleat should be 54 inches above the floor (assuming an 8 foot floor to ceiling height). Nail the cleat into the studs securely (otherwise, the weight of the cabinets will pull the strip out), and make sure it is level.
6. Line up all wall cabinets in a 'run' together on the floor. Using a drill, make pilot holes for

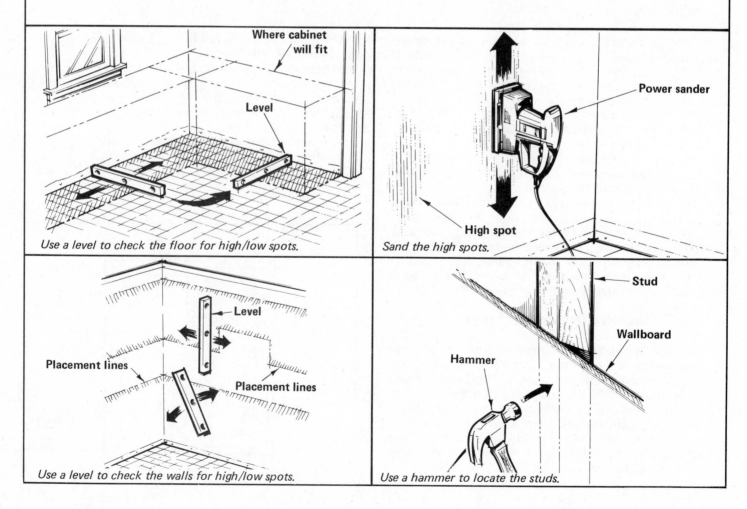

Use a level to check the floor for high/low spots.

Sand the high spots.

Use a level to check the walls for high/low spots.

Use a hammer to locate the studs.

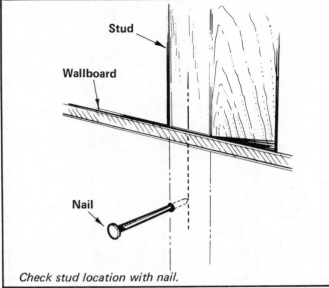
Check stud location with nail.

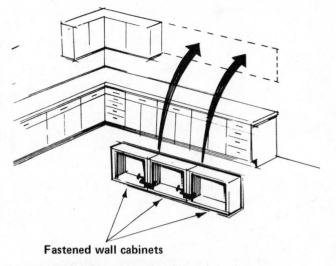
Line up wall cabinets as one unit.

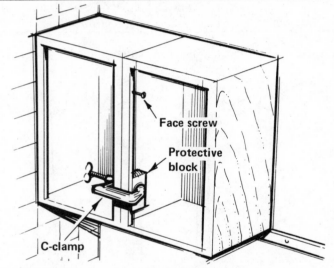
Clamp cabinets together and screw together securely.

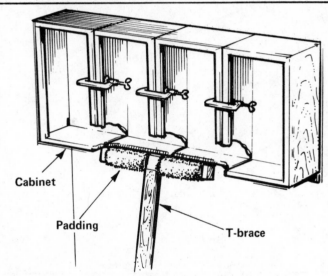
Use T-brace to help hold wall cabinets while fastening.

screws in the outside stiles of each adjacent cabinet; two for each pair of cabinets. Clamp with 2 C-clamps and screw them together securely. The purpose of this is to line up all faces in one level, straight run, making the cabinets a whole unit when you move them.

7. Have your helpers hold up the whole unit into the correct position on the wall, resting the backs on the cleat and using the T-brace to help hold it. Drill 1/8-inch holes through the mounting rail at the top back of the cabinet and into the studs. Then screw the cabinet to the wall with the No. 10 screws, four per cabinet. You may have to use the toggle bolts if there are not enough available studs.

8. Check with a level to make sure the unit is plumb, and do whatever shimming is needed before final tightening.

9. Follow the same basic procedure with the base cabinets; fastening them together as a unit and then moving them into the wall. You will not need a cleat or T-brace for the base cabinets; but make certain the whole unit is shimmed level so that a countertop will rest securely.

10. When you finish installing all wall and base cabinets, insert the drawers, hang the doors, and attach appropriate hardware.

How To Upgrade Your Old Cabinets

If your present kitchen cabinets are sound, solid, and agreeable in terms of styling, there is no need to replace them just because the finish has gone bad. You have three options open to you: 1) replace

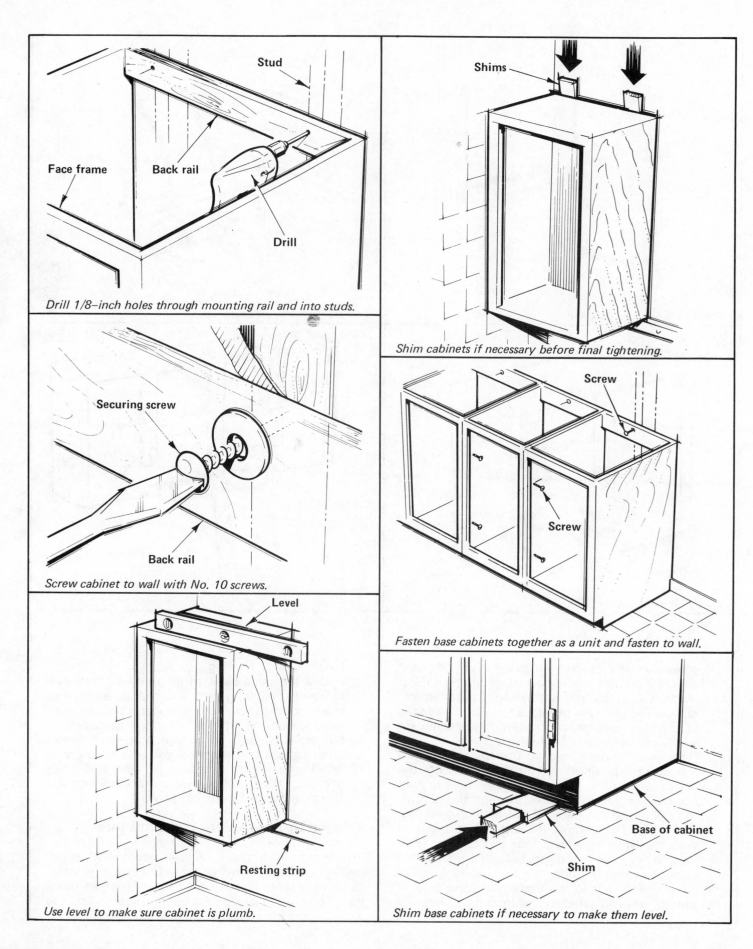

Drill 1/8–inch holes through mounting rail and into studs.

Face frame

Back rail

Stud

Drill

Securing screw

Back rail

Screw cabinet to wall with No. 10 screws.

Level

Resting strip

Use level to make sure cabinet is plumb.

Shims

Shim cabinets if necessary before final tightening.

Screw

Screw

Fasten base cabinets together as a unit and fasten to wall.

Base of cabinet

Shim

Shim base cabinets if necessary to make them level.

the doors and drawer fronts; 2) resurface them; or 3) paint them.

You can replace doors and drawer fronts no matter whether your cabinets are wood or steel. One system designed to fit all brands of steel cabinets consists of plastic-laminate surfaced doors and drawer fronts in a wide variety of colors and patterns. Matching laminate is supplied to cover all other exposed surfaces.

Any kitchen dealer can supply you with custom doors of the highest quality for your old wood cabinets, but naturally such doors are quite expensive. A less expensive alternative involves doors and drawer fronts of polyurethane, finished to look exactly like wood. You can do the work yourself or have it done by the dealer.

When installing new doors, you will notice that very little of the old cabinet surface is exposed. Most people simply apply a darker varnish over the exposed face frame because a darker finish will not make a sharp contrast with the new doors. Larger exposed surfaces—an end panel or the sides of wall cabinets framing windows—can be covered with panels that match the doors; the dealer who supplies the doors generally can provide the matching panels.

The cost of this replacement customarily runs less than half that of replacing cabinets, if you have the work done professionally. If you replace the doors yourself, the price would be only about 25 percent of full cabinet replacement. Differentials like these certainly make it worthwhile to consider replacing just the doors.

Resurfacing

Resurfacing old cabinets represents another popular alternative to the expensive task of installing new ones. Firms that do cabinet resurfacing come to your home, remove the old doors and drawer fronts, and take these parts back to the shop. There, they sand the doors and drawer fronts, and then apply new surfaces of plastic laminate. When the resurfacing work is completed, they bring the cabinet parts back to your home and remount them. Face frames and other exposed surfaces can be laminated in your home to match the doors and drawer fronts.

If you opt for this procedure, you can choose from more than 100 woodgrains, patterns and colors. You can even have the fabricator rout Provincial-style or V grooves (to simulate board-and-batten) in the doors or have him apply moldings to create a Traditional or Colonial style.

Be sure the fabricator applies laminate to both sides of the doors. You can have the same pattern on both sides or select a less expensive backer sheet. But you need the laminate on both sides to balance the door and thus prevent warpage. An uncovered back could cause the door to bow out in front.

Do-It-Yourself Cabinet Resurfacing

One of the easiest ways to resurface old cabinets and to give them an entirely different look is with tough and durable vinyl panels available from a number of manufacturers. The panels, which are very resistant to stains and scratches, come in a host of trimmable sizes that can be fitted to any cabinet door or drawer front. Matching material is available to fit rails, stiles, and other surfaces.

In addition to the vinyl panels, you'll need a screwdriver, sanding block, ketone solution for cleanup, a ruler and a pencil, utility knife, contact adhesive with spreading brush, wax paper, a small paint brush, and a trim paint in matching color.

Here are the steps to follow in do-it-yourself cabinet resurfacing.

1. Remove the old doors, and then take off all the hardware (pulls, hinges, etc.).
2. Sand the door surfaces until they are smooth.
3. Wipe the surfaces clean with ketone.
4. Measure the doors, and mark the dimensions on the panels with a pencil.
5. Trim the panels to size with a utility knife.
6. Apply contact adhesive to the backs of the panels and to the fronts of the doors. Then wait for the adhesive to become dry to the touch—usually about 15 minutes. At this point, the adhesive will not feel sticky, but it will grab to another adhesive surface.
7. Lay wax paper over about 3/4 of the door (it won't stick), and very carefully position the panel over the door on the wax paper. Don't let the panel and door touch because the two will adhere instantly and be very difficult to adjust. When the portions separated by the wax paper are perfectly positioned, press down all over. Then pull out the wax paper and press once again.
8. Paint the edges of the door with the matching trim paint.
9. If any surfaces of the face frame are exposed, paint them or apply flat strips to cover them in the same way you did the doors.
10. When all the paint is dry, rehang the doors.

Painting

If you want simply to paint your cabinets, you can do so effectively with a solid-color paint, either a gloss or semi-gloss enamel. You need the enamel to provide moisture resistance in the kitchen.

The cabinet surfaces must be clean and smooth before painting, but it is not necessary to remove the old finish. Just sand the rough spots to smooth

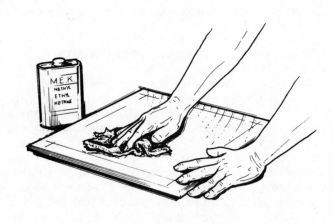

Wipe door surface with ketone.

Apply contact adhesive to back of panel and front of door.

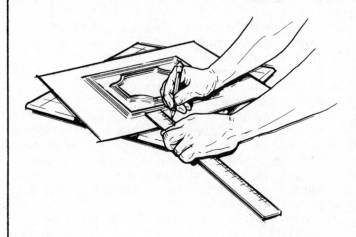

Measure doors and mark dimensions on panels.

Lay wax paper over about 3/4 of door and carefully position panel on the wax paper.

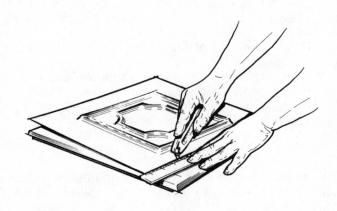

Trim panel to size with utility knife.

Paint edges of door with matching trim paint.

the finish, and wipe the surface clean and dust-free. Then paint the cabinets as you would any other wooden surface.

Refinishing

If you prefer to keep the natural finish of the wood visible, you can refinish your cabinets, but the job is much more complicated than painting. Simply stated, refinishing cabinets is an exhausting task. It can require many days, even weeks, if you have a large number of cabinets in your kitchen. Opting for a professional refinisher to come into your home and refinish your cabinets is a possibility, but having such work done for you is extremely expensive.

If you decide to do the work yourself, plan on carrying out bucket after bucket of "gook"—that is, stripper and the liquefied old finish. Be sure to cover and protect all areas on which the stripper could splash or drip, and wear rubber gloves because the chemicals could burn or discolor your hands.

It is essential that you do a thorough job, removing every trace of the old finish. Look at the area you have just finished from different angles so that the variations in light intensity can point out any areas you missed. There is nothing more disheartening than watching your new finish appear "blotchy" as it dries because you didn't remove all of the previous sealer.

Here are the steps you must follow to refinish your old cabinets.

1. Take off the old finish on the drawers and door fronts—after you have removed them from their mountings and placed them in a suitable place for such work—with a liquid stripper. If you cannot remove the doors and door fronts, use a heavy-bodied cream remover because you don't want the stripper running off the surface and onto something it could damage. With either type, be sure to follow the instructions on the label. If your cabinets are constructed of open-pore woods—such as oak or walnut—scrub the surfaces repeatedly with steel wool dipped in the finish remover.

2. When the old finish is gone, clean off all vestiges of the remover with lacquer thinner or mineral spirits. If traces of the remover remain on the surface of the wood, they will cause the new finish to become blistered or patchy.

3. Sand the surfaces by hand with fine sandpaper. If you discover dents or nicks in the finish, fill them with wood putty and then stain to match. Allow these treated areas to dry thoroughly before proceeding.

4. With open-pore woods, brush on a liquid wood filler both across and with the grain. When the filler dries (it will appear hazy), wipe with a rag across the grain to force the solution into the pores; then wipe lightly with the grain. Allow the wood to dry at least 8 hours before going to the next step.

5. If you wish to stain the wood, now's the time to do it. Follow the directions provided by the manufacturer of the stain.

6. Now seal the surface with shellac or a name-brand wood sealer. Apply two coats (via brush or spray) sanding lightly between coats. Once again, follow the instructions on the label.

7. Now give your cabinets a protective coat of resin varnish or lacquer. Remember, two thin coats are preferable to one heavy coat. Be sure to avoid drips, runs and brush marks in this final finishing procedure.

8. After the finish has dried sufficiently (one or two days), wax with a preparation containing carnauba wax. Do not use a liquid polish. Good grades of automotive waxes contain carnauba wax. Buff the wax application to a deep, lustrous sheen.

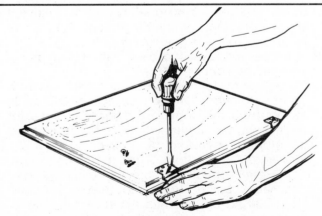

Remove all hardware from the doors.

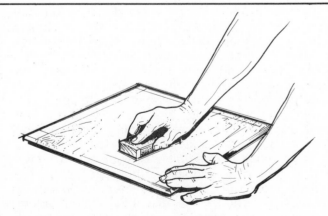

Sand surfaces by hand with fine sandpaper.

Doing Your Own Kitchen: Countertops

Thinking about replacing your countertop? If so, you have a choice of four basic materials: high-pressure plastic laminate, Corian, ceramic tile, and laminated hardwood.

High-pressure plastic laminate is the least expensive and by far the most popular kitchen countertop material. It comes in a tremendous range of patterns, colors and woodgrains. As countertop material, it measures 1/16 of an inch thick, although identical material 1/32 of an inch thick is available for vertical surfaces or table tops; the thinner type should not, however, be used on kitchen countertops. You can buy the high-pressure plastic in sheets and laminate it yourself to 1-1/2 inch plywood or particleboard, but it is far easier to buy prelaminated boards ready for installation as your new countertop.

Corian is a DuPont synthetic marble that differs from other artificial marbles in that it is drillable, cuttable and can generally be worked like wood. However, it is heavy and care must be taken since it chips readily. Considerably more expensive than laminates, Corian is a superb material for the kitchen countertop. You can even buy a Corian top with an integral sink bowl of the same material, all in one piece. If you install it yourself, put in the 3/4-inch thick Corian, using the 1/4-inch thick material for the backsplash.

Ceramic tile is the most expensive countertop material. Very popular on the West Coast and throughout the Southwest, it is very elegant and very durable, but it has some disadvantages too. Its very hard surface tends to reflect noise, and the grout between the tiles can pose a cleaning problem if it is not sealed properly. Tiles range in thickness from 1/4 to 3/8 of an inch and in size from a 1/2-inch to a 6-inch square. The 4-1/4 inch square is regarded as the most popular.

Laminated hardwood is the familiar butcher block material. Always popular on a limited scale—particularly for the food preparation section of the countertop—butcher block recently has come to be used throughout many kitchens. The hardwood involved usually is maple; thickness can vary, but the 1-1/2 inch material is quite commonly used for countertops. The wood must be well sealed to prevent excessive staining, and it requires a good deal of care and attention to look its best.

To enhance the flexibility of your new countertop, plan on including special-purpose inserts. The inserts most often are of butcher block, but an increasingly popular material is Pyroceram, a tempered glass ceramic that won't cut, stain, or scratch.

Stainless steel inserts are sometimes used, but stainless steel dents, dulls knives, and scratches.

How To Install A Plastic Laminated Countertop

Plastic laminated countertops can be self-edged or postformed. Self-edged tops have a square front and are faced with a separate strip of the same material found on the top. The backsplash is a separate piece joined at right angles to the top. In contrast, a postformed countertop is rounded over the front edge (often raised there for a "no-drip" top) and coved up at the backsplash and over the top to the wall.

Plastic laminated countertops are available in 6, 8, 10, and 12 foot lengths. If two lengths are to be joined to form an L, they must be joined with a 45-degree miter joint. Ask your dealer to cut the miter for you, and then you can put the two pieces together in your kitchen.

To install a plastic laminated countertop, you will need the following tools: a screwdriver, hammer, small wedge, level, tape measure, some 2x2 inch stock, nail, adhesive caulking, a pencil, wood screws, a drill, transparent tape, and—if there is a miter joint—an adjustable wrench to tighten bolts.

To replace an existing countertop with a plastic laminated postformed one, follow these do-it-yourself instructions.

1. Remove the old top. Since it probably is fastened to the base cabinets with screws, check inside the base cabinets for screws or nails. Remove the fasteners, and then lift the old top off. Be careful, though, because in addition to screws or nails, the countertop may be glued down, and pulling it up sharply could damage the base cabinets. A hammer and wedge may be necessary to free a glued countertop.
2. If necessary, level the base cabinets by shimming at the floor.
3. Place the new top in position, and then measure up from the floor. The top surface should be 36 inches from the floor to provide clearance for under-counter appliances and drawers. Most countertops need to be raised to reach 36 inches above the floor. Turn the top over and nail 3/4-inch thick, 2x2 blocks along the front and back, spacing them about every 8 inches. Use nails no longer than 1-1/8 inches; longer nails could penetrate the plastic top.

4. Assemble the miter joints by placing the sections together—bottom side up—on a soft surface that won't damage the countertop. Apply an adhesive caulking compound to the surfaces to be joined, and then use fasteners (I-bolts should come with the top and fit into special slots) to hold the sections together. Turn the fasteners snug but not tight. Check alignment of the front edges and top surfaces, and then tighten the front fastener. Now check again, and then tighten the next fastener. Follow this procedure until all the fasteners are tightened. When you turn the sections over and clean off the excess caulk, you should have a perfectly formed miter joint.

5. Push the postformed countertop back against the wall (or walls if an L). Then take a pencil, place it vertically against the wall with the point on the backsplash, and draw a line all along the top of the backsplash. If this line bows out, you know where you must file or sand away a little of the backsplash so that the countertop will fit flush against the wall.

6. Fasten down the top with wood screws through the triangular gusset plates in the corners of the base cabinets. If your cabinets do not have these gussets, you should find wood blocks in those corners through which you can drill holes for screws to hold down the four corners of the countertop. If you are certain that you will never want to remove the countertop, you can apply panel mastic—put on a continuous bead running around the entire perimeter—to hold the top in place.

7. For a sink installation, check the sink carton for installation instructions and a template for making the sink cutout in your new countertop. With a keyhole saw, you can make the cutout from the top; with a saber saw, you have to cut from the bottom or the laminate will chip. Draw the line for the cutout, use either a sharp punch or nail inside each of the four corners to make pilot holes for the drill, and then drill holes all the way through at each corner. Be sure your drill does not cut outside of your guideline, and be sure before you cut that you have spaced the sink properly from front to rear so that there is room for its rim in front of the backsplash.

8. Start sawing from hole to hole with the keyhole saw. To avoid chipping the laminate, it helps to put down transparent tape over your cutout line. Don't saw too hard; apply pressure only on the down stroke and none on the up stroke.

9. Lay a thick ribbon of caulk around the edge of the cutout where the sink rim will fit, set the sink in place, and press down all around. Wipe away the excess caulk. Follow the manufacturer's directions for fastening the sink to the countertop cutout.

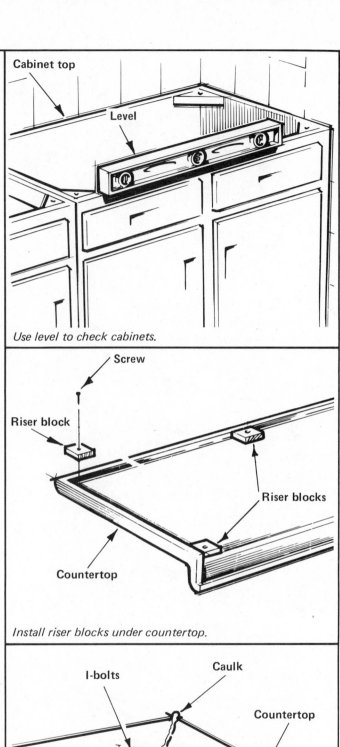

Use level to check cabinets.

Install riser blocks under countertop.

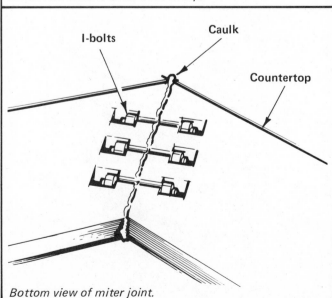

Bottom view of miter joint.

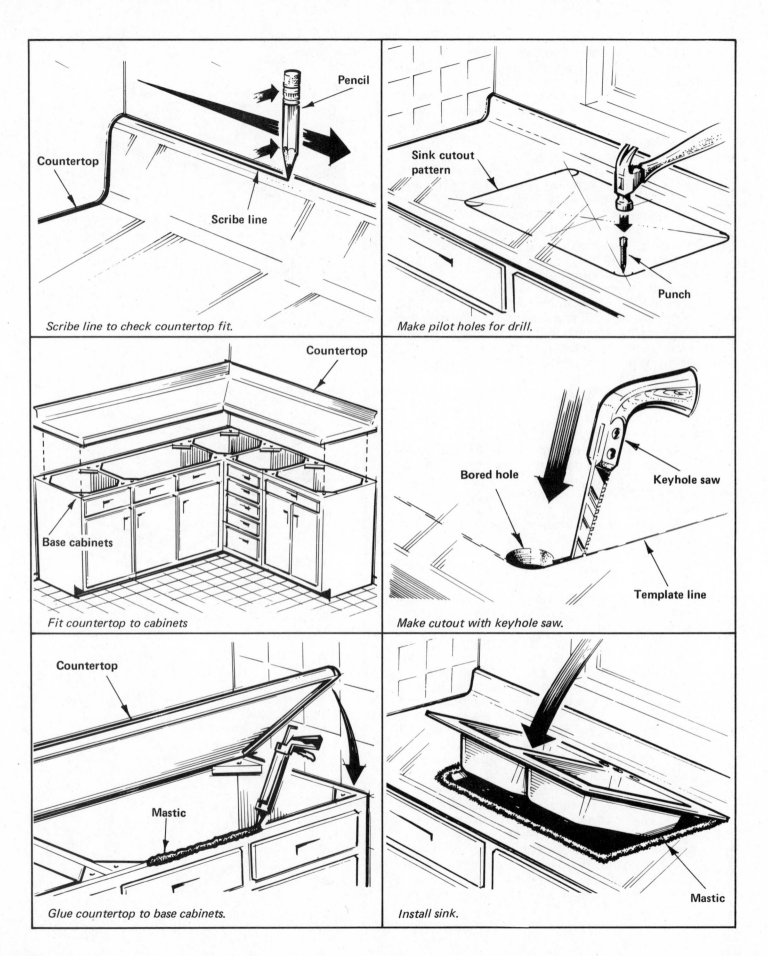

Scribe line to check countertop fit.

Make pilot holes for drill.

Fit countertop to cabinets

Make cutout with keyhole saw.

Glue countertop to base cabinets.

Install sink.

How To Install A Laminated Hardwood Countertop

The procedure for installing a laminated hardwood countertop is exactly the same as that for installing a plastic laminated unit, with three exceptions.

1. You will need help in handling the material because laminated hardwood countertops are extremely heavy, weighing up to several hundred pounds.
2. You must exercise greater care with a laminated hardwood countertop because the material can be chipped much more easily than high-pressure plastic laminate. It is much like Corian in this respect.
3. Corners are butted, not mitred.

How To Install A Corian Countertop

Corian can be worked just like plastic laminate even though it looks just like marble; however, care must be used in cutting it. Be aware of some difficulties in working with this material. It is heavy (so you will need a helper) and will chip or break unless care is taken with it. You should be very careful with this expensive material, for mistakes can cost money. If you lack the time or skill to do it carefully, have the top and cutout made by a professional.

You will need the following tools and materials: A screwdriver, hammer and wedge, level, circular saw (with a carbide blade), router, C-clamps, neoprene adhesive, turnbuckles and screws, scrap lumber, and sandpaper. To install a countertop of the DuPont material, follow these steps:

1. Remove the old countertop and level all the base cabinets. If your kitchen has just a sink front instead of a sink cabinet, you must provide extra support for the new countertop. Corian is quite heavy, and it needs support behind the sink. A wooden cleat nailed to the wall can provide support here and any other places —such as the corners—where there may not be adequate support. To provide extra support along the middle, lay a 1/4-inch board along the length of the cabinet run.
2. If you ordered a Corian top with an integral sink, the piece will be cut to the correct depth—*i.e.,* 25 inches front to back. But if you ordered a sheet of 3/4-inch Corian from which to make your own top and install a sink, you will have to cut the Corian to the correct 25-inch depth as well as to the proper length. The best way to cut Corian is to go very slowly with a circular saw (the blade should be as sharp as possible to

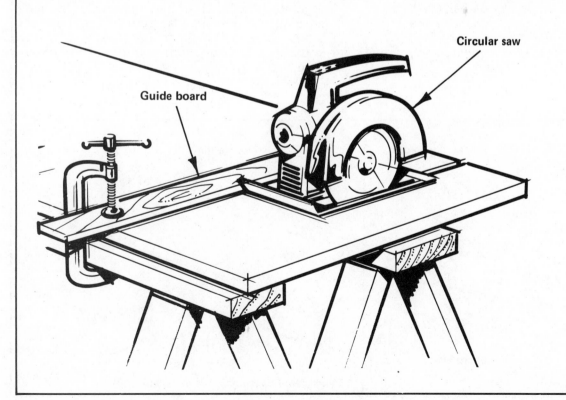

Guide board

Circular saw

The best way to cut Corian is to go very slowly with a circular saw. The blade should be as sharp as possible to avoid chipping.

avoid chipping). Since cutting will produce a "snowstorm" of Corian, plan on sizing it outside if possible.

3. To raise the Corian so that the top surface will be 36 inches off the floor, cut a strip 3 inches wide from the scrap to run the entire length of the top. Turn the Corian over and glue the strip along the bottom front, recessed about 1/8 of an inch, using neoprene adhesive. Be sure you glue so that the factory-finished front edge will face to the front. Then do the same along all sides. A ready-made top will already have this done for you.

4. If you must turn a corner for an L shape, make a butt joint rather than the miter joint you would make with a laminate top. Seal the butt joint with neoprene adhesive. If you wish to draw the two sections of Corian snugger (never tight), you can install a turnbuckle underneath attached to a recessed screw on either side of the joint. Ready-made tops will already have such turnbuckles installed.

5. You can make a sink cutout in Corian the same way as in a plastic laminate top, except that a router will do the job faster and better than a keyhole or saber saw. If you use a router, first make a jig of scrap lumber and fasten it down with C-clamps to guide the router. Despite the "snowstorm" of Corian, do not attempt to make the sink cutout outside. The strips at the front and back of the sink cutout would almost certainly break under the strain of supporting the weight of the heavy side portions. Once the cutout has been made, do not move the top without a helper. Corian fractures very easily.

6. Cutting Corian leaves sharp edges; sand the edges until the surface is smooth.

How To Install A Ceramic Tile Countertop

Installing ceramic tile is certainly the messiest approach to installing a new kitchen countertop, but it could well prove to be the most durable. You will need the following tools and materials: a hammer; a keyhole saw; notched trowel; tile cutter, or a glass cutter and tile nippers (both a tile cutter and tile nippers can be rented where you buy the tile); rubber trowel; and a pencil. A plywood sheet (if a new undersurface is required—3/4-inch CDX is best), epoxy or organic adhesive, grout, and a silicone sealer are also required.

Follow these directions for simple installation.

1. Make sure all cabinets are perfectly level, shimming at the floor if necessary.
2. Use a 3/4-inch sheet of exterior plywood as the base for the tile. Place blocks as necessary under the perimeter of the plywood so that the top surface of the tile will be 36 inches above the floor. If more than one sheet of plywood is required to form the base, leave a 1/4-inch gap between the sheets, and fill the gap(s) with epoxy.
3. Make the sink cutout in the plywood (and any other cutouts such as those for a built-in cooktop or counter inserts), following the same procedure described for a plastic laminate countertop.
4. You can lay tile "wet," which means in mortar, or you can fasten it down with an epoxy or organic adhesive. The manufacturer of the tile usually recommends a specific brand (or brands) of adhesive. Since the adhesive method is easier and faster, that is the one described here.

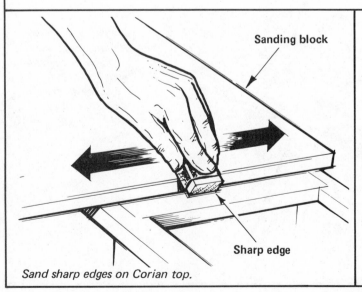

Sand sharp edges on Corian top.

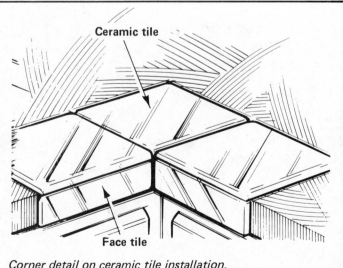

Corner detail on ceramic tile installation.

5. Determine the width of the grout line. With sheets of mosaic tile, the width of the grout line is already determined; with larger tiles, a small tab gives the correct spacing. If not, you must make the decision. To minimize cleaning problems, keep the grout lines narrow. The determination of grout width helps you calculate how much tile to buy. In buying the tile, incidentally, be sure to buy bullnose cap or cove pieces for the backsplash and edge pieces for the sink and front edge of the countertop. Buy a few extra because some are certain to break.
6. Lay the tile out on the counter and plan the grout gaps; then draw the pattern you will follow on the plywood.
7. Spread the adhesive evenly on the base with a notched trowel. Then lay in the tile, working on just a couple of rows at a time. Put each tile down flat and avoid sliding it; sliding thins the adhesive.
8. In all probability, you will need to cut some of the tiles to fit the pattern. A tile cutter is available to rent from a dealer. To cut tile without a tile cutter, first score it with a glass cutter and then nip the cut with the tile nippers, taking small pieces at a time.
9. Let the adhesive dry overnight before applying the grouting.
10. Apply the grout with the rubber trowel. Hold the trowel at an angle to force the grout down between the tiles. When the grout begins to dry, run the eraser end of a pencil down the grout lines to give them an even depth. Wipe off any excess with a damp rag. When the grout is completely dry, spray it with a silicone sealer to prevent oil or dirt from discoloring the grout.

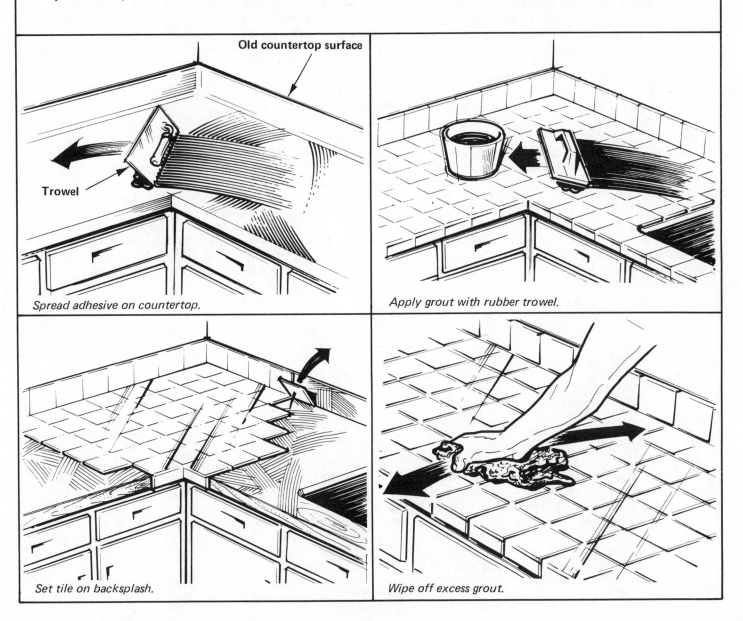

Old countertop surface

Trowel

Spread adhesive on countertop.

Apply grout with rubber trowel.

Set tile on backsplash.

Wipe off excess grout.

Doing Your Own Kitchen: Flooring

The right floor covering can change a dull kitchen into a bright and colorful one, or a plain kitchen into one that is elegant. Modern kitchen flooring can be either hard or soft, easy to care for or difficult, inexpensive or expensive. Yet the various materials have one thing in common: nearly all can be laid by the do-it-yourselfer.

Resilient flooring—which is the modern successor to linoleum (not manufactured in the United States since Armstrong abandoned it in 1974)—ranges from inexpensive asphalt tiles to somewhat more expensive vinyl asbestos sheets and tiles, to vinyl sheets and tiles that can range in price from moderate to expensive. Generally, resilients in tile form are less expensive than sheet goods. As you might expect, the resilient tile that comes with a self-stick backing is more costly than its plain counterpart, but that backing makes the tiles extremely easy to lay.

Asphalt tile is an inexpensive material that offers no advantages over the other resilients except price. Its colors are not as good; it is not as wear-resistant; and it breaks easily.

Vinyl asbestos tiles have less gloss than vinyl flooring, and the colors are duller. Their appeal lies in the fact that they offer no-wax ease of care at a moderate price.

The vinyls range from the least expensive rotovinyls to the most expensive no-wax vinyls. All vinyls are available with or without cushioning. The best, of course, are the well-cushioned no-wax vinyls. The old-fashioned shiny vinyls that were so hard to care for are now hard to find.

Cork tile actually qualifies as a resilient floor covering, but it is in a class by itself because it is a natural material. Soft and warm to walk on, cork deadens sound and is available with a clear vinyl surface that doesn't hide the beauty. In a kitchen, though, cork should not be laid in the work triangle because it stains more easily than the other resilients.

Parquet flooring consists of strips of natural wood glued together into squares. Oak is the usual material, although other woods are available. Manufactured in many sizes and thicknesses, parquet can be laid over a smooth subfloor or a smooth hardwood floor, and is particularly good for the kitchen eating area. The wood is, of course, susceptible to warping if subject to frequent soakings.

Carpeting can make an excellent material for a kitchen floor. Although not as easy to care for as resilient flooring, carpeting made especially for kitchen installations is not difficult to care for either. It has a synthetic nap, usually nylon, and a sponge rubber backing. Between the nap and the backing is an impermeable membrane that prevents spills from soaking through and makes the nap easy to clean with soap and water. Be careful, though, some carpet sales clerks often call indoor-outdoor carpet kitchen carpet. The two are not the same, and indoor-outdoor carpet should never be put in a kitchen. Kitchen carpet comes in self-stick tiles, 12-inch squares, and in rolls.

Ceramic tile can make an elegant kitchen floor covering, but it is hard on the feet and anything dropped on it will break or dent. If you opt for ceramic tile, though, you can choose from many colors and shapes, and create your own patterns when laying it.

How To Install Resilient Floor Covering

Resilient floor covering is nearly always installed with adhesive. Adhesive is especially needed on subfloors subject to seasonal changes in humidity.

Before buying the material, always check the installation instructions. You may find that the resilient flooring you want does not lend itself to easy do-it-yourself installation.

The following instructions apply specifically to Sundial, an Armstrong cushioned no-wax vinyl sheet, but the steps are quite similar for installing other types of resilient flooring. You'll need a chalk line, knife, straight edge, trowel, rolling pin or roller, the correct adhesive, and some cardboard.

1. Read the instructions that come with the flooring.
2. Measure the room as accurately as possible, and diagram the floor plan on graph paper, noting the position of cabinets, closets, doorways, offsets in the walls, etc. Measure twice to verify your figures.
3. Take the roll of sheet flooring into another room where it can be spread out. Use the chalk line to transfer the measurements from the graph paper to the flooring, allowing some extra for trimming. Put cardboard underneath the flooring to protect the floor. Then cut along the chalk lines with a sharp knife and straight-edge.
4. Carry the flooring back to the kitchen and put it in place; it should fit almost exactly. Trim all overlap with the knife.
5. Roll back half of the flooring and spread the

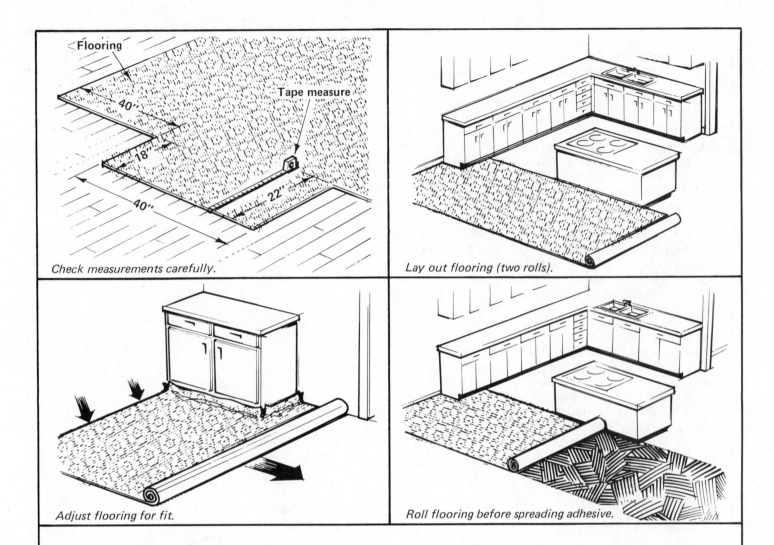

Check measurements carefully.

Lay out flooring (two rolls).

Adjust flooring for fit.

Roll flooring before spreading adhesive.

adhesive on the exposed floor with a trowel.

6. Press the flooring material back onto the adhesive before it dries.

7. Then roll up the other half of the flooring and repeat the procedure.

8. Finally, roll out the bumps in the material either with a rolling pin or with a special roller available from your flooring dealer. Trim edges tight.

How To Install A Ceramic Tile Floor

Installing a ceramic tile floor can be transformed from a very messy and difficult job to one that is relatively simple and clean. You can buy tile with a self-stick backing that requires just peeling off the protective paper and pressing the tile in place. Other tile comes in pregrouted sheets, containing hundreds of those little mosaic tiles that can all be laid simultaneously.

You can lay ceramic tile over gypsum board, exterior grade plywood, tempered hardboard, or almost any firm base. But never lay tile on a surface that is not perfectly firm or one that has dirt, wax, or

flaking paint. Always use the proper mortar, adhesive, and primer (i.e., those recommended by the tile manufacturer); the adhesive must be com-

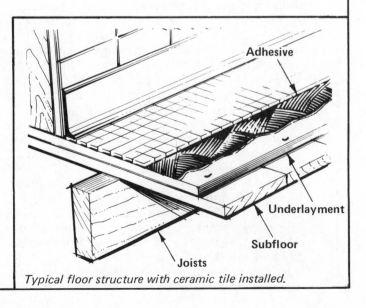

Typical floor structure with ceramic tile installed.

patible with the surface being covered and with any primer and grout.

If your present kitchen floor is wood, make sure it is sound and firm. Then cover it with 1/4-inch exterior grade plywood or underlayment board. Nail down the covering material every 4 inches with ring shank or ring-grooved nails. The nails must be long enough so that more than half the length of the nail penetrates the floor. Long (1-1/4 inch) staples will work as well and are less tedious to install.

If your present floor is linoleum, cork, rubber, vinyl, vinyl asbestos, or asphalt tile, you can apply the ceramic tile directly to it. But again, make sure the floor is structurally sound, firm, and free of any grease, wax, or dirt. The entire surface should be lightly sanded to ensure good adhesion, and badly worn spots should be leveled with underlayment cement.

To lay tile with pregrouted ceramic mosaic tile sheets you will need a tape measure, a chalk line, a V-notched trowel, a tile cutter, tile nippers, a razor knife, adhesive, and a carpet-covered roller. For caulking around the walls or any plumbing fittings, you'll need a tube of sealant and a caulking gun. For cleanup when finished, you'll need cheese cloth and high-flash-point mineral spirits.

Follow these steps for a neat and attractive ceramic tile floor.

1. Find the center of each of the four walls, disregarding cabinets, alcoves, etc. Snap chalk lines between opposing walls. The lines must be perfectly perpendicular to each other.
2. Starting at the center point, lay several sheets of tile along one chalk line. Then lay several sheets along the other line, all within the same quarter of the room.
3. When you approach the wall, overlap the last sheet to see where you must cut. If the cut line is in the middle of a tile, push all the sheets back so this cut will fall on a grout line. Do this with the two adjacent walls to minimize tile cutting.
4. Now go back and adjust the original chalk lines accordingly. If you are laying the tile sheets on a subfloor, adjust the sheets of subflooring so that the seams are at least 3 inches from any joints between tile sheets.
5. Starting at the intersection of the adjusted center lines, spread adhesive with the trowel over one quarter of the room—or over that part of it you can finish in one hour or less. If there is an area for which you will have to cut the tile (like a far corner), don't spread adhesive there yet.
6. Lay the first sheet of tile on the adhesive with its two edges precisely meeting the chalk guidelines. Butt each sheet tight against other sheets, holding the far edge upward so it doesn't get into the adhesive before the near edges are

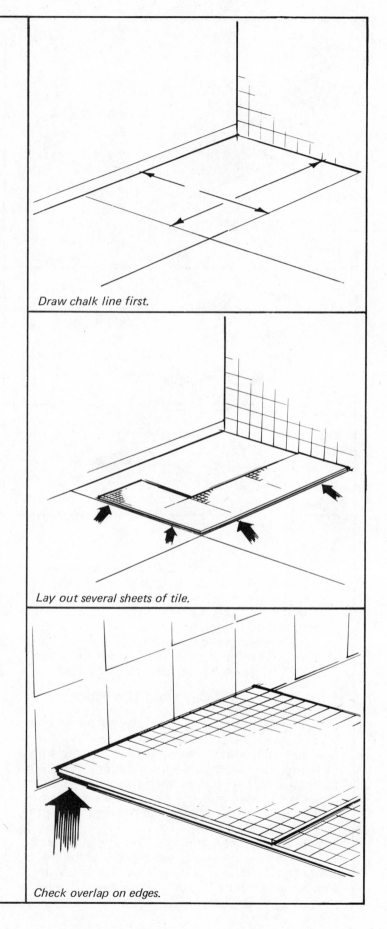

Draw chalk line first.

Lay out several sheets of tile.

Check overlap on edges.

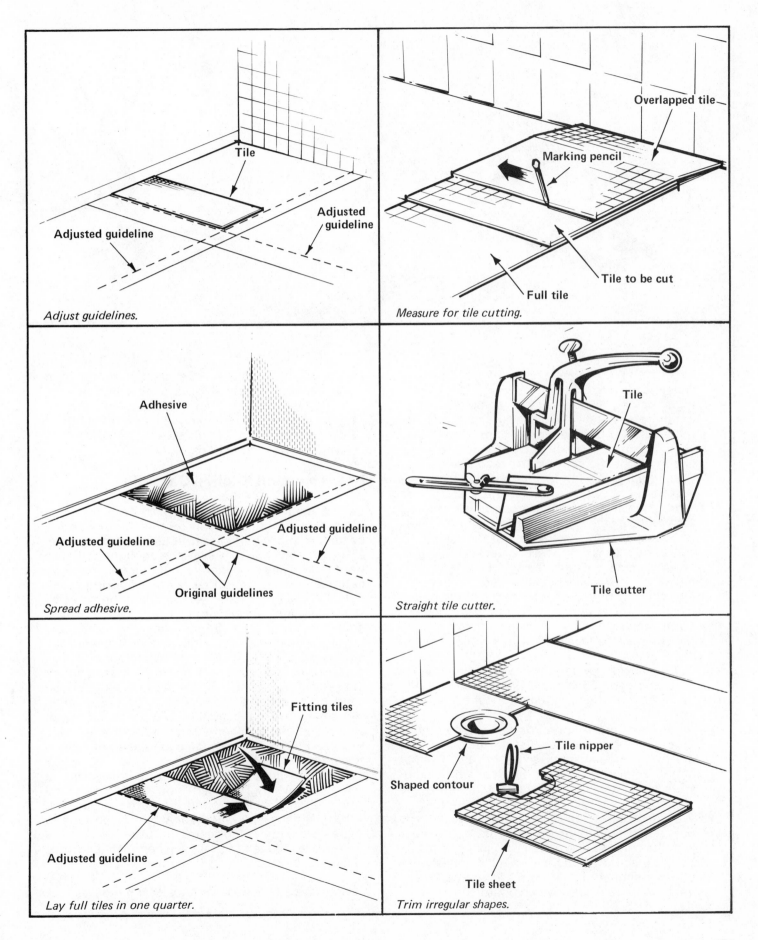

Adjust guidelines.

Measure for tile cutting.

Tile

Adjusted guideline

Adjusted guideline

Overlapped tile

Marking pencil

Tile to be cut

Full tile

Spread adhesive.

Straight tile cutter.

Adhesive

Adjusted guideline

Adjusted guideline

Original guidelines

Tile

Tile cutter

Lay full tiles in one quarter.

Trim irregular shapes.

Fitting tiles

Adjusted guideline

Shaped contour

Tile nipper

Tile sheet

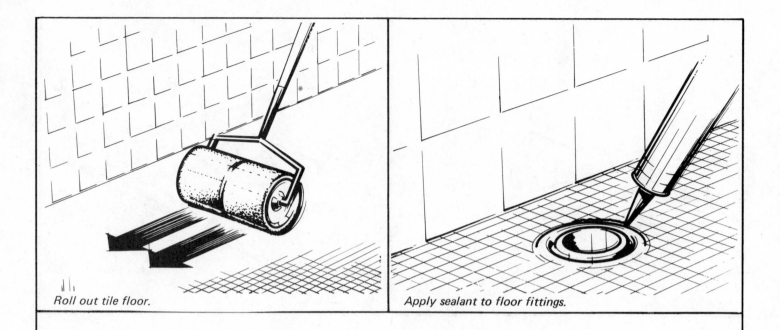

Roll out tile floor.

Apply sealant to floor fittings.

butted. Put the sheets straight down; never slide the tile into place.

7. Finish laying all the full sheets of tile before cutting any sheets. Next, fit all sheets that require cutting only at the grout lines. Butt the tile sheet against the wall to determine the grout line to be cut, then cut it with a razor knife.

8. Spread adhesive and lay the cut sheets, pressing them into place between the wall and the other sheets. If your measurement was slightly off and the space is too small, causing the sheet to buckle slightly, take it up and trim along the wall edge with tile nippers or a hacksaw.

9. To determine the cut line for tile sheets that must be cut with a tile cutter, place a sheet of tile precisely on top of the last full sheet of laid tile, and then lay another sheet of tile on top but butted against the wall. Use the edge of the top sheet as a straightedge to draw a line on the sheet below.

10. Cut the sheet along the line with a tile cutter (a tool which you can rent). Spread adhesive and lay in the cut sheet, putting the cut edge along the wall.

11. If you must make contour cuts, such as those around pipes or fixtures, use a soft pencil and draw the shape as precisely as you can. Cut out all the whole tiles within the line with a razor knife, and then use tile nippers to finish the contour.

12. Wait at least an hour after the installation is completed, and then go over the entire floor with the carpet-covered roller to make sure that the tile makes a good bond with the adhesive. In corners where the roller won't fit, pound the tile gently with a carpet-covered board.

13. Make a 1/8-inch bead of sealant along the joint at the wall. The sealant, available in colors to match the grout, prevents moisture seepage.

14. Seal around any plumbing fittings in the floor.

15. Clean any sealant or adhesive from the tile floor with mineral spirits or paint thinner.

How To Install Kitchen Carpeting

Carpet made specifically for kitchens has been around for about 10 years. Some daring homeowners put in nylon carpet in kitchens more than 20 years ago, but that is not recommended. The trouble with any carpeting is that there is no way to get it as clean as the other kitchen flooring materials. On the other hand, kitchen carpeting can be kept adequately clean with ordinary soap or detergent and water, and the impermeable membrane between the nap and sponge backing prevents any moisture from getting through to the floor.

The 12-inch squares with a self-stick backing are the easiest type of kitchen carpet to install. All you need do is remove the moldings or baseboards, clean the surface thoroughly, and press the carpet squares in place. When you come to the far wall, simply cut the last row of squares to fit with a scissors or utility knife.

Rolls of kitchen carpet do not come with a self-stick backing. Instead, you apply two-sided tape (2 inches wide) around the perimeter and—if butting is necessary—additional two-sided tape (5 inches wide) under the seams.

Here are the steps to follow when installing rolls of kitchen carpet.

1. Remove all baseboards and other moldings.

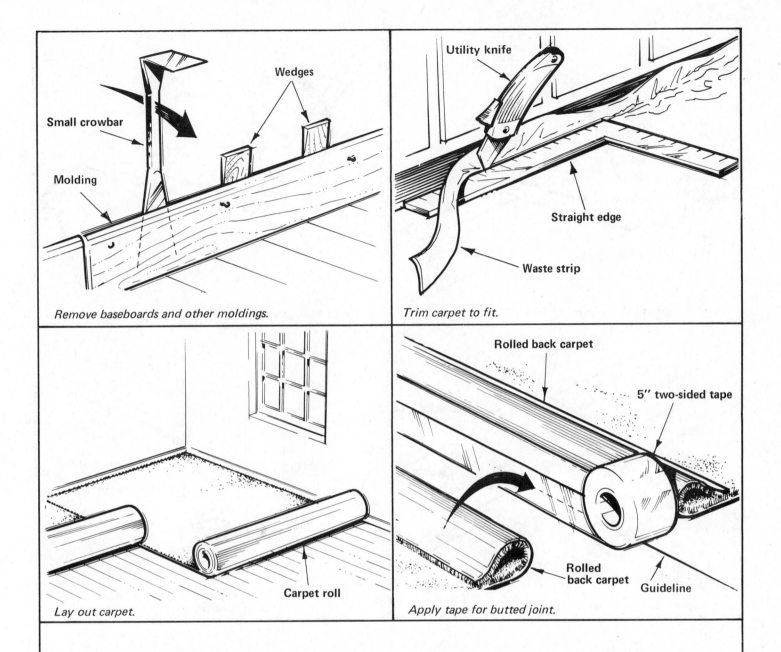

Remove baseboards and other moldings.

Small crowbar

Molding

Wedges

Trim carpet to fit.

Utility knife

Straight edge

Waste strip

Lay out carpet.

Carpet roll

Apply tape for butted joint.

Rolled back carpet

5″ two-sided tape

Rolled back carpet

Guideline

2. Lay out the carpet in the room if the kitchen floor is reasonably square. But if the shape of the floor is complicated, make a floorplan drawing of the kitchen floor. Measure with absolute accuracy, and then carry the carpet to another room to cut it.

3. Apply the 2-inch two-sided tape around the perimeter of the room, but leave the protective film on the upper side of the tape.

4. Lay out the carpet in the kitchen, checking for fit. Do any corrective trimming that might be necessary. If you discover spots where you cut the carpet too short, cut small strips from the unused carpet roll to fill in. If the carpet has a pattern, be sure to position the patches so that the pattern lines match.

5. When two pieces of carpet meet to form a butt seam, draw a pencil line on the floor between the two edges, roll them back, and apply the 5-inch two-sided tape. The tape should be centered on the pencil line so that each edge of carpet will adhere to 2-1/2 inches of the tape. Do not remove the protective film from the top of the tape yet.

6. Now go around the perimeter of the carpet, stripping off the protective film and pressing down on the carpet. If there are any butt seams, reach under the carpet and pull the film off the tape after the perimeter is secure.

7. Attach any patches.

8. Replace the molding and baseboards over the new carpet.

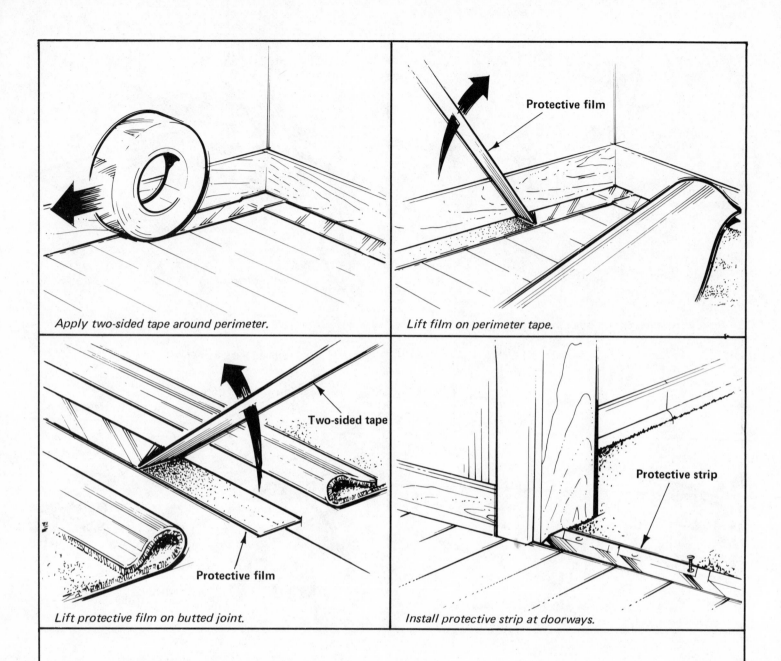

Apply two-sided tape around perimeter.

Lift film on perimeter tape.

Protective film

Lift protective film on butted joint.

Two-sided tape

Protective film

Install protective strip at doorways.

Protective strip

How To Refinish Hardwood Floors

Tired of floor coverings and want to restore the natural warmth and beauty of hardwood? It isn't easy, but it can be done. You will have to remove all vestiges of former finishes and adhesives and then strip the floor down to the bare wood. Only then can you apply the new finish.

Go to a tool rental store and rent a drum sander with a dust bag attachment. The store can also furnish sandpaper in various grit counts. Additional required tools include a disk sander, sanding block, hammer and nail set, paint brush, buffer, and a vacuum cleaner. In terms of materials, you'll need masking tape; open coat sandpaper in 20, 40, and 100 grits; turpentine; wax; and desired floor finish.

To refinish your hardwood floors, follow this step-by-step procedure.

1. Move everything out of the room. This includes curtains and draperies, pictures—everything. Floor refinishing is messy, with a lot of dust flying during the sanding operation.
2. Seal off all heating and cooling outlets with the masking tape, and around all doorways except the one you will use (seal that one, too, when you are ready to start). Some sanding dust will get into the rest of the house, but sealing doorways and duct outlets will help minimize the mess.
3. Carefully remove all quarter rounds, baseboards, or other molding at the floor.

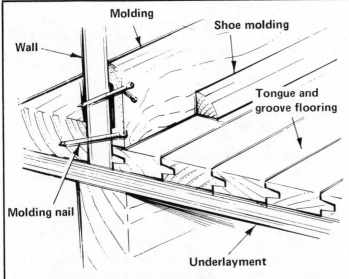

Molding

Shoe molding

Wall

Tongue and
groove flooring

Molding nail

Underlayment

Typical hardwood floor construction.

Typical floor sander.

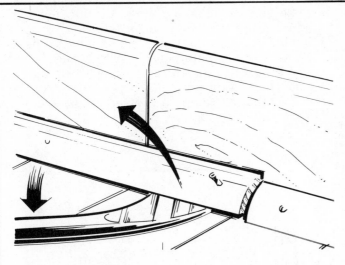

Remove shoe molding.

Floor sanding with hand sander.

4. Check the entire floor for nails, and countersink any that protrude, since they will tear your sanding belt or disk.
5. Open the windows.
6. For the first sanding pass, use 20-grit paper in the drum sander. Go back and forth over the entire floor, with the grain, overlapping about 3 inches. At the end of each pass, you will have to lift the sander and move it over—but be careful in doing this is avoid digging into the floor. Go slowly.
7. Use the disk sander and/or the sanding block in areas near the walls where the drum sander won't fit. Stay with the 20-grit paper.
8. Repeat the procedure with 40-grit paper, and then again with 100-grit. When you are satisfied that you have removed the old finishes, you can return the rental equipment.
9. Vacuum the room thoroughly, including the walls and around windows, to get all the dust out. Be sure to remove all dust or you will wind up with an inferior finish.
10. If your floor is pine (frequently the case in an older home), you'll have to use a special primer to seal the wood. Give the primer an hour to dry before applying your chosen finish.
11. If your floor is oak, rub some turpentine on a small section to see what the wood will look like with a natural finish. If you like the way the floor looks, you need not stain it. If you decide to stain the wood, wipe the stain on evenly and let it dry thoroughly according to the directions.

12. Among the easier clear finishes to apply are the plastic resins, one example of which is polyurethane varnish. The first coat will tack dry in about 15 minutes, and will be ready for the second coat in an hour. When the second coat dries, wax and buff. For a high gloss, wait overnight and apply a third coat using a mixture of one part reducer to four parts finish. Let this coat dry overnight before use. After the third coat, the floor will not require waxing and can be shined with a dry mop.

13. Natural varnish is a traditional finish coat that requires more care to apply. It is slower drying and there is more chance for dust to foul the finish. It is subject to checking as it grows older, though when applied properly it dries water clear for a beautiful finish. Follow it with a wax coat and buff.

A New Way To Install Parquet Flooring

A new method for floor refinishing can now give you the richness and elegance of parquet with surprising ease.

This new development is a self-sticking tile made with a hardwood face backed by moisture-proof plastic foam. The surface is rich grain hardwood.

These tiles can be laid over any clean, smooth floor. They are 9 inches square, and reducing strips are available for doorways that are beveled from the normal surface height down to the entry floor level. Though not preglued, they can be placed with a 2-sided tape. You will need a chalk line and a saber saw.

To install these parquet floors, do the following.

1. Remove any baseboard moldings, clean the existing floor and check it for smoothness. Build up any low spots and sand down high spots; if necessary, a new underlayment may be required.

2. When installing, it is easier to follow the same procedure as in tiling a floor, doing it by quarters from the center. This means that you may need to cut tiles around the perimeter of the room. The fractional pieces will then be the same size on opposite walls; making the job both neat and professional looking.

3. Simply peel off the paper backing and lay them down, butting them against each other. Make any required cuts with the saber saw. At the walls leave a gap of 3/8-inch for expansion. It will be hidden when you replace the molding, after the floor is laid.

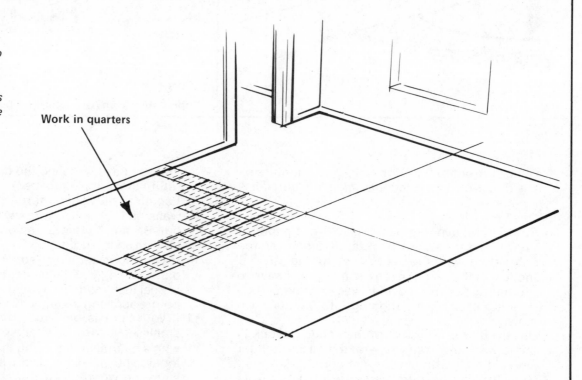

The proper method to lay out parquet tiles (or any other tile squares) is by quarters from the center of the room. First find the center of the four walls; draw floor lines after checking for squareness. Lay tile one quarter at a time, finishing all four quarters with full tiles before trimming perimeter pieces to fit. This will ensure an even look to the floor, since trimmed pieces will be of equal size.

Work in quarters

Doing Your Own Kitchen: Walls

Cabinets and appliances cover most of the walls in a kitchen. This would seem to leave little space for anything further. That's incorrect. There are a lot of things you can do and, with imagination, create something other than the usual flat white paint.

There's the backsplash area, for example, between the countertops and the upper wall cabinets. This is usually 5 inches high. Why not run this all the way up to the cabinets? It will look better and will be much easier to clean. Either match or contrast with the countertop surface or with the cabinets themselves.

Corian tops make it very easy to fill the rest of the area with the same material. This comes 1/4 inch thick and can be set on top of the counter and fastened to it with a bead of silicon sealer; or it can sit just as well on top of an existing backsplash.

You can also buy plastic figured sheets from your local countertop fabricator or from many lumber yards. This is applied directly to the wall with a mastic or contact adhesive.

Other options for walls include: Regular wall paneling, available in hundreds of patterns and colors; artificial or genuine brick veneer, vinyl wall fabric, self-sticking materials such as Contact paper, painted graphic kits, cultured (artificial) marble, and wallpaper murals.

Ceramic tile also can be used in the backsplash area or on other walls. They now come in self-sticking form to make installation a snap. You just pull off the paper backing and stick them on the wall.

The temptation with all of these options is to overdo it. It usually looks better to keep it relatively simple; but give it some thought before going to the same old paint. Wainscot treatment, for example, can sometimes add greatly to a kitchen dining area, as can a different wall covering; but too much will make a kitchen appear too 'busy.'

Paint In The Kitchen

Paints that work well in a kitchen include gloss and semi-gloss latexes, rubber-base paints, or flat and semi-gloss oil-based enamels. The latex materials are easiest to apply and clean up, are quick drying, and usually make the best choice in paints.

One of the first concerns in choosing a paint (or any other wall covering) is the color scheme. Color is largely a function of lighting. Before proceeding, be sure to read the section on lighting, which includes a discussion on color.

When painting walls, you can use either a brush or roller. The quickest method is to use a roller, but only after you use a brush to "cut in." That is, you put a few inches of paint around areas you don't want to touch or mark up with the roller. You should cut in a brush width close to all areas to be left unpainted; after shielding the area with masking tape or a hand-held sheet of cardboard. The ceiling is painted first, then work downward.

When using either brush or roller, make sure the walls are clean, smooth and even. Any old, flaking paint must be scraped, and the edges sanded or the new paint will not adhere. If you are right-handed, start at the left edge or corner and go to the right, working from the top down. A roller requires that you even the coverage by going crosswise after the up and down strokes. Go from one side to the other, from top to bottom, always painting against the wet edge. Try to time it so you can finish in one day. If you start wet paint against a dried edge it will show a mark.

Don't go too fast with either brush or roller. Speed causes splatters and makes for unnecessary cleanup problems.

Decorators usually suggest you paint the wood trim the same color as the walls, though you should use an enamel on the trim. If you choose to do this, then don't mask off the wood trim. Paint over it with the flat or semi-gloss wall paint, since it makes a good primer for the enamel.

Goof-Proof Wallpapering: How To Take It Down Or Put It Up

Most modern wallpapers are not really paper at all. The wallpaper often put up in your kitchen—where you have wide variations in heat and humidity—should be a vinyl-covered fabric, burlap, or metallic foil. You can buy these materials prepasted and some are even pretrimmed. It's a good idea, if possible, to buy one that's strippable, because these can be peeled off easily if you want to change later.

A standard roll of wall covering will cover 30 square feet, with 6 square feet in the roll that allows for overlapping, wastage, and so forth. Rolls come 24 inches wide x 18 feet long or 27 inches wide by 16 feet long. Both cover the same wall area. A few of the new metallic foils are 29-1/2 inches wide. You can also buy double and even triple rolls in the same widths but longer.

Before choosing the wall covering, measure the area you want to cover and add 20 per cent to that figure for wastage. You will then be prepared for any length or width your chosen material comes in. If you have one door and one window in the area to be covered, deduct one roll. For two doors and one or two average-size windows, deduct two rolls. If you want a border trim, this must be measured in feet, because such trim is sold in linear yards.

To prepare a wall that has a prior coating of flat paint, wash it thoroughly, fill all cracks, and remove any loose paint and sand the edges. Then apply a coat of wall sizing, a form of glue that makes wall coverings stick. Be sure to wash the walls because they often have accumulations of cooking grease.

If the wall is covered with gloss or semi-gloss paint, sand it down lightly with medium-grit sandpaper, just enough to remove the shine. Wash it with an ammonia solution made of one part ammonia mixed with six parts water. Rinse, apply sizing as above and proceed.

A textured wall surface must also be sanded reasonably smooth. Then fill any cracks or holes, rinse, and apply sizing. Bare wallboard or unpainted plaster, if smooth and sound, needs only a coat of sizing.

Should there be old wallpaper on the wall, it is best to remove it first. Vinyl paper will pull off easily; but often there are one or more layers of old paper. Many wallpaper stores rent steamers, and you will need a wallpaper scraper. Hold the steamer head to the wall and when the paste underneath has softened, use the scraper to peel it off. Wash the wall with steel wool and a washing compound to remove any old paste and sizing, rinse thorough-

ly, and patch any holes. Apply sizing and the wall is ready.

To hang the new wall covering you will need the following: A chalk line with a plumb bob at the end, paste brush, smoothing brush, seam roller, natural sponge and a razor trimming knife. You also will need a pasting table. This can be rented, or use a sheet of plywood—ideally about 6 feet long and 3 feet wide—resting on two sawhorses. If you can not do that, you can make-do with two card tables placed together, and covered with brown wrapping paper. If you are using a prepasted wall covering, the store will sell you an immersion tray. They are usually made of waxed cardboard or plastic, you can use a bathtub or large kitchen sink.

Though it seldom happens in a kitchen, if you are going to paper entirely around the room start in the most inconspicuous corner. This is because you will not be able to index (match the pattern) at the last seam. This usually is not a problem in a kitchen, because you normally will do only one or two walls.

Now, follow the steps below.

1. When hanging wallpaper, you should work from left to right if you are right-handed. Measure out from the corner along your first wall a distance of one inch less than the width of the roll. Mark the wall. Then tack your chalk line to the wall near the ceiling so it drops through the mark, hold the weight steady, and snap the line against the wall. This gives you a true vertical on which to line up the paper so it will be straight.
2. Lay the first sheet of paper on the pasting table, and cut it lengthwise to 4 inches more than your

Wallpapering tools surrounding cutting table: (clockwise from upper left) seam roller, plumb bob, utility knife, toothed cutter, paste bucket, razor blade, smoothing brush, paste brush, and scraper.

floor-to-ceiling height. Hold it up to the wall to check. There should be about a 2 inch overlap at the ceiling and floor.

3. If it is right, lay it back on the table face up and unroll paper for the second strip. Make sure that the pattern matches at the left edge of the new strip and the right edge of the first strip. Don't cut until it indexes. Repeat this to get a stack of several strips ready to hang. Turn the stack over pattern side down and you are ready to start.

4. Mix your paste according to the manufacturer's instructions. Avoid lumps. Tying a string across the top of the paste bucket to hold the brush will keep the handle clean.

5. Apply the paste first on the top half of the roll in a figure 8 and then the remainder, making sure to cover the whole surface. Any unpasted spot will make a blister. Fold the top half over, paste to paste, and apply paste to the bottom half. Fold this in the same way. This will make it easy to carry the strip to the wall.

At the wall unfold the top half, carefully and accurately position the edge next to the chalk line, and start smoothing toward the corner with your hand. Smooth it well into, and an inch around, the corner. When finished, unfold the bottom half and smooth it the same way.

6. Use your smoothing brush to work out excess paste and air bubbles, always working toward the edges. Use the edge of the brush to ease the material tight into the corner along the ceiling and the floor or baseboard. Turn the brush vertical to smooth the paper into the vertical corner. Make sure the material sticks.

7. Proceed as above with the next panel, butting it against the edge of the first, and so on, working along the wall.

8. Roll the seams with the seam roller about 15 minutes later. Do not roll hard, but firmly. Rinse each strip after rolling with a natural sponge and clear water, squeezed dry enough so the water will not run. Trim off any excess material at floor and ceiling with the razor knife. Have plenty of blades on hand so you can throw the blade away after five or six cuts. They dull rapidly, and when dull will easily tear the material.

9. When you reach a corner, measure from the edge of the last strip to the corner, and add a half-inch. Subtract the total from the width of the roll strip. Measure this total along the new wall, make a mark, and snap a new chalk line to be sure all strips on the new wall will be vertical.

For example, say you have 15 inches from the edge of the last strip to the corner. Add a half-inch and you get 15-1/2 inches. Subtracting this from the width of your roll (say it's 24 inches) and you get 8-1/2 inches. Measure along the new wall a distance of 8-1/2 inches

and make your mark for the new chalk line.

When you hang the last sheet on the first wall (the sheet that turns the corner), butt its left edge against the right edge of the previous strip. Smooth it and tap well into the corner, then trim it vertically a half-inch from the corner on the new wall. Slide the remaining section to

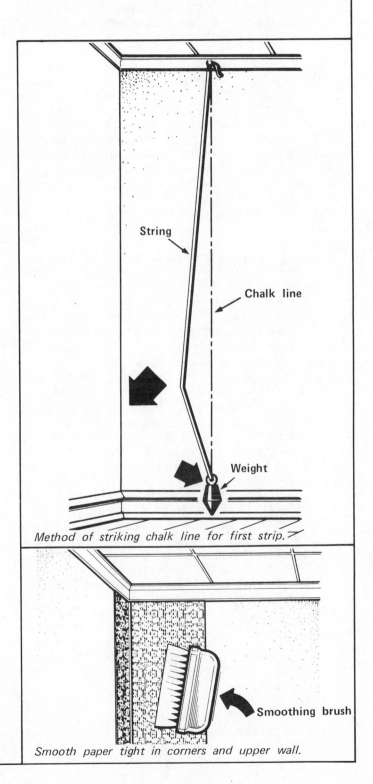

Method of striking chalk line for first strip.

Smooth paper tight in corners and upper wall.

the left, into the corner and over the half-inch you already have pasted. Line up the right edge with the new chalk line on the new wall.

10. Do not try to piece small strips in over windows and doors. Hang a full strip just as though the window or door was not there. Use scissors and cut diagonally from the inside of the door or window and across the corner like a miter joint. This will let you paste the paper flat against the wall around the corner, and you can trim off excess paper with your razor knife.

To hang prepasted wall covering, follow the same procedure as above, cutting strips to length and indexing them. To apply a strip, reroll it from bottom to top with the glued side out, loosely, and immerse it in the tray. Follow directions on immersion time. Then carry the whole tray to the wall, lift the end of the roll to the ceiling, index to the line, and stick it down. Again rub and brush out air bubbles; then trim as before.

How To Install Wood Paneling

Wood paneling is popular for kitchen walls. Relatively easy to apply, especially using the new paneling adhesives, paneling does not require a lot of wall preparation and covers up many flaws. The variety of patterns and wood finishes is almost limitless. However, some of the less expensive panels are not moisture resistant and for that reason are not suitable for the kitchen. It may be better to choose a good plastic-surface paneling instead. Most panel sheets are 4x8 feet. Sheets are available in 4x10 or 4x7 feet for higher or lower ceilings.

To apply, follow these steps.

1. Remove all moldings from the lower edge and check the wall for high or low spots. Sand down any high spots. If the wall is reasonably smooth, you can apply the new panels directly to the old wall. If it is uneven, you will have to use furring strips (1x2 inch slats of wood) to provide a plumb, level surface. Locate your wall studs, which probably will be 16 inches apart center to center, and nail the furring strips horizontally, every 16 inches to the wall. Cut furring strips to fit vertically every 16 inches and nail along the studs between the first set.

2. Since this will make any wall outlets or switches inaccessible or too deep for their cover plates; remove the cover plates and reset the boxes out. The edge of the box should be almost flush with the room side of the panel. Be sure to shut off the current first.

3. Before paneling is installed, it should be brought into balance with the temperature and humidity conditions in the room. Panels should spend at least a day in the room in which they are to be installed stacked flat with full-length furring strips separating them so air can circulate between the sheets.

4. Carefully check ceiling height at several places before cutting panels to fit. Often there are slight variations. If such variations are no more than 1/4 inch you can then cut all panels at once. If you are using a circular saw, cut slowly against a guide strip C-clamped to the stack because circular saws often tend to wander. Cut panels 1/2-inch short to allow 1/4-inch gap at floor and ceiling for expansion.

5. Stack all panels in position at the wall to check for pattern or woodgrain color. Woodgrains may vary considerably from panel to panel. Place them for the most pleasing combination, then move them aside and out of the way.

6. If the first panel will fit into a corner, place it there and check the far edge for plumb. Corners are seldom completely straight, and you may have to sand or file the corner edge of the panel to conform. Do this carefully, for if the first panel is crooked, the entire wall will look uneven.

7. Apply adhesive to the first panel, going around edges and then in three wavy vertical lines between them from top to bottom. If you are using furring strips, only apply adhesive to the strips.

8. Press panel into place, with a 1/4-inch gap at top and bottom, and wedge it up from floor with wood shingles. Put in a couple of panel nails at the top to hold it in place. Press all over the face of the panel to spread the adhesive. Now repeat with the second panel, butting it carefully to the first.

9. Go back to the first panel, put your fingers under it at the floor and pull it out from the wall about 6 inches. Brace it there with a small piece of wood. It will be hinged from the top by the nails you put in. The purpose here is to let the adhesive get tacky. This will take about 10 minutes, during which you can glue and put up the third panel. Then remove the block of wood and press the first panel to the wall, and use a hammer and cloth-covered block of wood to spread adhesive fully and glue panel to wall. Pull out the second panel and brace it and put the fourth panel in place, following this sequence as you move along the wall.

10. When you come to panels where you will have to cut holes for switches or outlets, measure carefully from ceiling, floor and the edge of the preceding panel. Mark for the cutout on the new panel. Drill pilot holes within each corner of the mark and saw it out with a keyhole saw.

11. Finish the job off with matching moldings at top and bottom and the outer edges. Where the moldings meet, miter them or use a coping saw to make them fit together.

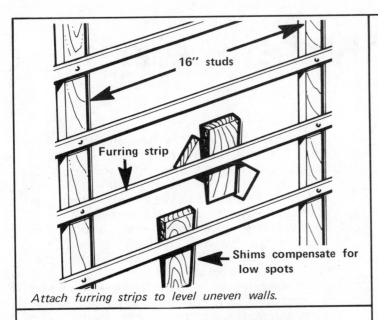

16" studs

Furring strip

Shims compensate for low spots

Attach furring strips to level uneven walls.

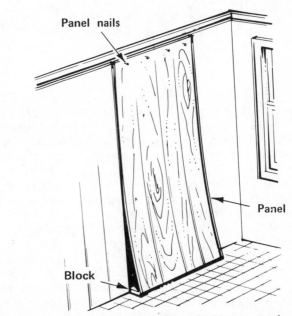

Panel nails

Panel

Block

Pull out panel and allow adhesive to become tacky.

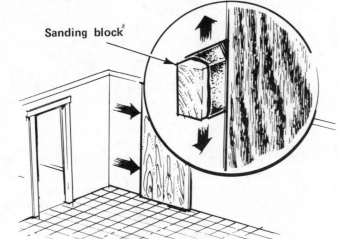

Sanding block

Sand corner panel to conform with uneven wall.

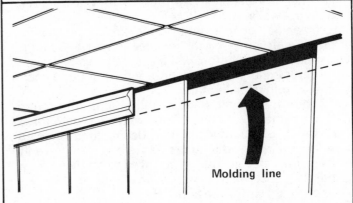

Molding line

Install moldings to cover up uneven panels.

Wilder Things To Do With Walls

The conventional wall treatments already covered—painting, paneling, papering with vinyl or plastic laminates—are suited for kitchens because all are easily cleanable. But there are also artificial brick and stone veneers, popular for other rooms of the house, though they are harder to clean because they easily pick up kitchen grease. In a kitchen that opens to a dining or living area they can be excellent on a far wall. Easily applied with a mastic; they come with directions and you need only be sure to keep bricks reasonably level and plumb, with the lines straight.

More interesting in the kitchen, where there is often a blank wall in a dining nook, are painted graphics and murals.

Painted graphics are available in kits, some just for the wall and at times including the ceiling. If you have a flair for this kind of decoration, you can create your own graphics. If you do, always draw in miniature first so that pattern and colors are pre-established. Outline on wall, then do it color by color within the masked areas, leaving ample drying time between each color application. Remember, also, that you are doing this in the kitchen, so use gloss or semi-gloss paints.

Murals come in rolls like wallpaper, and you buy the necessary rolls to create the mural in one package. They come in specific widths and heights, though this is not as critical as for wallpaper. If, for example, your mural is a wooded scene, you can use all or any part of it depending on wall dimension. Murals are also available in vinyl-coated, prepasted, and even strippable designs. All of them are hung roll by roll as with any wallpaper.

Doing Your Own Kitchen: Ceilings

The easiest way to renew an old ceiling is to repaint it. A more difficult way is to apply a wallcovering, either matching the walls or harmonizing with them. You can put up acoustical tile, which not only makes a very attractive ceiling, but also can cut noise levels by from 55% to 75%. Kitchens do get noisy, what with appliances, running water, and many noise reflecting surfaces.

Most kitchen ceilings are painted white or off-white because one of the primary decorating principles is to put light colors high, dark colors low. A darker color on a ceiling tends to lower it and make the room seem smaller, and usually kitchens are too small already. Very light pastels in the same color family as the walls or countertops can be very pleasing, as long as they are lighter than the walls.

To paint a ceiling, first protect all kitchen equipment with drop cloths or newspapers. Ceilings should be done before walls, but if the walls are not to be painted protect them around the upper perimeter with masking tape.

Using a semi-gloss latex paint, "cut-in" around the perimeter of the ceiling with a brush for a distance of about 4 inches. Use a long-handled roller for the wider areas. Go slowly and evenly from one side to the other, always applying new paint against the wet edge. When finished, it is easy to clean up with soap and water.

How To Wallpaper A Ceiling

If possible, pay to have it done by a professional. Applying a wallcovering to a ceiling is backbreaking work and, since you will work on a makeshift scaffold, it is very dangerous. By having it done professionally, you may save a hospital bill.

If you want to try it, do the following:

1. You will need a vinyl-surfaced wallcovering, paste and other materials used for paperhanging on walls. In addition, you will need two ladders and a plank to make a scaffolding. Position them so you can work with your head about 6 or 8 inches below the ceiling. Use the two ladders as horses to support the plank, and the plank must be long enough so you can work from one side of the room to the other without getting down. You will also need a helper to hold the paper as you apply and smooth it down.

2. Always hang paper across the room, not lengthwise, because the linear distance is shorter. Snap a chalk line on the ceiling as you would for a wall so you can line up the first strip.

3. Cut all paper until you have the correct number of strips the right length to go across the entire ceiling. Allow an inch of overhang at each end of the strips for even trimming. If there is a pattern, be sure to index the strips before cutting them so the pattern matches.

4. If not prepasted, glue up the first strip, then fold it loosely like an accordion, starting at one end with each fold about 14 to 16 inches wide. Hang the smoothing brush around your neck with a string so it will be handy when you need it.

5. Get up on the scaffolding near the edge where you will start the first strip. Have the helper also get up on the scaffolding. Unfurl the first couple of folds of paper while holding it up near the ceiling, and have your helper move the rest of the strip right or left so that you start straight along your chalk line. Smooth it to the ceiling with the brush. Check for straightness as you finish applying the strip. Slight unevenness in the corner along the ceiling line won't matter. However, if it is uneven enough to show, apply the first strip so it overhangs the wall by about a half-inch and trim it with a razor knife. Be sure you stay aligned with your chalk line.

6. Move the scaffold over, paste and fold the second strip in the same way. Proceed with the other strips until the room is finished.

7. When you come to a light fixture, cut off the current and remove it. Hold the paper up close and slit it to fit over the wiring. Slit from a central point and outward like rays so you can smooth the strip flat, then go back and trim. Replace the fixture when finished. Trim off all excess around walls, sponge down the surface, and the job is finished.

How To Install Ceiling Tiles

The standard way to install ceiling tile in a kitchen has been to nail up 1x3 inch furring strips on 12 inch centers across the joists. You then staple or nail the tongue-and-groove tiles to the strips. A new method uses metal furring channels. They are self-leveling and hide beneath the tiles, making the ceiling look like one continuous piece.

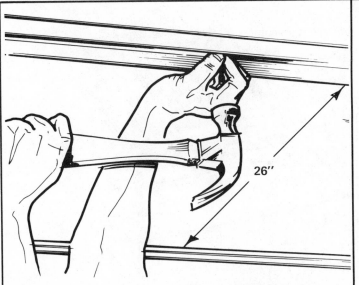

Measure out 26 inches from wall for first furring strip.

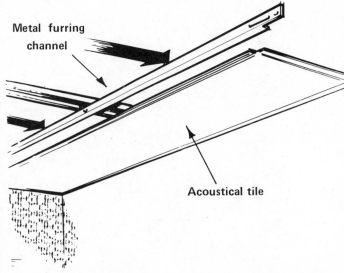

Metal furring channel

Acoustical tile

Typical suspended tile system (dropped slightly).

This is the Armstrong Integrid system. It uses 12x12 inch or 12x48 inch tiles and furring channels that are manufactured in 12 foot lengths. These are designed to hold metal cross tees from which the tiles are suspended.

The ceiling is installed like this:

1. Nail molding to all four walls, 2 inches below the level of the ceiling.
2. Nail the first metal furring channel to the ceiling, 26 inches out from wall. A nail goes every 48 inches along each channel. Remaining channels are spaced 4 feet apart from the first one.
3. Bend the sides of each channel slightly inward and clip on cross tees. When clipped in, tees will slide easily along the channel.
4. When all channels and tees are in place, start installing tile in a corner of the room. Just lay the tile on the molding and slide the tee into concealed slot on leading edge of tile.
5. Continue across room installing full tiles. When a tile must be cut to finish a row, save the remainder and use the leftover piece to start the next row. The tiles hide all supporting members except for the perimeter molding.

Other ceiling tile systems use hanging wires to support the strips and cross tees. They are excellent for dropping high ceilings, or if you want to include luminous ceiling lighting fixtures. These fixtures are engineered to fit with the ceiling system and are the same size as the ceiling panels. Fixtures are dropped and installed with a panel beneath them wherever you need a light. The result is a continuous, integrated system.

Other Ceiling Ideas:
Skylights, Beams, And Hooks

A skylight can add both magic and natural daylight to the kitchen of any one-story house, even when it has a gabled roof. Best of all, it can be installed fairly easily in a day, if the roof is flat.

If the roof is gabled, the way to do it is to construct a "light shaft" from the skylight in the roof, through the attic and to a hole in the ceiling of the kitchen. The light shaft can be made of 3/8-inch plywood—just four walls attached on the outside corners with strapping and screws—and painted white on the inside.

First, though, check the ceiling and the attic to make sure there is a place for a skylight. You might find cooling ducts, wiring or other mechanical elements that can't be moved out of the way. If the way is clear, buy the skylight to fit between the rafters. These can vary from 16x16 inches to 48x48 inches. The roof opening generally will be cut about 3 inches less on both dimensions. Try to find a skylight that is doubled-glazed with a dead air space between, to avoid heat loss in winter or summer cooling problems.

To install a skylight, do the following:

1. Up in the attic, drive a 3-inch nail up through the roof at each corner where you want the opening. Follow the same procedure with gabled or flat roofs.
2. Climb onto the roof and locate the nails. Remove the roofing material about 12 inches all around the skylight area. Drill pilot holes within

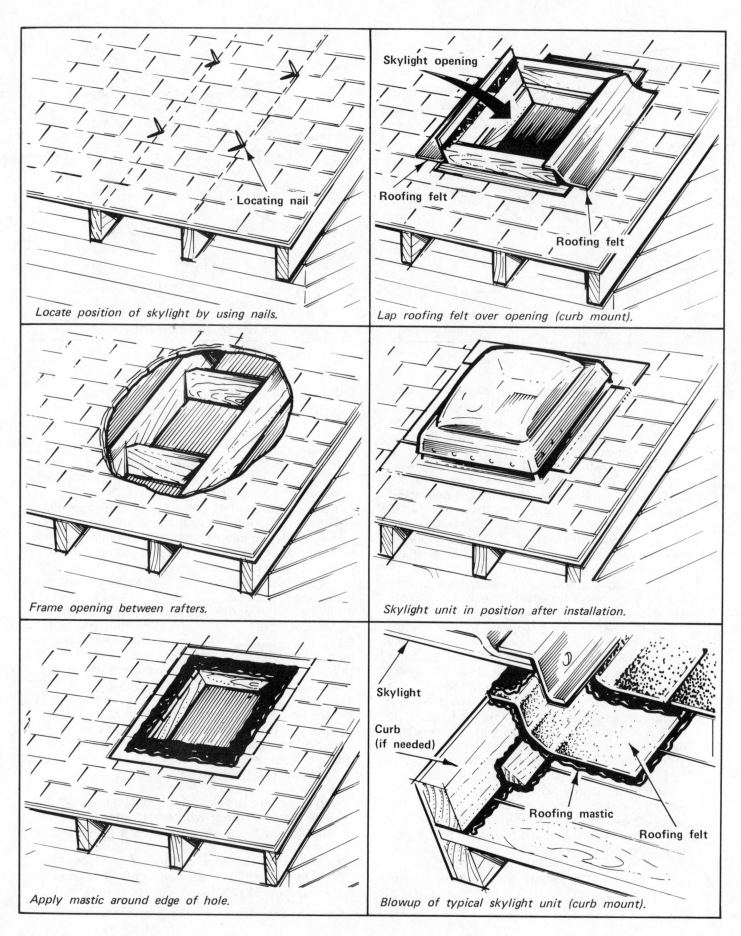

Locate position of skylight by using nails.

Lap roofing felt over opening (curb mount).

Skylight opening

Roofing felt

Roofing felt

Frame opening between rafters.

Skylight unit in position after installation.

Apply mastic around edge of hole.

Blowup of typical skylight unit (curb mount).

Skylight

Curb
(if needed)

Roofing mastic

Roofing felt

the corners of the cutout and cut the hole for the skylight with a keyhole or saber saw. You may have to cut one rafter in doing this.

3. Frame the opening at top and bottom between the rafters with the same size stock as used for the rafters. Normally these will be 2x6 inch pine. If the rafters are too far apart to align with the skylight, add framing at the sides. If it was necessary to cut a rafter, you will have to tie it into the framing with other 2x6's.

4. Apply roofing mastic around the entire opening, about 1/4-inch thick. Cover all exposed wood surfaces.

5. Position the skylight over the opening, drill small holes for nails, and nail each corner down into a rafter using 8 penny nails. Use rustproof roofing nails around the flange itself, spaced about 3 inches apart.

6. Apply more mastic over the edge of the skylight. Stop short of the cutout and any parts that will be visible from below. Cut strips of roofing felt wide enough to go from the flange to overlap the felt on the roof decking. Put the side pieces on first, then the top piece;   and then a piece at the bottom overlapping the sides to prevent a moisture trap.

7. Apply another coat of mastic over the felt strips and replace the roof shingles. When all shingles have been replaced, apply a bead of mastic across the bottom edges of the skylight. The result will let light in and keep moisture out.

The above instructions are for a low-profile skylight, mounted flush to the roof. Others are mounted on a curb. The process is the same except that you build a "curb," a box of 2x6 inch lumber to fit on top of the cutout. The skylight fits over the top of the curb.

Ceiling Beams

Ceiling beams can be constructed of 1/4-inch plywood or hardboard, miter-jointed where the edges meet and held together with glue blocks inside. Once installed, they can be painted to match the ceiling, or covered with woodgrain self-stick vinyl.

Another easy way to get realistic ceiling beams is to buy them ready-made of polyurethane plastic. These are finished to look exactly like wood, come either smooth or carved, and are so light that a child can easily lift a 12 foot length with one hand. They can be attached to the ceiling with mastic and, once in place, even an expert can find it difficult to detect that they are not wood.

Cut the foam beams either with a knife or a hand saw. If you want cross beams, they can be lap-jointed where they cross. This means you cut a section out of the bottom half of the beam you put

up first and half section out of the top of the beam that crosses it. Measure carefully before making the cuts and make them a half-inch too small. Shave them to fit tightly. This is extra work, but the joinery is critical to their appearance, especially on patterned, preformed beams.

You should cut the long beams to fit tightly. To place them, have a helper pull the center down while you slightly bend the ends up into place. Then push the center up. Shave slightly if the beam is too long.

Hooks And Hanging Implements

Decorative and sturdy hooks are available to hold pots, plants, or what have you from the ceiling. Do not use ordinary hardware; instead go to the lighting department of a good home center or any place where they have parts for swag lights. Buy the hooks used for these hanging lamps. These hooks come in silver, brass, black and white. They screw directly into the joists above your ceiling wallboard or plaster.

The problem here is to locate the joists and then to be sure you get solidly into wood for firm support. Swag lighting hooks have little base plates, 1 inch or more in diameter, that fit tightly against the ceiling when screwed in. This means that once you locate the center of the joist you can drive a finishing nail in on either side of the spot where you want to place the hook, and make sure there is enough wood to hold it. The nail holes will then be hidden by the decorative plate. Use a drill to make a pilot hole for the hook. Without this it is very easy to screw the hook in crooked.

Do not depend on molly or toggle bolts in the ceiling wallboard for any real weight. Over a period of time it will slowly pull the wallboard down until it is noticeable, and may pop the nails. Be sure by screwing into a joist. If this is impossible for correct placement, screw a solid 2x3 inch furring strip across two joists for the hook, and paint it to match the ceiling.

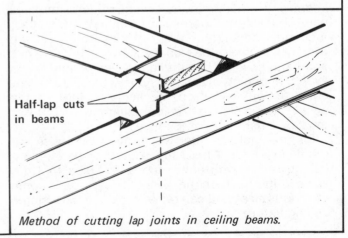

Half-lap cuts in beams

Method of cutting lap joints in ceiling beams.

Doing Your Own Kitchen: Electrical

Lighting in the kitchen must be planned from two points of view, the decorative and the functional. The decorative aspect is important not so much for the shape of the fixtures, but rather for the way the light affects color rendition. Different types of lighting definitely affect the overall decoration scheme, the appearance of foods, and perhaps even the mood of those who are using the kitchen.

From the functional point of view, you need general illumination for the entire room and localized illumination in the work areas. Such 'task' or directional lighting supplements the general lighting and is needed over counter spaces and other work/activity areas in the kitchen.

Artificial light in the kitchen can be either incandescent or fluorescent. Bulbs are incandescent and tubes are fluorescent.

Incandescent light is 'warmer'—that is, it is more flattering to skin tones, natural woods and the color of food. The light always comes on immediately, can be hooked to a dimmer switch to control its strength, and the bulbs or fixtures are less expensive than fluorescent tubes. Incandescent bulbs do generate more heat, however, and they consume more electricity to put out less actual light per watt than a comparably sized fluorescent tube.

Fluorescent lighting is more efficient than incandescent, producing about 250 percent more light for the current used. Service life is about seven times that of an incandescent bulb. Cooler in heat output and color rendition, fluorescent tubes provide more even illumination with less glare. There can be a slight flicker or hum, however, this can be partially alleviated with diffuser panels and proper installation.

An excellent form of general illumination for the kitchen is a full luminous ceiling, which simulates natural daylight. When such ceilings are installed, they must be situated along the centerline of the room, with the tubes spaced at least 10 inches apart and covered by diffusers. Keep in mind, however, that luminous ceilings (unless installed in new construction) will drop the actual height of the ceiling. The distance from the ceiling to the diffuser must be a minimum of 15 inches.

Fixture makers offer what they call false luminous ceilings. These are square or rectangular ceiling boxes with either tubes or bulbs that are surface-mounted on the ceiling. These boxes come in various sizes and can replace the standard single ceiling fixture.

Besides general illumination, you will need task lighting for counter work surfaces and at the sink and range. Counter areas can be well-lighted with undercabinet fluorescent fixtures. Fixtures should be 12 to 18 inches long and spaced about 30 inches apart. Use 15-watt tubes.

When the sink is under a window, you can create enough light for it by using two 40-watt tubes recessed in a soffit and shielded with a diffuser. An alternative would be to use a 75-watt incandescent downlight centered over the sink.

Lighting at the range is usually solved by lights that come installed in the ventilating hood. Typically, such fixtures take a 25-watt incandescent bulb or a 15-watt fluorescent tube; the latter should be the Deluxe Warm White type for better color rendition. An alternative would be to use recessed lighting or a soffit downlight with a 75-watt incandescent bulb focused down on the range top.

What Do-It-Yourselfers Should Know About Wiring

If you plan to install lighting yourself—or make other sorts of electrical connections—the first thing you must know is whether you are permitted to do any wiring at all. Most communities have wiring and electrical codes, and many of these specify that all wiring and electrical work must be done by a licensed electrician. The first step, therefore, is to go to the town hall or county seat and get a copy of the electrical code to check whether you are permitted to do the work.

Also, the editors recommend that unless you know something about electrical work, have it done for you by a licensed electrician. Wiring is dangerous, and electrocuting yourself is not a good tradeoff for saving money.

In nearly all cases, no matter who does the work, the local authorities will make at least two inspections. One comes when the preliminary work is completed, another when it is finished. When obtaining the code, ask if you will need a permit. Ignorance is no excuse, and you can be subject to fines later if you fail to do something that local law requires.

Here's how your electrical system works:

The power company supplies electricity through

its wires, this passes through a meter in your home and then to a service panel. The power company's responsibility ends at the meter. The service panel is the start of a number of separate, discrete circuits. Each circuit is a small electrical system with a variety of electrical outlets, and each circuit is guarded and controlled by either a circuit-breaker that trips or a fuse that blows in case of overload.

Terms you should know:

A volt is the unit used to measure electrical pressure or current strength.

An ampere (or "amp") is a unit used to measure the rate of flow of electricity or intensity of current draw.

A watt describes current drain relative to voltage. For example, 120 watts at a pressure of 120 volts is one amp (W/V = A). Watts divided by volts equal amperes. Amperes multiplied by volts equal watts (A x V = W).

A typical 15-amp circuit in a home can deliver 1800 watts (A x V = W, or 15 x 120 = 1800). In your kitchen, this could mean a television set that takes 300 watts, a mixing center that takes 400, a toaster that takes 980, and four 30-watt under-cabinet tubes. This adds up to 1800 watts and that should be the maximum for that circuit. Before adding outlets on a circuit, you have to know what the load already is on that line. You can do this only by checking circuit by circuit. Take out the fuse or trip the circuit breaker to see what doesn't work. You can not assume everything in one room is one the same circuit. One side of the kitchen might be on the same circuit with that side of the upstairs bedroom; another side may share a circuit with a room on the first floor.

The service panel will be found in a metal box near the meter. Called the panel box, it usually has blank spaces for additional circuits. Check to see, since it may be possible to add another circuit.

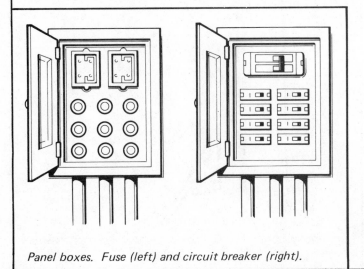

Panel boxes. Fuse (left) and circuit breaker (right).

Junction Boxes And Cable

If you wish to install a new switch or receptacle outlet, you will have to cut into the existing wall or ceiling to mount a junction box. This box provides an anchor point for the electrical cable and the actual fixture. Cable will have to be run from an existing circuit to this new box. Often, it is possible to drop a wire through into the basement or go up into the attic; if not, you will have to do some 'fishing.' This process is what happens when you put a wire through a blind wall or other location where you cannot conveniently reach to pull the cable. Fishing tape is springy, flat steel wire 1/16 X 1/8 inch that comes in coils of 50 or more feet. With a couple of 12-foot lengths, you can do about all the fishing you need to do.

To fish for a wire, you will require the following equipment: A keyhole saw, brace and bit, some fish tape (sold in rolls in the hardware store), the proper cable, junction box, patching plaster and the wall finishing materials. To install a new box:

1. Locate where you want the new junction box, mark and then saw out that section of the wall or ceiling. Mount the box securely to the stud. Determine where the cable will run from the existing circuit. Try to have it come up through the basement or directly through a party wall.

2. Cut a hole in the wall beside the existing circuit. Determine how many studs will have to be bored in order to route the cable; then drill the holes with the brace and bit. It may be necessary to locate additional access holes in order to do this. Be careful to avoid plumbing and electrical lines that are already in place.

3. Bend hooks at the ends of the fish tape by applying heat from the gas stove or a propane torch. This will prevent it from catching on obstructions and will give you a place to attach your cable. Run the tape through the holes and along where the cable will run. It may be necessary to use two tapes from opposite sides before you have a sufficient length.

4. Pull cable through with the fish tape and make the necessary connections into the junction box using the appropriate connectors. The fishing holes should then be covered with plaster. Refinish the wall and/or ceiling.

Junction boxes come in standard sizes, and there are special ones to fit into the ceiling. All general-purpose circuits require at least No. 12 two-conductor wire; a three-way switch will require three conductor wire with an attached ground. If you are installing an appliance receptacle, heavier gauge wire will be required if the appliance takes 220 volt current. Your electrical code will tell you what type of wire and/or conduit to use and should always be consulted prior to any installation.

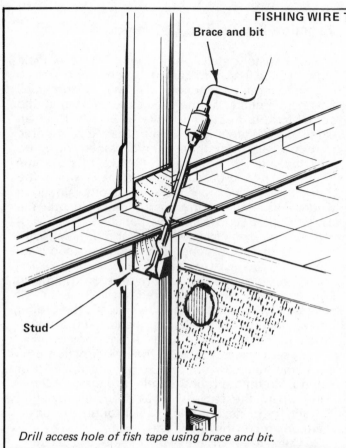
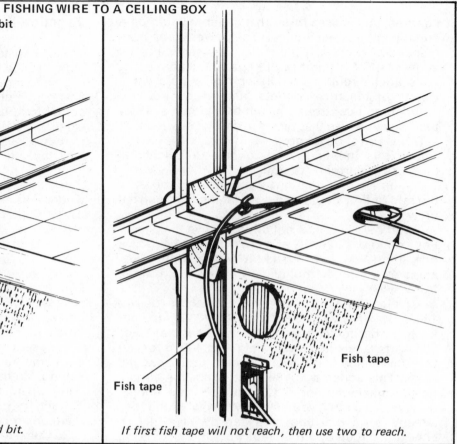

Drill access hole of fish tape using brace and bit.

If first fish tape will not reach, then use two to reach.

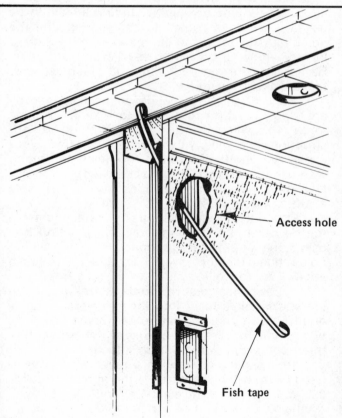
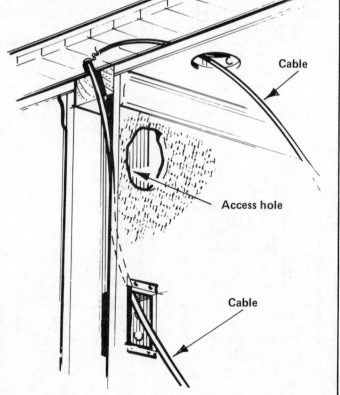

Insert fish tape through holes and around to second hole.

Once fish tape is through, hook cable onto end and draw into place.

Single-pole switches control a single outlet or fixture, while three-way switches control a fixture or light from two locations (as on opposite doors in the same room). Standard plugs are called duplex receptacles. Any of them will fit into a standard junction box.

Wire nuts are solderless connectors for joining two or more wires. These are available in many sizes and are simply screwed over the exposed ends of the wires.

There are several types of electrical cable. Depending on your local code, standard in your area may be Romex or BX cable. The latter is in a metal sheath; the former typically is run through conduit or is stapled directly to the stud in such a way that no staples pierce the cable. If you strip the outer covering from the cable, you will find one bare wire, one with black insulation, and a third with white insulation. The black wire is the hot wire. It attaches to another black wire or to the brass-colored attachment screw in the device you are hooking up. The white wire is neutral and attaches to another white wire or to the silver-colored screw in the device. The bare wire is the ground and is attached to the green screw.

If your electrical code calls for conduit to route the cable to the outlets, you must install such conduit first. Take care to make accurate bends in the tubing. Fish tape is the method by which the Romex cable is led through the conduit.

Replacing A Single-Pole Switch

If you need to replace a switch because it no longer operates or because a newer type would fit your remodeling plans, here is how to go about it:

1. Shut off the current to the switch. Remove the cover plate, and use a voltage tester to make sure the switch has been deactivated. Touch one probe of the tester to the brass hot screw and the other to the metal box. If the light is dark, the current is off.
2. Remove the two screws at the top and bottom of the switch that hold it to the box. Pull the switch completely out, loosen the screw terminals, and remove the wires.
3. Align the new switch so the lever is down in the off position. Attach the wires in the same sequence as in the old switch. Replace the entire switch into the box and secure with the same mounting screws. Replace the cover plate and restore the current.

Replacing A 120-Volt Receptacle

If a receptacle cracks and you wish to install a new one, the procedure is as follows:

1. Be sure the electricity is shut off. Test with a voltage tester to make sure no current is going to the receptacle.
2. Remove the mounting screws and pull the receptacles from the box. Check carefully to see how many wires are attached to the receptacle. With four or more wires, there will be two cables entering the box. This is the "middle-of-the-run" type and means other receptacles are on the same circuit. If there is only one cable, then the receptacle is an "end-of-the-run" type and represents the end of a circuit.
3. Remove the wires by removing the attachment

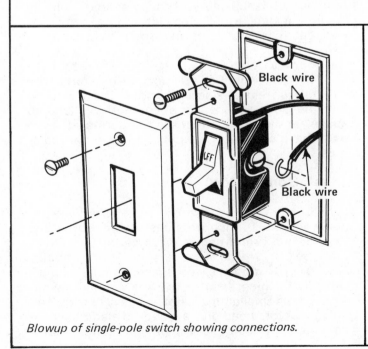

Blowup of single-pole switch showing connections.

Black wire

Black wire

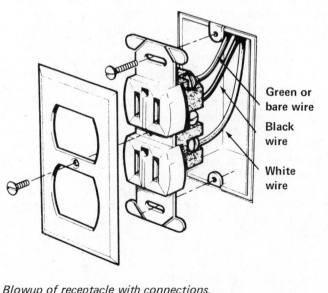

Blowup of receptacle with connections.

Green or bare wire

Black wire

White wire

screws on either side. Wire up replacement in the exact same manner as the original receptacle. Make sure all screws are tight.

4. Remount receptacle in the box with the mounting screws. Replace the cover, and turn on the current.

Ranges

With the exceptions of built-in ovens and cooktops, most ranges are relatively easy to install. Built-in ovens need special cabinetry with cutouts for the oven. Despite the fact that the ovens come in standard nominal widths, there are dozens of different sizes for the cutouts. Some are a single cavity, double ovens have two cavities, and more expensive models have two cavities plus something else, such as a warming drawer. The size of the cutout must be made according to the manufacturer's specifications for the particular oven model.

In replacing a built-in oven, the cutout may have to be made bigger. It can simply be cut larger, provided the oven cabinet will accommodate the new size. Check not only the cutout size, but also the width and height of the front frame of the cabinet. If either are too wide for the old cabinet, you will need a new oven cabinet. If the new oven takes a smaller cutout size, you often can add lumber framing in the cutout to scale it down.

With all gas ranges, you will have to shut off the gas and have a pipefitter make a new gas hookup. For electric stoves, have an electrician make a new electrical hookup. Most ranges take a separate circuit of 220 volts. For the light circuit or the new pilotless ignition in a gas range, an existing circuit will usually do.

In replacing a built-in cooktop, you will have to check cutout size for the specific model. Here you will have to worry about the cutout size in both dimensions and also the depth below the top flange, which can vary from 2-7/8 to 14 inches. This depth will affect the cabinetry below the cooktop.

You can make the cutout wider if you are replacing with a larger model, but you can not easily make it smaller. Some kitchen specialists will cut out an entire section of countertop a few inches wider than the new model, then install the cooktop in a new section. This is very effective if the new section has a contrasting pattern, such as butcher block. A metal T-molding can be used to join the new section to the old at either or both edges.

Other ranges, which have the cooktop and oven or ovens all in one unit, are much easier to install. The free-standing models simply have to be pushed into position, and gas and/or electrical connections made. Slide-in models are similar to free-standing but do not have finished sides. Kits are available to finish the sides if you want to use them free-standing. Slide-ins usually are flanked by cabinets on either side and must be placed to fit up close to the cabinets so they have a built-in appearance. They come in standard sizes, so there is little difficulty in replacement if needed later.

Drop-in models do not go all the way to the floor. They usually have one oven and a cooktop, and the bottom rests on a shallow base cabinet. Cabinet manufacturers make base cabinets for this purpose. Some drop-ins hang from the countertop by protruding flanges, and these have the most effective built-in look; though this calls for a very tight fit at countertop level.

Remember, in installing a range you will want a matching ventilating hood over it, between 22 and 30 inches above it. Cabinet manufacturers make special cabinets to accommodate hoods above the range.

Refrigerators

Most refrigerators are free-standing. There are only two built-in brands in the U.S. (Sub-Zero and Defiance), but several offer built-in trim kits to make free-standing models look built-in. Free-standing models can simply be pushed into place and plugged in. Then they should be leveled with the screws at the bottom so that the door swings shut gently when opened to a 45-degree angle.

There might be a problem getting a new refrigerator through a door, depending on the front handle and/or the coils mounted on the back. If this is so, nearly any model will go through a doorway if the door is removed. In rare instances, it might also be necessary to remove some of the doorway trim.

Built-in models require a special cabinet. Usually you will not be able to buy built-in models from a regular appliance store. They are sold only by kitchen dealers, and the dealers will have the custom cabinets made for the specific refrigerator models.

If your kitchen has the space, you can achieve a built-in look simply by framing the opening with cabinets on either side and above. But if you do this, be sure you retain a countertop "landing space" at the latch side of the refrigerator door so as to have someplace to put food or other materials.

Trash Compactors

A built-in trash compactor in the kitchen will replace either a 15-inch wide base cabinet or, in the case of two brand names (Thermador and Waste King, both by Norris Industries), a 12 inch cabinet. The 12-inch model saves space and has ample capacity for most families, with the added advantage that its smaller bag is not as heavy to carry out.

Compactors need only a standard electrical connection. They do not have to be built-in nor located in the kitchen although they should be handy to it. A built-in installation in the kitchen is simply the most desirable of the options. A compactor could go in a stairway, back porch, a breezeway or in a garage. But, like most kitchen appliances, it should be near the point of first or last use. This means near the kitchen or the garbage cans.

How To Ventilate Your Kitchen

Cooking produces most of the pollutants found in the normal home, and if these pollutants are not exhausted to the outside they will come to rest on all surfaces in the kitchen and in other rooms. The pollutants are grease, moisture, smoke, and odors. Since their source is the range, the best place to put an exhaust system is above the range. Methods of venting a kitchen include ducted range and oven hoods, wall fans, ceiling fans, and—in warmer climates—window fans.

Most production range hoods are rectangular metal units measuring up to 21 inches front to back and 5 to 9 inches high. They come in standard widths from 24 inches to 48 inches to fit under a wall cabinet. Taller canopy-type hoods are often used over island or peninsula ranges; some have sufficient power to be used for indoor barbecuing.

Most special order cabinet companies make hoods to match their cabinets. Regular hood-type blower units are mounted in these wood hoods by the kitchen dealer or the installer.

Hoods usually are placed 22 inches above the cooking or stove area. They can go as low as 18 inches, although this brings a possibility of head bumping. They should not be more than 30 inches above the cooktop for proper exhaust.

Ducted hoods have either a 8 inch round opening or a rectangular 3-1/4x10 inch discharge opening. These openings connect to standard ductwork and are equivalent in air movement volume. Adaptor units are available to change the discharge opening from round to rectangular or vice versa.

Ceiling fans mount between joists and usually discharge vertically through a round duct. Air is exhausted through a roof jack. Some ceiling fans have side discharges for use through an outside wall, or they can be installed in a wall with the duct (3-1/4x10 inches) running vertically between studs.

Wall fans usually are the most economical (if relatively inefficient) way to vent the kitchen. Installation on an outside wall requires no ductwork and is fairly simple. A wall fan should not be mounted in the wall over the range, since an accumulation of grease on the wall or fan is a potential fire hazard. The farther the fan is from the main source of pollutants, however, the less effective it will be in removing them.

You can reduce kitchen noise with a remote blower. As opposed to a hood or ceiling fan, such centrifugal or "squirrel cage" blowers can be placed outside to pull, rather than push, the air out. Remote blowers are much quieter than fans, and move more air.

Vent hoods, fans, and blowers are rated both in sones and air movement by the Home Ventilating Institute. Sones are internationally recognized

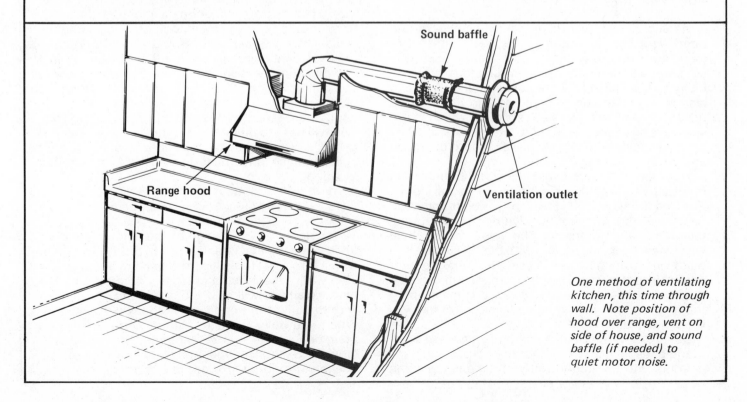

One method of ventilating kitchen, this time through wall. Note position of hood over range, vent on side of house, and sound baffle (if needed) to quiet motor noise.

units of loudness. For example, one sone is equivalent to the sound of a modern refrigerator operating in a quiet kitchen. HVI sets a limit of 8 sones for kitchen fans of up to 500 cubic feet per minute (cfm) capacity.

For good performance, a hood must have a capacity of at least 300 cfm; this kind of power calls for a blower, which is much quieter than a fan. Fair performance would call for a 200 cfm fan, with 140 cfm representing the minimum.

In an island or peninsula, cfm ratings must be about 25 percent greater because of air movement. For example, HVI recommends a minimum of 40 cfm per lineal foot for a standard range hood and 50 cfm per lineal foot for a peninsula or island hood. Thus a 36-inch range hood must have a minimum capacity of 120 cfm, while an island hood of equal dimensions must have a minimum capacity of 150 cfm.

Duct work must take the shortest, straightest route to the outside. Every foot of ducting length and every turn reduces ventilating performance. Where ducting is impossible—as in an apartment—ductless filter hoods can be used, but ductless filter hoods do not remove heat and moisture, and they are far less effective in removing smoke, grease and odors. On the other hand, they do filter the exhaust before returning the air to the kitchen, and thus are better than nothing. Ductless filter hoods are easy to install, requiring nothing but an electrical hookup.

Intercoms—To Do The Talking Without The Walking

A neglected or overlooked convenience in the home is often an intercom system. These are packaged radio systems that permit two-way communication from the central station in the kitchen to as many as 20 remote stations. They can also be a music center with AM and FM radio, a turntable and/or casette recorder with stereo speakers and even carry a fire/intruder alarm. They can even be bought with foldaway record changers and 8-track tape players.

With all of these capabilities, intercoms can function as an entertainment center in the home. The most favored is to plan a communication center in the kitchen to include a desk area, telephone and intercom. The telephone is best when wall-hung, in keeping with the thesis that you build in everything you can to keep counter surfaces clutter free. The intercom system can also be built into the wall, the foldaway features keeping the record-changer and tape player out of the way when not in use.

Obviously, none of these belong within the work triangle, especially with records or tapes, because it would add to kitchen traffic. Kitchens are often the most heavily used room in the house, however and an intercom system could prove useful and a definite time and work saver.

When you talk on a kitchen or other master station, you press a talk button and the message goes out on all remote stations. Then you push a"listen" button and you can be answered from any remote station. Usually remote stations have no buttons for talk or listen (though some expensive models will have them). According to NuTone, a leading manufacturer, the electrical cost of such a system if left on continuously is only about a penny per day and usually less.

These systems take special wiring. The wiring is available from the intercom manufacturer, along with rough-in and finish kits, all available through your dealer. Running wires through existing walls, especially from one story to another, is not difficult but it can be tedious. You will have to install a complete circuit from the central station through all remote stations.

You can get a wireless system that simply plugs into house current. The trouble with these is that they are subject to radio interference and will work only on 110 volts. Many houses are wired for 220 volts, so some circuits would be out of phase with the intercom and would work only in certain rooms. A simple system with just two or three stations might do to eliminate this, but not in an elaborate setup with stereo, record player, intruder/fire alarm and so forth.

In a deluxe, fully-wired unit, you have to figure out where you want the stations and then how to get the wire to them. Sometimes you can run wire along baseboards, or under a molding. In going from floor to floor you must look for gaps along the walls. Often it is easier to drop a wire through into the basement or go up through the attic and drop it down to another room. A couple of locations where you can usually go from floor to floor are along the plumbing waste stack or the vent that goes from your water heater all the way up through the roof. You will have to do some "fishing." That's what it is called when you put a wire into a blind wall or ceiling space and must fish for it from another location.

To do this, you must buy fishing tapes—springy, flat steel wires 1/16 x 1/8 inch that come in coils of 50, 75 or 100 feet. Ordinarily if you cut a couple of 12-foot lengths, you can do all the fishing you need to do. Heat the end of each tape over a gas range or with a torch, get it red hot, and bend in a small loop. This will prevent its catching on obstructions behind a wall and will give you a place to attach your wire to pull it from one hole in the wall to another. When you have to make fishing holes, try to cut them behind baseboards, moldings, door trim or in closets. Skillfully done, the wires will be unnoticeable throughout the entire system.

Doing Your Own Kitchen: Plumbing

As with electrical work, most localities have codes for plumbing that govern what can or cannot be done. Before doing anything, check with your local governmental unit, obtain a copy of the code and find out if you require a permit. You may find that a licensed plumber is necessary. Also, in some areas disposers are mandatory, where in others they are prohibited. Only a copy of the code can tell you these things.

To put it simply, plumbing is putting pipes together so they will not leak while conducting water to a given point. Though it takes skill to plumb out an entire house, the do-it-yourselfer can handle smaller jobs and produce a serviceable addition that will stand up to normal use. However, before attempting even smaller jobs, you should be familiar with general plumbing work. Plumbing can be complicated in older homes, so unless you are sure you know what you are doing, it might be safer to have the work done by a licensed plumber. A burst pipe can be not only messy but costly to rectify.

Over the years, many types of pipe have been used to conduct water; common in most homes are galvanized iron or steel, copper or, the greatest boon for the do-it-yourselfer, plastic pipe. There are several types of the latter; which kind you use depends on the type of material being carried. Chlorinated polyvinyl chloride (CPVC) takes both hot and cold water; polyvinyl chloride (PVC) is used in drainage and waste systems; polybutyl (PB) is flexible and easy to route into difficult areas. All can be interconnected with copper, or steel/iron. However, plastic pipe frequently leaks, even when installed by a plumber. You must be sure to cement it properly if you are using it. Check the code first, since plastic is not allowed in many areas.

The advantage of plastic piping is that a torch or solder is not required for fittings (as it is with copper) and this eliminates much difficulty. All plastic pipe joins together with a solvent cement; an operation called 'solvent welding.' You must make the joints quickly since the welding action is extremely fast, and once welded, the joint is permanent. You cannot take it apart to try again.

Before working with any plumbing, you will have to find the main water shutoff, which is normally located near the water meter where the water enters the house. Once the main water shutoff is closed, open all valves in the cold water lines to drain them. Hot water should be shut off where it leaves the water heater, then drain those lines. Otherwise, you may destroy your hot water heater. Once drained, the lines will not drip when you disconnect any pipe. This will also allow you to 'sweat' fittings if you are working with copper tubing, a process using solder to seal the joints.

If you are working with cast iron or steel pipe, you will need two pipe wrenches. Because of the nature of piping systems, you must hold one pipe (cast iron or steel) firmly while you unscrew a fitting from it, or you can loosen the whole section. Threaded iron pipe is fitted one section at a time and each is screwed tight in sequence; you cannot start from the middle and work toward either end—a disadvantage with iron or steel piping.

For copper, you will need a tubing cutter, hacksaw, a cleaning tool (steel wool or a wire brush is fine) and something to bend the tubing. Flare fittings require a special tool, though most gas stations have the flaring tool to do it if you are using this type of connection.

Copper pipe or fittings should not be joined until they have been 'brightened' with steel wool to remove any oxidation. You will also need a small propane torch, solder, and flux. Be sure to carefully solder any joints and use plenty of flux to ease the action, as this is crucial to the operation.

Copper tubing itself comes in two basic varieties: rigid and semi-flexible. The latter is easier to work

Three standard indoor piping systems and their joints - iron/steel (top); copper (middle); plastic (bottom).

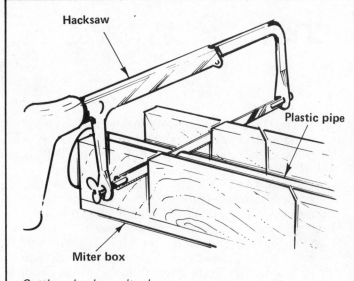

Cutting pipe in a miter box.

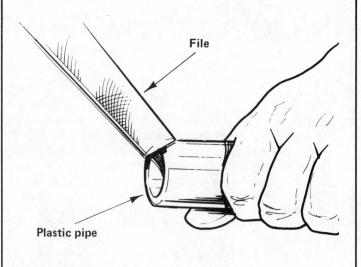

Remove all burrs before solvent welding.

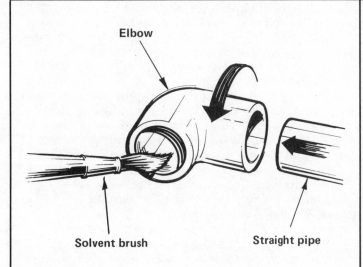

Typical solvent welding operation with plastic pipe.

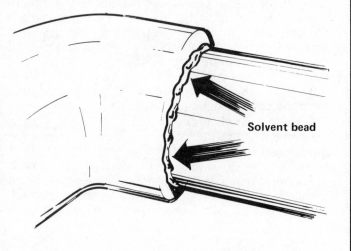

Finished solvent-welded joint. Note bead of fused plastic.

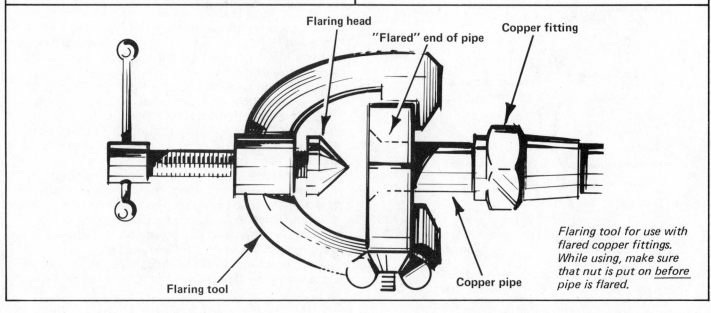

Flaring tool for use with flared copper fittings. While using, make sure that nut is put on before pipe is flared.

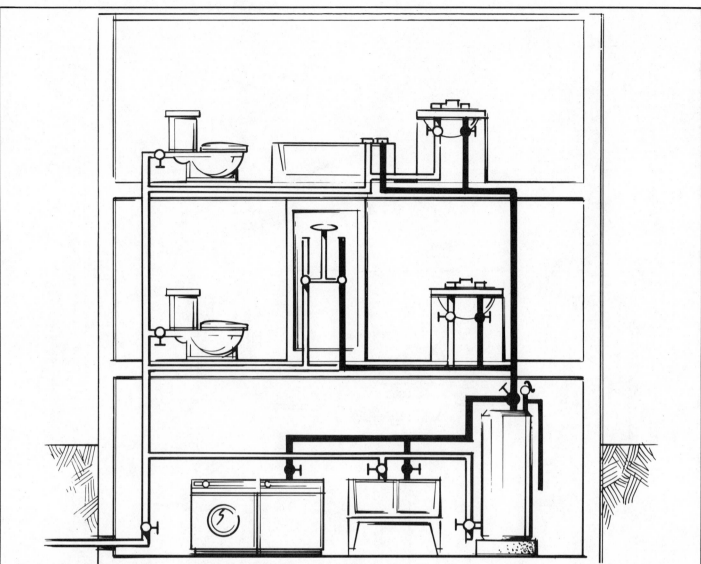

Typical hot and cold water system in home; white for cold, black for hot. Note position of hot water cutoff, placed on house side of water heater.

with, though you must exercise care to avoid kinking. It is especially useful when doing installation work in cramped or confined spaces.

Installing A Kitchen Sink

One of the easiest and quickest ways to give your kitchen a new look is to put in a new sink. These always come with full installation instructions, and the following directions should supplement them. Sinks come in two types—those with a separate steel rim or those that are self-rimming. Both are connected to the countertop with clamps provided with the sink; you must follow the instructions that come with the sink. All types require that a mastic or sealant be placed under the rim to provide a watertight seal between the countertop and the sink edge.

1. If installing in an old countertop, first turn off water supply and remove the old sink. In a new countertop, make the cutout with the template provided, or have it done wherever the top is made. Be careful to go slowly and use a router or saber saw. There will be a slight clearance for the sink to fit in, but it is not much. Try the rim after the cutout is made to make sure.

2. Install the faucet body you have chosen on the sink. It will tighten down through the use of large lock nuts at the bottom of the hot and cold water faucets. Make sure the rubber washer is in place around the rim of the faucet body, so

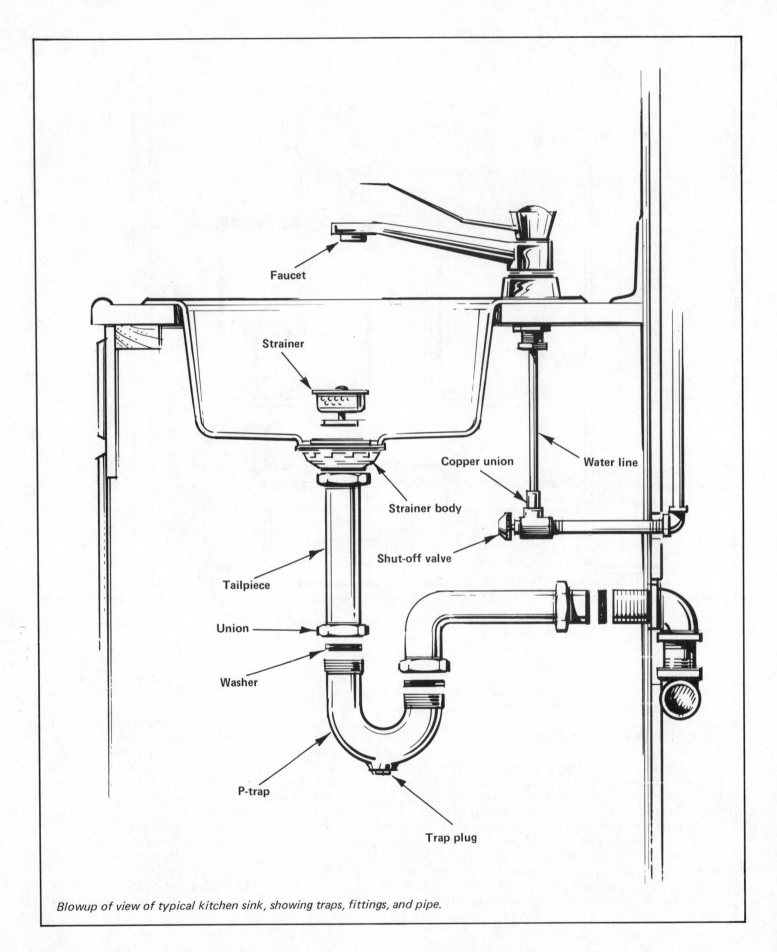

Faucet

Strainer

Copper union

Water line

Strainer body

Shut-off valve

Tailpiece

Union

Washer

P-trap

Trap plug

Blowup of view of typical kitchen sink, showing traps, fittings, and pipe.

126

water will not leak under the sink later.

3. The strainer body goes into the drain hole, after first placing a 1/8-inch bead of plumber's putty around the underside. Set the whole unit in the drain hole and attach the metal and rubber washers over the screw threads, followed by the large locknut. Slide on the strainer sieve, tighten on the next locknut, and insert the tailpiece that connects the strainer body with the drain pipe. Tighten all the nuts with a large pipe wrench, but be careful that you do not tighten them so hard as to chip the porcelain on the sink.

4. Lay a bead of plumber's putty 1/4-inch thick around the rim of the countertop opening. If using an old countertop, make sure all old putty has been removed from the rim surface.

5. Lift up the sink and put it into the countertop opening. Slide the clips into the grooves or channels underneath. If this particular unit requires fasteners to be located on the counter rim, do this before dropping in the sink (the installation instructions will so specify). Tighten all screws firmly, but not tightly; overtightened fasteners may crimp or bow the sink top. Check for a tight fit between sink and countertop on all sides before going further.

6. There should already be valves on the water pipes coming from the wall; if not, now is the time to install them. They will save you later aggravation if a sink washer needs replacing.

   Iron or steel pipe simply requires tightening of the unions and pipe sections after liberal application of pipe joint compound. Work from the wall pipe union to the faucet heads.

   Copper pipe requires that all joints be soldered or 'sweated.' Flux is applied to each joined surface, the joint heated, and then solder applied. It will draw itself into the joint. Compression fittings in copper tubing have only to be tightened securely, but be careful not to overtighten as the metal is soft and will twist out of shape.

7. Lastly, install a P-trap from the tailpiece of the strainer body to the drainpipe. Tighten all sections of the assembly securely, then turn on the water supply and check for leaks.

Garbage Disposer

Disposers come with a sink flange to fit the disposer to the sink at the drain and with full instructions on how to install the unit. Models vary, but the procedure here is typical.

First, check the code to find out if the unit is permitted in your area and if you are permitted to install it. If you are, get the necessary permit. This installation calls for plumbing and electrical work.

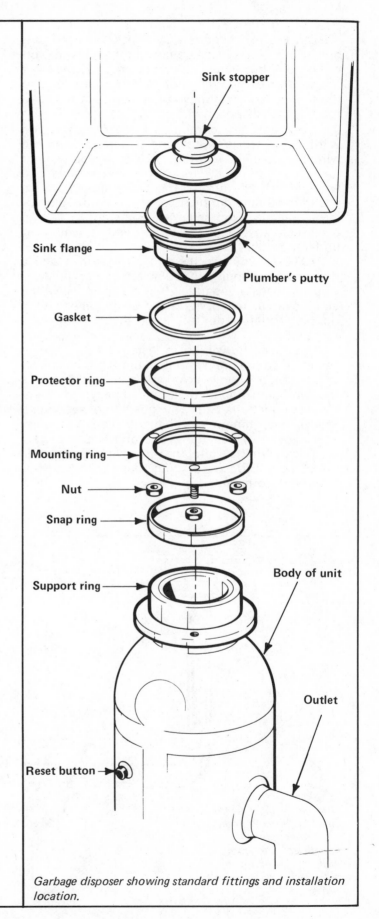

Garbage disposer showing standard fittings and installation location.

Read the instructions fully and spread the unit out to see what pieces come with it and what you will have to buy. Make all measurements, and note the position of incoming hot and cold water lines to the faucet. You may have to move them to make room for the disposer.

If your unit is a continuous-feed disposer, you will have to buy a switch and switch box and the wiring to connect it. If it is batch-feed, you will not need a switch, as the top of the unit acts as one when closed and turned. Disposers should have a separate 15-amp circuit. Even if you do the plumbing installation yourself, you may want to call an electrician to put in the circuit with a wall plug under the sink.

(**NOTE**—If you do this and also plan to add a dishwasher at some other time remember the dishwasher needs a separate 20-amp circuit. Have the electrician install both at the same time with a double outlet under the sink to accommodate them.)

The procedure will be to install the sink flange assembly to the drain and then mount the disposer to the flange. Then cut the pipe pieces to fit, make the plumbing connections and, finally, the electrical connections. Study the position of everything first to determine accessibility. In your particular case, you may see that you can't reach certain electrical terminals after the piping is in, so this will affect your procedure. With many models, it is necessary to make all electrical connections first.

Note also that the disposer has a plug that, when pushed out, can take a drain line from a dishwasher. If you plan a dishwasher now (or later), this drain plug will have to be pointed where the dishwasher will go.

Sink flange assemblies vary widely by manufacturer, so you will have to follow the directions for your unit. The better units will have quiet rubber and neoprene mounts to cut down on noise when the disposer is in operation. Once you get the flange installed, the disposer itself will simply snap into place. Just be sure you get a tight, waterproof seal between the sink flange and sink, using enough plumber's mastic or caulking compound. Once you set the flange, do not try to turn it. Don't do anything to disturb the mastic until it all is firmly tightened down.

In attaching the drain, you will use a P-trap if the drain goes into the wall or an S-trap if it goes down into the floor. These traps prevent backup of sewer gases and odors. Watch that you do not allow the upsweep of the trap to get as high as the outlet from the disposer. The P-trap entry into the wall also must be slightly lower than the drain from the disposer or it will malfunction or back up.

For continuous-feed disposers, you will have to install a switch to turn it on. The most convenient place is on the bottom of the top rail of the sink cabinet, so when you open the cabinet door, the switch is at your fingertips. However, if small children might pose a problem, mount the switch up in

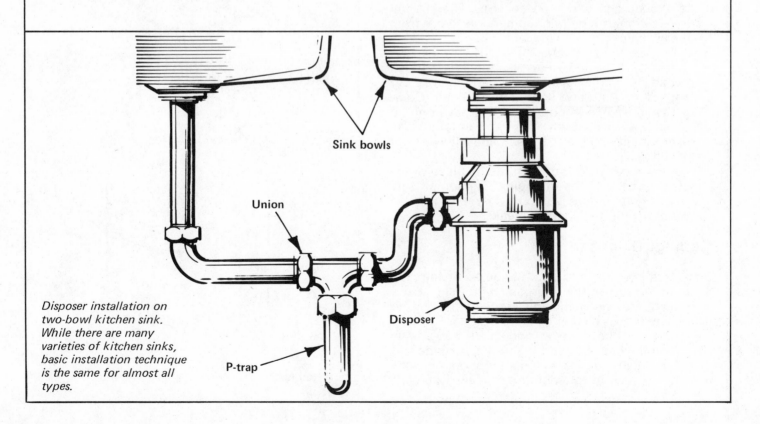

Disposer installation on two-bowl kitchen sink. While there are many varieties of kitchen sinks, basic installation technique is the same for almost all types.

Sink bowls

Union

P-trap

Disposer

the backsplash area more than an arm's length from the disposer, where it can't be turned on when a hand is in the disposer.

Dishwasher

While dishwashers may vary in quality and operation, they are pretty uniform in installation procedure. Built-in models are 24 inches wide and a minimum of about 34 inches high, with leveling legs to bring them up so they can attach to the bottom of the countertop. All of them are about 24 inches deep to conform with the depth of standard kitchen base cabinets.

The dishwasher should be adjacent to the sink, on either the right or left side. If there is a 24-inch-wide cabinet next to your sink, it might indicate the kitchen was designed with a future dishwasher in mind. You may be lucky enough to find the electrical rough-in already there. If you do not have a cabinet there, you will still have to provide a 24-inch hole, or buy the only brand that comes in an 18-inch size (Sears Kenmore). You may have to take out a bigger base cabinet, or two smaller ones, then replace the remaining hole with a new cabinet.

Another alternative is to buy a portable or a convertible dishwasher. The portable can be rolled into place when needed, and it hooks up to the hot water faucet and drains into the sink. The convertible is sized and designed so it can be built in at a later date. The only trouble with both is that you need a place to put them. Do not try to build in a dishwasher more than a step from the sink, or rather than solving your problem, it will become one.

To install a dishwasher, do the following:

1. Assuming you have a 24-inch cabinet to take out, first look for screws fastening it through the face frame to cabinets on either side. Remove them. Check for screws fastening the cabinet to the wall and take them out. There may also be screws through the corner gussets that fasten it to the countertop; these must also be removed.
2. This cabinet will be fitted tightly and you may have to take up the floor covering to slide it out. In pulling it out, be very careful not to chip or mar the cabinets on either side. In rare cases, you may find that the cabinet rests on a kick rail, rather than the kick rail being a part of the cabinet; the cabinet will come out more easily and won't disturb the floor covering, and you can simply saw out the piece of kick rail, flush at either side.
3. If you are going to slide the dishwasher into place under a tiled countertop, don't remove any wood strips supporting the tile. Check the

floor and wall first for any cracks that should be sealed to prevent insects from entering the house. Make sure you have a solid wood base under the countertop for fastening the dishwasher at the front. Usually there is ample room and screws will go directly through the tabs on the dishwasher into the countertop. If your countertop is Corian, pilot holes will have to be drilled for the screws.

4. Now check your space. Then measure the dishwasher to make sure it will fit. You will also need a separate 20-amp circuit for the dishwasher. You may want to call an electrician to put the circuit in, as it can be a dangerous operation.
5. Hot water supply line to your dishwasher should be 1/2-inch flexible copper tubing, and it should have a shut-off valve in a place where you can reach it. A good place for this shut-off valve is in the sink cabinet, near where you attach your new supply line to the existing hot water line that serves your faucet. Use compression fittings for easy installation. If you find the dishwasher inlet valve is 3/8-inch female thread, install a 1/2-inch compression elbow with a 3/8-inch male pipe thread (which might come with your dishwasher). Be sure to use sealing compound on all threads.
6. Drill a 1-inch hole through the side of the sink cabinet about an inch from the wall and 6 inches above the floor. Measure down from the existing hot water shut-off valve, across and through the 1-inch hole and 8 inches into the dishwasher area. Add 4 feet to this measurement. That is the amount of copper tubing you will need.
7. Shut off the main water supply and hot water

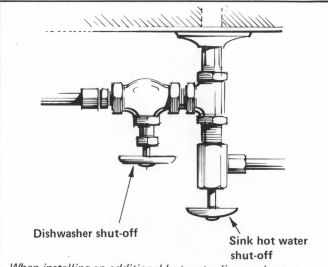

Dishwasher shut-off

Sink hot water shut-off

When installing an additional hot water line, make sure that a shut-off valve is put in on the new line.

valve on the house side of the water heater. Open all faucets in the house to drain, remove the existing hot water shut-off valve in the kitchen cabinet and install a new 1/2-inch pipe tee behind it. Reinstall the old shutoff valve that goes to the faucet, and put a new shutoff valve for the dishwasher line direct to the bottom of the tee. Now run your copper tubing from the new shutoff valve, through the 1 inch hole and to the inlet on the dishwasher, which usually will be at the right front corner beneath it.

8. The drain line can feed directly into your disposer—attaching to a plug provided for that purpose—or into the sink drain pipe. The drain hose must be routed up to above the highest level of water in the sink, to prevent siphoning. For this, hand-screw a hook into the bottom rear of the countertop, loop the hose over it, then drill a 1-inch hole in the sink cabinet for the drain hose to enter. You might prefer to install an "air gap" anti-siphon device on the sink, routing the dishwasher drain up to it and then down to the disposer or drain. For this, you need a fourth hole in the deck of the sink, which might already be there. It can also be cut in a stainless steel sink. Alternatively, it can be mounted in the countertop. While plumbers recommend this device, kitchen installers usually find looping the drain will do the job. Behind the rear of the dishwasher, there will be room to run the loop up to the countertop and then down to the hole in the sink cabinet.

9. With all connections made, slide the dishwasher into place and screw it to the countertop through the two front tabs. Adjust the leveling legs at the bottom to make sure the unit is level.

10. Turn on the main and hot water at the shutoff valves and check all fittings for leaks. Run the dishwasher through a full cycle, again checking for leaks.

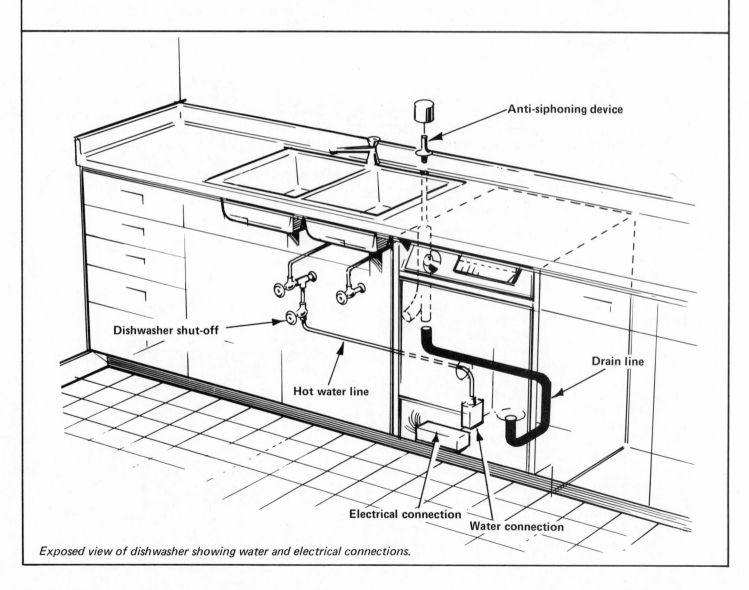

Exposed view of dishwasher showing water and electrical connections.

Doing Your Own Kitchen: Storage

There are times when the kitchen is too small for the things you want to put into it. A kitchen cabinet is a box that can make very efficient use of space; unfortunately, cabinets come in set sizes. There are better ways to take advantage of the smaller spaces commonly available in the kitchen.

Open shelving is one answer. A wall cabinet is normally 12 inches deep, but you can get good use from shelving 6 to 10 inches deep. The one problem with open shelving is that it requires attention and good housekeeping. Dishes and other things that are on display must be kept clean and orderly.

Hanging curtains in front of the shelves can relieve cleaning chores to some extent.

Potracks are a space saver. Potracks are normally suspended from the ceiling and can be used to hang pots, utensils, plants and other odd objects. Here again, these items will be on constant display and they also demand good housekeeping.

Cabinet organizers are commercially available in many houseware departments. They fit inside the cabinets and increase their storage capacity. This makes the existing space more efficient.

Wall cabinets on an unused countertop can also

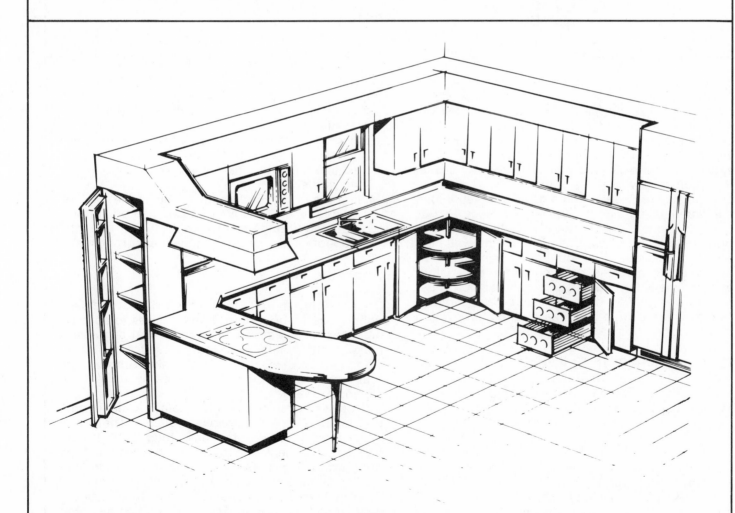

Typical kitchen installation showing some storage possibilities -- shelf storage in closet, Lazy Susan shelves in corner cabinet and hidden bread/produce drawers.

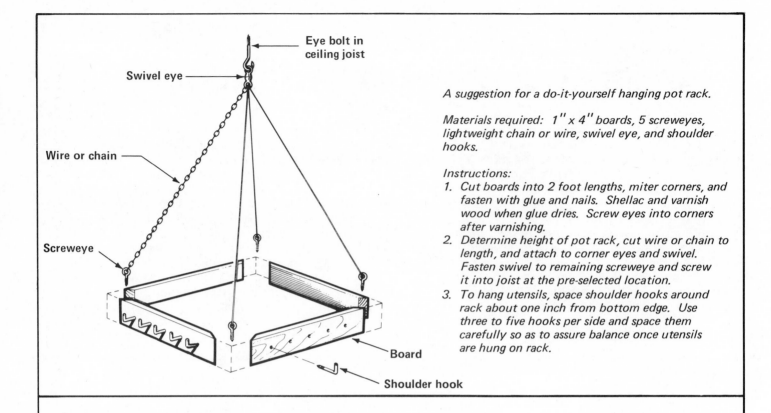

Eye bolt in ceiling joist

Swivel eye

Wire or chain

Screweye

Board

Shoulder hook

A suggestion for a do-it-yourself hanging pot rack.

Materials required: 1" x 4" boards, 5 screweyes, lightweight chain or wire, swivel eye, and shoulder hooks.

Instructions:
1. *Cut boards into 2 foot lengths, miter corners, and fasten with glue and nails. Shellac and varnish wood when glue dries. Screw eyes into corners after varnishing.*
2. *Determine height of pot rack, cut wire or chain to length, and attach to corner eyes and swivel. Fasten swivel to remaining screweye and screw it into joist at the pre-selected location.*
3. *To hang utensils, space shoulder hooks around rack about one inch from bottom edge. Use three to five hooks per side and space them carefully so as to assure balance once utensils are hung on rack.*

provide more added space. A wall cabinet is usually 12 inches deep, and if placed on top of a base countertop (normally 25 or more inches deep) this will leave at least 13 inches of usable counter space. If you are blessed with extra counter space, this could be a workable solution.

Peninsula or islands in the center of the kitchen can sometimes be added for extra storage and/or counter space. This can be especially useful in a one-wall kitchen where there is one long wall covered with cabinets. If all you require is more counter space, it can consist of a countertop only. Other alternatives would be to put a wall cabinet(s) beneath this or, if you have the room, base cabinets below. There should be at least an inch of overlap of the countertops on all free sides.

Between The Stud Storage

Between-stud cabinets are designed to fit between standard wall studs and are available in different heights. Installation is simple if you follow these directions:

1. Check for piping, outlets or electrical conduit behind the wallboard so that you have enough room to install the stud-cabinet.
2. Cut out the wallboard in the area where the cabinet will fit with a keyhole saw. The stud-cabinet will usually have a flange that will

cover up any cut marks in the wallboard after installation.
3. Insert the cabinet into the wall and nail from the inside into the two standing studs. You may have to shim if there is any free play along the two studs.
4. If you can not find room to insert the cabinet inside the wall, many units can also be surface mounted (though this will make it protrude into the room and may add to movement problems).

Door Shelving

Door shelving mounts to the back side of a closet door. It can be bought in different sizes to accommodate shallow (can size) storage. You can easily make such shallow shelving yourself out of plywood and brackets, but do not make it more than four inches deep or it will be in the way of the door closing properly.

Drawer kits that enable you to put drawers in odd places are also commercially available. These are made to fit between standard studs, though you first should check the depth of the wall before purchasing. These kits also have brackets for installing under a counter or into a wall. Most require at least 17 inches of space for the drawer clearance. If you have the room, they can also be combined side-by-side or one under the other for a built-in appearance.

Buyers Guide: Materials

Cabinets

Aside from appliances, there is no category of kitchen furnishings where you will spend more money than on kitchen cabinets. If carefully selected and properly installed, good cabinets will last as long as the kitchen itself. Neither price nor appearance is a reliable indicator of cabinet quality. The significant factor is workmanship in the construction and the fit into the kitchen when they are installed. You have to know what you are buying.

Style and design factors are a matter of personal choice. Apart from that, cabinets can be divided into three general categories. These are called stock, special-order, and custom. The main difference between the three is in cabinet construction. Price is not a good criterion. A top-line stock cabinet can easily cost more than a cheap custom model, and their appearance will be the same.

Stock cabinets are what their name implies: mass manufactured cabinets in a variety of standard sizes. Size is based on 3-inch standard modules. The smallest is 9 inches wide, and each cabinet will be wider by 3 inches until the top width of 48 inches. Stock also means that they are kept in a warehouse for immediate delivery. What you are getting in stock cabinets is delivery convenience, a name-brand manufacturer, and a number of choices within preset limits. If a run of cabinets will not fit the available space, a stock filler strip will be used to make up the difference.

Special-order cabinets can be any standard size, shape, or finish. They are available with a wider choice of accessories than stock. A large manufacturer makes the cabinets to your order in the sense that the 'whole' kitchen is made at one time. They will still be a standard size box cabinet, but the finishes are sure to match exactly. For this service, you will pay a premium of 20 percent or more and there will usually be some delay in delivery. You will get a set of cabinets that will last, in the finish you desire, and with a fairly precise fit to the kitchen. Their general appearance will not differ substantially from that of the stock cabinets which the same manufacturer will make.

Custom cabinets are usually

Stock wood cabinets can be very functional and decorative.

made by a local craftsman within your area. The construction is different because the entire face frame of a run of cabinets is made in one piece and then the box built around that. You will get an exact fit to your kitchen and the spacing between the doors will be even, creating a uniform appearance. You will not get as wide a choice of additional accessories, nor will the finish be as good. The small craftsman cannot afford to stock the wide variety of accessories a large manufacturer can and his finishing line will not have as good a quality control system. What you are paying for is that 'built-on-the job' look that only custom work can give you.

The difference between a good cabinet and a poor one is in materials and the workmanship.

Here are some things to look for:

● Hardware, especially the interior parts of the cabinet. Drawer slides are important, since they are the main wearing parts of the system. Cheap construction slides the drawers directly on wood; better quality will have metal slides. The best drawer systems will have double metal tracking with nylon and ball bearing rollers. Shelves should be removable, attached by clips, and carefully constructed. All hinges should be strong, swing freely without binding, and be silent in their operation.

● Joinery, especially where stiles and rails (the vertical and horizontal framing) come together. The corners should be braced for dimensional stability. Drawers and shelves should be carefully put together with mortised joints. The whole box of the cabinet should look and feel sturdy.

● Materials. Solid wood is not the best material for certain purposes, since large pieces are subject to warping; if plywood is used it should be a good grade and thick enough for stability. Cabinets with unfinished plywood shelves or flimsy backs are not recommended. Wide shelves should have support in the center to bear any expected weight.

● Style and finish are relatively unimportant, unless you choose a cabinet with a laminated surface. Laminates can splinter and their wearing qualities are only as good as the substructure beneath them. Molded or plastic drawers, for example, can break if a heavy weight is dropped in them. Any edges on laminated cabinets should be clean and neat, and the laminated surface as thick as possible.

● Steel cabinets are available from only one national manufacturer, St. Charles. They are durable and easy to clean. They can also be purchased with a laminated or wood finish. One drawback is that they weigh more than wood and this may be a difficulty if you choose to put them up yourself.

Some special buying tips you should look for when purchasing kitchen cabinets are:

1. Take note of whether the manufacturer is domestic or foreign. Some kitchen dealers will carry foreign, chiefly German, cabinets as one of their display lines. These are usually of very high quality and extremely expensive. Most are in a contemporary style and finished in bright, plastic laminates. Delivery time could be a problem, however, particularly if you choose something unusual in fittings. Warranty service is generally good, but service is a definite question when buying imported cabinets.
2. Know something about quality cabinet construction when you go to make your selection. It may be better to spend a few dollars more on a special order cabinet rather than a special offer the dealer may be having. Good cabinets are built to last and their price will reflect this.
3. Both knock-down and unfinished cabinets are available. The price differential in either case is only about 10 percent.

Special-order cabinets offer features such as adjustable shelves.

With a knock-down cabinet what you are saving on is the shipping cost, but it takes time to design a good one of any variety and to build it. Self-finishing is another matter; but you will have a mess. For uniformity of finish, only a large manufacturer can get consistent quality control, either in stock or special order work. Neither you nor a custom craftsman can afford the large finishing equipment necessary to do the job perfectly.

4. Carefully check any warranty on cabinets you buy. While it is a federal requirement that all dealers just give you a set of installation instructions if you choose to do the work yourself, this may void the guarantee. Look for as long a period of time as possible because cabinets require use before they show any flaws.

5. No matter what kind of cabinets you buy, they must all be installed correctly. The best cabinets will show 'racking' or other flaws if they are not set right. If you feel hesitant about tackling this job, have it done by a professional.

CABINET BUYING RECOMMENDATIONS

In the cabinet trade there are several national manufacturers that are widely recognized as offering excellent construction and warranty service. The categories below mention only special-order or stock cabinets. Custom work is usually done at a local plant and the price will be set for the work you want done. All of the manufacturers listed offer quality work for the various price lines that they offer.

Wood Cabinets

Special order. These will have special features like adjustable shelves, many choices in available accessories, and selected woods. Since time must be taken to build these cabinets, there will be a wait for delivery of anywhere from six weeks on up. Manufacturers in this category are: Wood-Mode, Coppes, Quaker Maid, Mutschler, Rich-Maid, and Rutt. All special-order cabinets are available unfinished.

Stock. Cabinet makers in this category offer a more limited selection of door styles, one or two standard finishes, and no changes in size from the standard module. Stock cabinets are kept in a warehouse and are available for immediate delivery.

Top lines include Merillat, IXL, Excel (some series), Scheirich (some series), Brammer (some series), Del-Mar, and Long-Bell.

Acceptable lines include Boise Cascade, Brammer's Peppermill, Connor, Aristokraft, and Kitchen Kompact.

Two stock lines—Excel and Overton—are available unfinished at a lower price.

Steel Cabinets

Steel cabinets for the kitchen are made by only one national manufacturer—St. Charles. Available as stock or special-order, steel cabinets from St. Charles are of very high quality, but also very expensive.

Laminate or Plastic Surfacing

Though there are several regional lines, the best national brand in plastic laminate cabinets is Nevamar. Other available lines are St. Charles' Bellaire and Scheirich's Gardencourt.

European Imports

As a class, all the available imports are equivalent in price and quality and offer the popular plastic laminate surfaces. The leader is Allmilmo, simply because it has the largest dealer network; but equally good cabinets are those offered by Beckermann, Poggenpohl, and Tielsa.

Cabinet type	Price, per 18-inch base cabinet	Do-it-yourself installation	Durability	Cleanability	Do-it-yourself repair
Wood					
Stock	$ 60.00-150.00	Difficult	Good	Good	Fair
Special order	$125.00-170.00	Difficult	Very good	Very good	Easy
Custom	$130.00-300.00	Difficult	Good	Good	Easy
Printed finish	$ 50.00- 75.00	Difficult	Good	Fair	Poor
Laminates					
Domestic	$ 40.00- 80.00	Difficult	Excellent	Excellent	Difficult
Foreign	$140.00-300.00	Difficult	Excellent	Excellent	Difficult
Steel					
Stock	$ 40.00 and up	Difficult	Excellent	Very good	Fair
Special order	$150.00 and up	Difficult	Excellent	Very good	Fair

Countertops

Countertops are available in many materials, surface textures and styles. They share one feature in common—the ability to withstand punishment. Appearance is not the essential feature of a good countertop. The question that should be asked is: How will this material stand up to heat, stains, abrasion, cutting, or weight? All are very common conditions in the kitchen. While most countertop materials are dependable in this respect, you should be sure of these qualities in the countertop you select. Appearance is no indication of how the material will react in use. By choosing carefully, you will have a furnishing that will give good service and add beauty in the kitchen.

Plastic Laminate

The most popular material for the tops of counters and other work spaces is plastic laminate. This material is available in many colors, patterns and textures, and is one of the best countertop coverings.

The top is really a layer of plastic bonded to a core stock, a bond that will last almost forever if not abused. The actual plastic layer is very thin, only a sixteenth of an inch or less; while the core stock can range from 3/4 of an inch on up. The purpose of the core is to give dimensional rigidity to the top surface. The material from which it is made is relatively unimportant as long as it is solid.

There are two basic varieties of laminate countertops, post-formed and self-edged. The difference depends upon the way in which the laminate is formed over the core material. Post-formed tops have rounded edges on all front and back surfaces and are made of a single sheet of laminate. There will be a 'no-drip' bullnose edge on the front and a 'cove' up to a backsplash in the rear. Self-edged tops are square edged in both construction and appearance. Separate sheets of laminate are used for the edges and the backsplash areas. There may also be a dark line of laminate thickness to show where the edges have been joined.

Self-edged tops take more skill to make and more handwork, while post-formed tops are cheaper due to mass production. Both are made and sold as 'slabs' in 6 to 12 foot lengths. These are cut to dimension later as kitchen space requires. While it is possible to laminate your own top, this is a very difficult job. It is not easy to get perfect adhesion of the laminate, the edges will chip readily, and a large countertop is unwieldy to work with. If you wish to do it yourself, use a stock slab. You will have to make the sink cutout yourself and cut it to length. Both post-formed and self-edged tops will have to be mitred. It is best to have these cuts done professionally, particularly for post-formed tops where everything has to be rounded. A professional will have the equipment to do the job correctly. If he ruins the slab, he'll absorb the cost.

Some buying tips for laminate tops are:

1. Industry sources indicate that the average life of a laminate countertop under normal use will be from seven to ten years. Plastic laminate surfaces come in several thicknesses; the thicker the layer, the longer it will last. Buy the thickest one you can afford.
2. Plastic laminated tops are resistant to most household stains, but not to high heat or sharp knives. You should not put a hot pot directly from the stove onto the plastic surface, nor use it as a cutting board. Consider putting in an insert of butcher block to take this punishment and form a central working space.
3. A new development in laminated tops is the "Suncraft" edge. A bevel replaces the square edges of the self-edged top. This process eliminates the dark line characteristic of the self-edged top while maintaining the crisp outline.

The self-edged laminate top has both cleaning ease and a crisp appearance.

4. Plastic laminate countertop slabs can be worked by the do-it-yourselfer, but it is not an easy job. Think about having it cut professionally if you are not familiar with power tools.

Cultured Marble

Artificial marble, under the trade-name Corian, has become popular in the countertop market in recent years. It can be worked with carbide-tipped power tools in much the same manner as wood. Scratches or nicks can be removed with sandpaper, knife cuts with a scouring pad, and burn marks can be simply wiped off. It is also available with a sink molded directly into the countertop to form one integral unit. Drawbacks with Corian are its limited color range (usually solid white or with faint mottling) and premium expense. Of all the countertops you can buy, Corian has the highest price per square foot.

Buying tips for Corian are:

1. Corian is a difficult material to work with. It is extremely heavy and will break or fracture if it is handled carelessly. You must be prepared to take great care in working with it. Though it can be machined to fit odd walls, this is definitely a job for the craftsman.
2. Base cabinets beneath Corian tops must be sturdy. All the framing members must be strong enough to hold the weight, especially down the center. Corian can break down inexpensive cabinets if it is not supported correctly.
3. Corian is not indestructible. The surface will abrade if it is continuously rubbed in one spot. If you need a countertop cutting board, have a wooden insert placed in a section.

Ceramic Tile

The various types of ceramic tile are described more fully in the

A Corian top can also make a breakfast or lunch counter.

flooring section of this Buyers' Guide. A few points can be made about the use of ceramic tile as a countertop material. Ceramic offers the widest choice of colors and patterns of any countertop material. It is easy to install yourself. It is reflective and introduces a lot of glare into the kitchen. Though it will stand up to normal use, heavy objects dropped on it will shatter and could damage a tile. This can be a problem to repair if you do not have several extra tiles.

Some buying tips for countertop tile are:

1. Tile is not a light material. Make sure that the base on which you are installing it has enough support to take this weight, is clean, and free from surface irregularities.
2. Tile installations have joints between the tiles which must be grouted. Grout stains easily, can be cut, and will allow water to seep through if it is damaged. Make sure that any

Ceramic countertops are not difficult to install or to keep clean.

3. Buy a tile with a glazed surface, rather than the unglazed. Countertops are sure to have spills and unglazed tile will pick up stains and grease. Glazed tile is like glass and is almost impervious to common household materials.
4. If you want to have a cutting board in your top, have an insert put in. The glassy surface of the tile will dull knives and if you catch the edge of the grouting it is easy to damage the seal, allowing water to seep through into the back of the tiles.

Butcher Block

Butcher block countertops and inserts are made of the same material as the old-time chopping block. All acceptable grades of block must be made of maple or other hardwoods and be well laminated. They will be very heavy. One single drawback with butcher block is that it shows wear immediately. Because of the expense, there are not many countertops made exclusively of

tile installation is properly sealed with a silicone sealer over the grout. Alternatively, buy tiles mounted on a backing sheet with the waterproof sealer already in place. These are easier to lay, the grout is waterproof, and they come in a wide choice of colors and patterns.

Corian countertops are available with a molded bowl.

butcher block, but it is popular as a work insert. There is no material better suited for the work areas in the kitchen.

Some buying tips for butcher block are:

1. Get a good grade of block, well-sealed on all sides, and at least 1-1/2 inches in thickness. All butcher block will require care and periodic resealing to retain its appearance, but it will still show wear. This is inescapable with the material.
2. All butcher block is heavy. The base cabinets must be able to support the weight, plus the pressure of work on the surface. If you buy a block and cut it to size yourself, be careful to reseal the ends or it will warp.
3. Quality butcher block is expensive. If it seems thin or the finish is poor, do not buy it. It must be a hardwood, unstained, laminated under pressure, and sealed properly. There are no short cuts for this quality product.

COUNTERTOP BUYING RECOMMENDATIONS

Plastic Laminate Tops

Plastic laminate material is man-ufactured by many national corporations. This product is made of the same materials and methods and is equivalent in quality. The actual thickness of the plastic surface, which can range from a 1/16 of an inch or thinner, is what governs cost. You will want to buy the thickest you can afford. Patterns, colors, and surface textures do vary among the various manufacturers, and every brand name will have at least a 100 choices. Of all the national brands, Formica is the leader. Essentially the same product can be had from Wilsonart, Consoweld, Textolite, Pionite, or Micarta.

Aside from the actual surface material, an important consideration is the subsurface upon which it is bonded. Local fabricators do most of the work in any given area. You will want to be sure that the subsurface is clean, smooth and free of all holes or other damage. It must be at least 3/4 of an inch thick to add dimensional strength. If available, try to have this made of particleboard. Plywood must usually be layered and the glue bond is a point of weakness.

Corian Tops

Corian is a tradename of a DuPont product. It is available as either a stock slab or with a molded bowl. Almost all kitchen dealers carry Corian tops or can get them for you. If you choose to install your own sink, you must get one that is made to fit this particular material. It is not recommended that you work with it yourself unless you are handy with power tools.

Ceramic Tile

The choices in ceramic tile are so numerous that it is difficult to make product recommendations. The manufacturing process is much the same in all cases. Price differentials are based on patterns and glazing. The most widely available is American Olean; but acceptable tiles are made by Amsterdam, Lusterock, Trayco, and U.S. Ceramic. Make sure that you get enough to do the job, as they will not guarantee that the colors will be consistent between lots.

Butcher Block

The best of butcher block comes in laminated maple and is available from several manufacturers. Recommended are Bally Block, Michigan Maple Block, and Sensenich. All of them provide acceptable grades of this material and will back their product if it splits or warps because of some manufacturing defect.

Material	Price, per foot (2-foot width)	Do-it-yourself installation	Durability	Cleanability	Do-it-yourself repair
Laminated slab					
Post-formed	$ 7.00-12.00	Fair	Very good	Excellent	Poor
Self-edged	$ 5.00-12.00	Fair	Very good	Excellent	Poor
Custom	$15.00 and up	Fair	Very good	Excellent	Poor
Corian					
3/4-inch	$ 40.00-60.00	Difficult	Very good	Excellent	Excellent
1/2-inch	$ 30.00-45.00	Difficult	Very good	Excellent	Excellent
with integral bowl	$800.00-1000.00 for 10'	Difficult	Very good	Excellent	Excellent
Ceramic tile	$3.00-10.00	Fair	Excellent	Good	Fair
Butcher block	$18.00-25.00	Fair	Poor	Fair	Poor

Flooring

Anyone interested in kitchen flooring has a wide selection of materials from which to choose. Ranging from the hardness and durability of ceramic tile to the warmth of cork, flooring differs (aside from style or color) in terms of foot comfort, ease of maintenance, and compatibility with the other furnishings in your kitchen. The following is a guide to the varieties of floor coverings available and their general characteristics. Only by visiting a number of kitchen or general flooring stores, however, will you be able to determine what is right for your kitchen and, most importantly, what is right for you.

Resilient Flooring

By far the most popular choice in kitchen floor covering is resilient tile or sheeting. It is available in hundreds of patterns, colors and textures, but all types of resilient flooring share several common characteristics. They are all relatively soft underfoot (as opposed to ceramic tile or wood), need a minimum of care to look their best, and most can be installed easily by the do-it-yourselfer. Properly installed, any quality resilient flooring will provide years of beauty in your kitchen.

One major consideration in the selection of resilient flooring is wearability. The kitchen is a high traffic area and requires a sturdy material on the floor to handle such abuse. Resilients are available in different gauges up to 1/4 of an inch (thickness of the actual flooring material), with the thicker gauges providing better wearability. Differences in gauge, unfortunately, are almost indetectable to the eye, and the only way to make certain of a particular flooring's thickness is to examine the manufacturer's specifications; price is not always an indication of thickness. In any case, try to buy the thickest resilient flooring available within the limits of your budget.

In addition to thickness, quality resilient flooring is characterized by its ability to withstand indentations. Floors are not only indented by static loads like refrigerators or tables, but also by momentary impact from shoe heels or dropped articles. An average person can exert tremendous pressure on a floor, and that pressure per square inch is increased enormously if the person is wearing pointed heels or has a nail protruding from a shoe. Good flooring, therefore, has cushioning to lessen the effects of momentary impact and to provide greater comfort underfoot.

In terms of wearing quality—*i.e.,* the ability to withstand the constant abrasion of foot traffic while maintaining their appearance—sheet resilients are better than tiles simply because there are fewer seams to catch dirt and wear down.

All resilients, even those labelled "no-wax," require regular cleaning, and most no-wax materials need refinishing after several years of steady foot traffic. Manufacturers recognize this problem and provide a special refinishing solution for use on no-wax floors. This solution does much to restore the original shine of the floor. Some patterns, of course, disguise scuffing and scratches better than others. Textured flooring and busy patterns with dark or multicolored backgrounds look the best. If the kitchen is going to be subjected to an extensive amount of foot traffic (for example, if it serves as a walk-through corridor into another room), you should investigate the darker or more textured surfaces available in resilient flooring.

Resilient flooring includes the following basic types:

Asphalt Tile. The least expensive resilient, asphalt tile (and it is usually available in tile form only) looks good, but it is definitely not as easy to clean as the other resilients. In addition, it is brittle. It cannot withstand impact loads (those which might catch an edge, for instance), and it sometimes breaks under normal traffic.

Vinyl Asbestos Tile. Slightly more expensive than asphalt tile and easier to clean, vinyl asbestos tile has a slight cushioning built into it and thus provides a softer feel underfoot. It is available in a no-wax version for easy care, and some versions come with a self-stick backing for easy installation by the do-it-yourselfer. The material is sometimes referred to as "vinyl composition" tile by manufacturers who shy away from mentioning the hazardous substance asbestos. As used in tile, though, asbestos poses no danger, and it contributes significantly to the flooring's wearability.

Vinyl Tile or Sheet Goods. Generally the most expensive of the resilient floorings, the vinyl tile or sheets come in the brightest colors and the most realistic simulations of natural materials (*e.g.,* stone and wood). Vinyls frequently come with "extras" like cushioning and no-wax urethane surfacing, but such extras can drive the price of the material up to almost double that of vinyls lacking these features.

Vinyl resilient is available in rotovinyl and inlaid versions. With rotovinyls, the pattern is reproduced on the surface by a process much like printing. This process is used extensively for reproduction of natural finishes like parquet or brick, after which the printed pattern is protected by a vinyl coating to keep the material shiny. Of course, periodic waxing is necessary to maintain the rotovinyl's appearance.

With inlaid vinyl, the design extends completely through the tile or sheet. Inlaid is richer and deeper in pattern and color than rotovinyl, and the design wears better. Regular versions still require waxing to look their best though. While available in tiles, inlaid vinyl is more often sold in sheet goods 6 feet wide or wider. Unless you are handy with tools, it is recommended that sheet goods be laid by a professional installer. Matching patterns is difficult and the rolls themselves are unwieldly and difficult to handle.

The no-wax feature involves the application of urethane onto the top of the vinyl flooring, either rotovinyl or inlaid. The surface shines due to a series of tiny ridges, the tops of which wear down while the valleys retain their original luster. The no-wax finish, however, is not permanent, and a dress finish is available to restore the shine that wear has reduced. The dress finish will not last as long as the original finish.

Buying tips for resilient flooring:

1. For maximum wear, see if the flooring you like is available in a gauge for "light commercial use." Though the patterns are more limited, flooring made for commercial purposes are thicker and made to withstand heavier impact loads—definite advantages in a heavily traveled area like the kitchen.
2. Examine the warranty that comes with the flooring, since a defect may only appear after several months or years of installation. Read the warranty carefully, and then make sure the flooring is installed according to the manufacturer's instructions. Improper installation can void the warranty.
3. Cushioning and a no-wax finish are features that boost the price of the flooring without contributing to its wearing quality. If you do not require additional cushioning in your kitchen and do not mind some additional care, such features may not be for you.
4. If you are not doing your own installation, buy the sheet resilients. The absence of seams will make cleaning

Self-stick vinyl tiles can simulate heavier materials such as natural slate.

Vinyl sheet flooring offers both no-wax care and cushioning.

Vinyl sheet is offered in many designs - including ceramic tile.

Ceramic tile flooring is both attractive and durable.

easier and reduce the risk of heels getting caught.

5. Resilients are relatively soft and cannot withstand excessively heavy traffic. If your kitchen is subject to such traffic going through it. you should consider other flooring materials.

Hard Tile Flooring

Ceramic tile and its close relatives like slate, brick, and quarry tile share certain characteristics: They are small pieces of material inlaid in adhesive or mortar to create some kind of decorative design. Grouting material is placed between the individual pieces to finish off the design, and — if done properly — the result is a floor that is durable, colorful, and able to outlast just about any other flooring.

On the other hand, a hard tile floor is expensive, and it can be very hard on feet. In addition, objects dropped on such a floor will almost certainly break. In terms of attractiveness and durability, though, a ceramic or other hard tile floor is hard to top.

Tile is available in two types: glazed or unglazed. The glaze, fused into the tile body during firing, is what gives the hard shine and color to the tile. Also suitable for walls and countertops, glazed tile has a finish that is almost impervious to stains and marks. Unglazed tile has a flatter sheen and is therefore the choice in cases where reflection could be a problem. When used on the floor, moreover, unglazed tile provides a much firmer gripping surface for walking (provided it is not waxed).

Mosaic ceramic tile, available glazed or unglazed, differs from regular ceramic in that it is smaller and is mounted on a mesh back or paper sheet for easier installation. It can also be purchased pregrouted with a waterproof grout/sealant already between the tiles. Pregrouted mosaic sheets make do-it-yourself installation much easier, and the waterproof grout/sealant protects against staining. Of course, having the tiles spaced to the correct distance takes a great deal of the hard work out of the installation. You pay extra for such convenience, but few do-it-yourselfers object to the additional outlay.

Quarry tile is another popular flooring material. Often used outside or in commercial applications, quarry tile is available in either glazed or unglazed types and commonly in muted earth colors. The square tiles can range in size from 4 to 9 inches, and curved or geometric pieces are available. They should be installed in wet mortar to ensure a firm bond, and they should only be installed over extremely sound subflooring that can support their extra weight (3 or more times heavier than ceramic tile). As a consequence, quarry tile is not recommended for most kitchens.

Slate or brick are just what their names imply: structural materials commonly used for walls that can be laid on a floor. Very heavy, slate or brick is not recommended for use in the average kitchen. If you wish to simulate natural brick or slate flooring, then seek out a ceramic tile or a resilient flooring that approximates the look without the additional weight.

When shopping for any variety of hard tile flooring, be sure to purchase enough so that you will not have to go back later to get more. There will always be some breakage and waste in installation, and tile in any one run will differ slightly in color from another kiln batch. It is better to buy extra pieces initially than to find that you cannot match the color of the broken pieces.

When choosing a color or pattern in ceramic or other hard tiles, try to be conservative. Tiles are permanent and difficult to cover later if you decide that you do not like them. You can eliminate one source of dissatisfaction by making certain to seal the grout. Unsealed grout material will quickly become discolored.

Buying tips for hard tile flooring:

1. Unglazed tile is porous and thus can be stained. Grease will soak into unfired tile, which can make the material a problem in the kitchen; glazed tile, on the other hand, has a slick surface and may cause people to slip and fall. Because of these liabilities, you may want to consider having tile around the kitchen perimeter and installing a matching resilient in the high traffic areas of the work triangle.
2. The smaller tiles are easy to lay if they are already attached to a mesh or paper backing. Since the larger quarry tiles should be set in wet mortar, they are messy and require some skill to lay correctly. If you are using them in a large area, therefore, consider having the work done professionally.
3. Though it may look good in your kitchen and require a minimum of care, tile is hard on feet. Its reflective surface, moreover, will cause noises to echo. Since the kitchen is a noisy place anyway, you may want to avoid adding to the din.
4. Try not to buy tile that is "on sale" unless you are sure you can get enough to do the job, plus extras. A given run of tile will usually be the same shade, but anything else —even if labeled the same color from the same manufacturer—will differ. Such differences are characteristic of the manufacturing process and cannot be helped.

Kitchen Carpeting

One interesting material for use as a kitchen floor covering is carpeting. An adaptation of the popular material used on patios or in breezeway areas, kitchen carpeting is easy to install by the do-it-yourselfer, looks attractive on the floor, and is extremely easy on the feet. In addition, it absorbs sound. Its wearing characteristics are about the same as the better quality resilients and it is slightly more expensive than the lower grade resilient flooring.

On the other hand, carpet is more difficult to keep clean. Spills are a good deal harder to remove from a carpet than from resilient or hard tile flooring. One can quickly lose patience with a material that must be cleaned constantly or one from which stains cannot be removed effectively.

Kitchen carpets are made of three layers of synthetic material: a nap with a loop or tuft construction, a sponge backing, and a waterproof membrane to prevent any seepage from soaking into the floor. The thicker the construction, the easier on the feet and the more noise-absorbing the carpet will be.

Kitchen carpet is available in self-stick tiles 12 inches square or in long rolls. The tiles are easy to lay, and any fitting work can be done with a utility knife or a pair of scissors. The problem with tiles involves the joints between the squares. Spills can seep through the seams to the floor underneath, and the joints may become unsightly.

Rolled carpet, which can be laid either loosely (with two-sided tape to hold it around the perimeter of the room) or glued down with an adhesive, is better than the carpet squares because it has fewer seams. It also permits a nice continuous pattern, and is less expensive than the self-stick tiles. Smaller rolls, though, may have to be butt-jointed, and such joints can catch heels or other objects crossing the floor. If the kitchen is filled with sharp angles, moreover, cutting the rolls to fit can cause problems.

Some tips for buying kitchen carpeting:

1. Make sure that you are getting kitchen carpeting and not indoor/outdoor material.

The latter is porous and made so that water will soak through and drain away, making it unsuitable for the kitchen. True kitchen carpet should have a waterproof layer built in to protect the underlying floor from damaging spills.

2. When deciding between carpet tiles or rolls, remember that tiles are easy to replace should something happen to one or two. You simply remove the damaged tiles and replace them with identical ones. Rolled carpeting requires more effort to repair, and the seam where you make the patch will probably be quite visible.

3. Rolled carpet can be laid with two-sided tape, but is more permanent when it is laid with an adhesive. This is a messy task at best, and the carpet is heavy and difficult to handle. If you lack the necessary skills but still wish to install kitchen carpeting yourself, opt for the squares.

4. Stick with medium or dark colors. Not only will they not show dirt as readily, but they will also disguise wear. Carpet, in spite of its synthetic nature, is a soft surface and can wear.

5. A busy carpet pattern can clash with the rest of the furnishings in the kitchen. Therefore, try to get a sample to take home and match with the rest of the kitchen; you may be surprised to find a pattern that you thought looked wonderful in the showroom does not blend well with your other furnishings. Since carpet covers such a large surface area, it immediately attracts the eye and the careful effect you labored to achieve may be completely undermined by the wrong material on the floor.

Kitchen carpeting comes in many patterns and colors.

Wood And Parquet Flooring

Wood is probably the most traditional of all floor coverings. With the right finish and proper care, it will last as long as any flooring available on the market. Yet that beautiful appearance will last only as long as the material that protects the wood, and that material must be renewed fairly often in a high traffic area like the kitchen. If you are prepared to spend a great deal of time caring for your kitchen floor, wood may be the material for you; you will sacrifice time and work for the beauty that you get.

Regular wood flooring, made of tongue-and-groove strips about 2 inches wide, is normally installed when the home is constructed. This sort of installation requires a great deal of work and is best left to a professional. Traditional parquet flooring (individual strips of wood laid in various patterns) is also a tedious and exacting process that requires skill to do properly. In fact, any wood flooring that is laid is exceedingly expensive and difficult to maintain. Therefore, most people opt for a resilient flooring that simulates wood rather than the real thing.

Some manufacturers market parquet flooring that comes in tiles or long planks backed with foam cushioning and coated on the top with vinyl. Some have a self-stick backing for installation by the do-it-yourselfer. Actually a cross between traditional wood and the resilients, these hybrid parquet floors offer the beauty of the one and the ease of maintenance of the other.

Buying tips for wood and parquet:

1. If you are going to have a regular tongue-and-groove wood floor laid, make sure that the installer will guarantee his work. Wood floors expand or contract depending upon the moisture conditions, and expansion areas and a solid underlayment are necessities. If the floor starts to warp six months later, you want that installer to stand behind his work.

2. Wood, like ceramic tile, is hard. Things dropped on it will break, your feet will tell you that you are not standing on a cushioned surface. Think carefully before having a wood floor installed, since the result is expensive and relatively permanent. You will not be able to change flooring as easily as you can with resilients.

3. If you must have a wood floor in the kitchen, investigate the wood tiles with a vinyl or urethane finish. They are not only easier to care for, but they also permit you to replace a damaged area without difficulty.

Special Types Of Flooring

Plywood. Plywood and particleboard can be used as flooring materials, but they are more often used for the subfloor or underlayment. Both can be stained and varnished or sealed and painted. Not as tough and durable as other flooring materials, they need constant care and show wear and stains readily. Therefore despite their low costs, plywood and particleboard cannot be recommended as kitchen flooring materials.

Seamless Flooring. Seamless (or poured) flooring is not widely used in the home, being designed for heavy-traffic commercial application. It is the ultimate in no-wax durability. The actual flooring consists of an epoxy base, some kind of inset pattern or vinyl chips, and a urethane or acrylic top coat. The material will bond to anything, flows readily around the obstructions, resists everything except industrial acids, is waterproof and requires neither waxing nor buffing. Its chief drawbacks are that it is hard, relatively permanent, and for good results must be installed by a professional.

Cork Flooring. The nature of cork—a soft and basically spongy material—would make it seem unsuitable for floors. Yet, it offers great beauty and a pleasant cushioning effect. Recently, some manufacturers have made cork floors more practical by creating cork floor tiles. These tiles have a self-stick backing, come in standard squares, and the top surface is coated with a long-lasting urethane finish. If you like the look of cork, then these tiles—which come in a variety of colors—may be what you need to do the job while avoiding the inherent shortcomings of the natural material.

FLOORING MATERIAL RECOMMENDATIONS

Resilient Flooring

This category contains the largest selection you can find in flooring material, with additional features like cushioning and 'no-wax' finishes. Gauge (thickness) is the principal difference between high, medium, and low

TILE COUNTER FOR FLOOR TILES OR CARPET SQUARES		
Room area	Number of tiles needed (includes wastage)	
(square feet)	9x9 inch tiles	12x12 inch tiles
40	80	46
80	144	88
100	192	110
150	280	160

prices. Another price difference can be in pattern or types of inlaying, since some require more effort in the manufacturing process. All of the national brand names will offer many different series with various features and patterns. They will also have an explicit guarantee for their products.

Among the various types of resilient flooring you will find are:

Asphalt tile. Kentile is the only remaining manufacturer of asphalt tile squares, and even this company has dropped them as a regular product line. They are manufactured solely as a replacement for existing flooring. They have poor wearing qualities, and it is likely that you would not be able to replace any broken or defective tiles. Not recommended.

Vinyl asbestos tile. The key factor in pricing vinyl asbestos tile is the thickness of the material. Low-priced vinyl asbestos is 1/16 of an inch thick; medium price is 1/8-inch thick; and higher priced material has a continuous pattern throughout the tile and is even thicker. All manufac-

turers have standard patterns, you must specify the thickness that you want when ordering it. Kentile, Asrock, Amtico, and Armstrong all offer vinyl asbestos tiles in various thickness and all are about equal in quality and price.

Self-stick tiles are available from the same manufacturers for do-it-yourself installation. These are sold by the carton in the standard 1/16 of an inch thickness.

No-wax tiles are also available in vinyl asbestos in a gauge of 3/32 of an inch. Difference among the manufacturers is in pattern selection, the quality and wearing characteristics are about the same. Amtico's "Sunbeam" and Kentile's "Bright 'n Shiny" are acceptable no-wax vinyl asbestos tile.

Vinyl tile and sheet goods. There are really no low-priced straight vinyl tiles or sheet goods because the manufacturing process is the same for all brands. Pricing here is based on gauge, pattern, and extra features like no-wax or cushioning. Most patterns can be ordered in any gauge. The type of manufacture

(whether rotovinyl or inlaid) will also affect price, with inlaid vinyls costing more.

Vinyl sheet goods are offered by Armstrong, Congoleum, Goodyear, and Mannington; straight vinyl tile by Armstrong, Amtico, and GAF. All are equal in quality and there is not much difference except for pattern.

Cushioned vinyl tiles or sheet goods come both with or without seaming. Medium priced lines are Congoleum's "Prestige" and "Shinyl Vinyl," and Armstrong's "Quiet Zone." At a much higher price are Congoleum's "New Dimension" (no seaming) and Amtico's Sundance Series.

No-wax tiles or sheet goods offer maintenance ease, but the finish will not last forever. Armstrong, Amtico, and Congoleum all offer a no-wax feature in their vinyl resilients; price is dependent upon the thickness of the wearing finish (urethane).

Only Armstrong makes a cushioned, no-wax flooring. There are two lines of this type; Premier Sundial is the medium priced series and Solarian is the top-of-the-line.

Hard Tile Flooring

Ceramic tile is not graded according to material composition, but on added features like design, glazing, size and a backing sheet (if present). All tile will wear about the same if properly installed, but you must be sure to obtain enough when you buy them. Each kiln lot will differ slightly in color from the next, and it is better to be sure that you have a few spares for later use.

Leading tile brands sold include Agency, American Olean, Amsterdam, Michigan Brick and U.S. Ceramic Tile. All of them are nationally available and you will be able to see a wide selection. Pregrouted tile on backing sheets is more expensive, but the grout is waterproof and they are easy to install by the do-it-yourselfer. They are available from American Olean and H & R Johnson.

Vinyl resilients come in self-stick tile form for easy do-it-yourself installation.

Kitchen Carpeting

Carpeting for the kitchen is offered by several national manufacturers. Price differences are based on thickness, pattern, and if the carpet is on rolls or offered in tiles for do-it-yourself installation. Leading national brands are Mannington, Mohawk, Viking, and Congoleum Industries. All offer a guarantee when installed according to the manufacturers instructions.

Wood And Parquet Flooring

Regular wood flooring laid in the traditional manner can be expensive. Aside from the material cost, there will be the wages of the woodworker and that will not be inconsiderable. Any carpenter contractor will come in and quote you a price, but be prepared for a stiff figure (especially for parquet). The work takes time to do correctly, and any short-cuts will appear in the form of warping, squeaks and a poor finish.

A better alternative to traditional installation are those wood floors that are made in tile form. Long planks and random widths are also available; but the central feature of these products is their ease of installation. Like resilients, some offer cushioning, and several of these are wood surfaced tile with a self-sticking back. Leading manufacturers of hardwood floor and parquet are Bruce Hardwood Industries, Hartco tiles by Tibbals Flooring, and PermaGrain Products. Their prices are comparable and the floor will have the traditional wood look at a fraction of the price you would pay for the installed variety.

Special Types Of Flooring

A poured or seamless floor can be installed in the kitchen, either as a do-it-yourself project (not recommended) or by having an installer come in to do it. You must be sure of the number of top or surface coats that the installer puts on (at least five and preferably more) and the guarantee. Materials used by the local installers vary only slightly in the embedded material, but you may have difficulty in finding an installer if you are far from an urban area. Poraflor (Woodside, NY), Dur-A-Flex (Hartford, CT), and Cambridge Tile (Cincinnati, OH) are all names to look for if you wish this kind of flooring installed.

Cork tiles are available with a vinyl bonding and surface under the trade name Cork-O-Plast from PermaGrain Products. These are laid like resilient tiles and have much the same feel underfoot. Though higher priced than a regular resilient, they combine the beauty of the natural material (which is too soft for floor wear) with the easy floor care of the resilients.

Material	Price, per square foot	Do-it-yourself installation	Durability	Cleanability	Resilience
Asphalt tile	$0.35-0.50	Easy	Poor	Fair	Fair
Vinyl asbestos tile	$0.45-0.55	Easy	Excellent	Very good	Good
Self-stick	$0.55-0.70	Easy	Excellent	Very good	Good
No-wax	$0.90-1.20	Easy	Excellent	Very good	Excellent
Vinyl tile	$0.50-1.20	Easy	Excellent	Very good	Good
Self-stick	$0.50-1.50	Easy	Excellent	Very good	Good
No-wax	$0.70-1.50	Easy	Excellent	Excellent	Excellent
Vinyl sheet	$0.70-0.90	Difficult	Excellent	Very good	Good
Cushioned	$0.70-1.00	Difficult	Excellent	Very good	Excellent
No-wax	$1.00-1.50	Difficult	Excellent	Excellent	Excellent
Cushioned, no-wax	$1.60-3.00	Difficult	Excellent	Excellent	Excellent
Ceramic tile	$0.70-4.00	Fair	Excellent	Good	Poor
Pavers	$1.00-2.50	Difficult	Excellent	Excellent	Poor
Quarry tile	$4.00	Difficult	Excellent	Excellent	Poor
Carpeting Roll	$1.00-3.00	Fair	Good	Fair	Excellent
Tiles	$1.00-3.00	Easy	Fair	Fair	Excellent
Parquet wood-tiles	$2.25-5.00	Good	Good	Fair	Good
Seamless, poured	$1.00-5.00	Difficult	Excellent	Excellent	Poor
Cork tile	$1.00-2.00	Easy	Very good	Good	Excellent

Walls

Kitchen walls can be split into functional and decorative areas. Functional walls are covered with cabinets, windows, or shelves. The wall areas between and above are usually filled with backsplashes and soffits. The other walls can serve a decorative function, complementing and enhancing the total kitchen. If what you put up does not blend well, though, it could negate the whole appearance. Your new decorating scheme may be with you for some time and if it has a

jarring effect, it may make you unhappy with your new kitchen.

Many kitchens open out into other parts of the home. If there is a dining nook or a work area, you should consider the decoration as a whole. A wall that may look great in relationship with the kitchen furnishings may not blend with other areas within visual scanning range.

Let's look at some of the available materials and products that might decorate your kitchen walls.

Paint

Paint is the most common wall covering. Basic paint types include latex (water-based), alkyd

(oil-based), and rubber. The finish can be flat, semi-gloss, or gloss; the latter two are best because of cleaning ease. Latex paints are the easiest to apply and clean up. Properly applied, a good paint will last for years and blends with almost any style or furnishing.

Graphics are a variety of painting technique in a preset pattern. The pattern is transferred to the wall and the marked areas are filled in. The work can be time consuming and messy, but you may be delighted with the effect.

Some buying tips for paint are:

1. When buying latex, read the label. Fifty percent or more of the pigment base should be latex solids, and the main pigment ingredient should be titanium dioxide. This gives the paint covering ability. Single-coat coverage paints are more expensive because they use more of both.
2. If you plan on hanging other materials, look for a neutral color to harmonize with everything. Cool colors recede and should be used for a small room, warm colors do the opposite.

Paneling

Paneling is popular, especially in a dining nook. Excellent simulations of brick, stone, wood, or even marble are available. Wood veneers are the most expensive. Types vary, but a vinyl top surface is best for easy care. This type is washable, and the surface won't pick up grease or other stains in the kitchen. Paneling normally comes in 4-X-8-foot sheets and in a variety of thicknesses. Good paneling is not cheap, but there is no better material to use if the wall is unsightly and has many imperfections.

Some things you should look for are:

1. Avoid rough or grained surfaces in kitchen panels, especially in light colors. They will

One of several available graphic systems for use with paint.

collect dirt and can be difficult to clean.

2. Cheap paneling may look good, but it is unreliable. It is usually on a hardboard base that can chip in installation. It is better to buy quality material; it will last longer and has a richer appearance.

3. Paneling is easy to do yourself. Dealers will always have full installation instructions and will gladly provide this to you.

Wall Coverings

So many products are marketed under the name wallpaper that it is simpler to call them all 'wall coverings.' Common characteristics are that they come in rolls and must be put up with glue as individual strips onto the walls. The best product for the kitchen are the waterproof vinyl coatings. These are usually strippable (you can easily take them down later) and are prepasted. The thicker the actual fabric or paper design, the more expensive the wall covering will be. Always ask for the vinyl coating because you will want to wash the wall covering.

Consider murals as one alternative. These are really large, space-filling designs in wallpaper form. They come in one size in a prepackaged kit, and you trim the design to match the size of the space you want to cover. These are relatively expensive, but they offer some unusual decorating ideas.

When selecting a wall covering, look for the following:

1. Wall coverings can be difficult to put up. If you do not have time to do it carefully (and they can be messy), have somebody come in and do it for you. Professionals will usually guarantee the job for some time.

2. Most murals are not vinyl coated. If you use one, seal the final product with a clear silicone finish. This will protect it.

Artificial brick paneling often makes an attractive backsplash.

Simulated stone paneling can beautify an unsightly wall.

3. You will find it easier to work with a prepasted and strippable wallpaper, despite the larger expense. Mistakes can be taken down and put back up again, and it can be easily changed as your needs require.

Laminates

If you select plastic laminate countertops, consider doing the area between the wall cabinets and the backsplash in a laminate material. These are available to match in a thinner gauge. It is best to have this installed profes-

sionally. They are easily cleaned and will last as long as the kitchen.

If you decide to do this yourself, you should look for the following:

1. It may be that your countertop fabricator has a piece of the same material from which he covered your countertop. If so, he may sell it to you at a reasonable price.

2. Often a countertop will be fairly long. A sheet of laminate does not come longer than 12 feet. You may require molding at the resulting

Vinyl wall coverings create a bright and airy look.

Patterned ceramic tile is both decorative and durable.

seams and this can detract from the smooth effect.

Corian

The 3/4-inch thick material that is used for countertops is available in a 1/4 inch thickness for walls. Corian sheets are 30-inches wide and are sold in up to 10-foot lengths. They can be cut to fit. Corian is quite expensive. Easy to clean and extremely durable, Corian may require special bracing and gluing on a vertical surface because of its weight. With a countertop of the same material, however, nothing beats the match you can achieve by using it.

Several points you should know about Corian is that it will chip or break until it is supported. Should you do any work with it yourself, you will need a helper, maybe even two. It is safer to have an installer come in to put it up.

Ceramic Tile

There is an extensive description of tile in the flooring section of this buyer's guide. A few things may be said when it is used as a wall covering. Ceramic tile has been used on many walls in the area between the backsplash and the bottom of the wall cabinets. It is durable, easy to keep clean, and has a good appearance. Ceramic tile can be highly reflective, especially the glazed ones, and the grout can be discolored by stains if not sealed properly.

Some buying tips for wall tile are:

1. All tile except that laid in wet mortar is not difficult for the handyman to put up. Look for tiling systems that offer tile in prepatterned sheets, some of which are pregrouted. They are easier to work with and the finished product is waterproof.

2. Buy enough to do the job and a few extras. Some will break in application and if you need to replace one later it will be difficult, if not im-

possible, to find an exact color match.

WALL MATERIAL RECOMMENDATIONS

Paint

All top quality latex paints are equal in quality and coverage among the various manufacturers. All will offer a limited warranty. Despite their higher price and more limited wall coverage, 'one-coat' coverage paints are superior because they contain more pigment material and are a better product. You will pay less in the long run for a one-coat-covering latex at $15.00 a gallon than you will for one costing only $8.00 or $9.00. It will cover the walls in a shorter time, last longer and be easier to clean.

Graphics

Graphics are basically a variety of painting technique, but there are products on the market that can make your job easier if you choose to put one up. One example, The Supergraphic kit (Supergraphic, Inc.) has a template, preset designs, and a specialized applicator brush that can make applying these moddish designs

a snap. Graphics can be added as an accent to any wall in the kitchen (or any other room of the home).

Paneling

There is a wide choice of style, color and surface texture among the various panel manufacturers, and most national brands have wide distribution. Often, paneling is used as a loss-leader in building supply centers and a few sheets can be picked up to refinish one or two walls in the kitchen at a nominal cost. National brands of paneling are available from Weyerhaeuser (w), Wilsonart (p), Pavco (w), Marlite (p), Formica (p) and Allied (w). (p or w after manufacturer means plastic or wood panels.)

Wall Coverings

Wall coverings are usually selected by pattern and their compatability with other kitchen furnishings rather than by manufacturer. Best for the kitchen is a polyvinyl chloride laminated to a lightweight fabric. The thicker the vinyl surface, the more expensive it will be. Expect to pay from $10.00 a roll on up, especially if the paper is imported, or has extra features like pregluing.

Murals

Typical murals will vary in height and width for the finished design, but they will come in rolls like any other wall covering. Scandecor, Environmental Graphics, and Marlite Corporation all offer acceptable products; another manufacturer, Imperial Wallcoverings, offers graphics that are vinyl coated, fully washable, preglued and strippable.

Laminates

All the manufacturers of laminate products (see countertop section for a list of them) make smaller sized sheets for installation on walls. Laminate is usually used between the backsplash and the underside of the wall cabinets. If you decide to have it there, put it up before the cabinets are installed. This will eliminate later cutting and fitting.

Corian

Corian sheets are available in 1/4-inch thicknesses for wall coverings, 30 inches wide and in up to 10 foot lengths. It is quite expensive ($5.00 a square foot), but makes a nice match when combined with a Corian top.

Material*	Price per square foot	Do-it-yourself installation	Durability	Cleanability	Do-it-yourself repair
Paint	$0.03-0.10	Easy	Good	Very good	Easy
Vinyl Wallcovering	$0.25-0.70	Fair	Very good	Good	Fair
Plastic laminate	$0.75-1.00	Difficult	Excellent	Excellent	Difficult
Ceramic Tile	$1.50-5.00	Fair	Excellent	Good	Fair
Corian, ¼-inch thick	$5.00	Difficult	Very good	Excellent	Excellent
Paneling	$0.25-1.00	Easy	Good	Very good	Fair
Real Brick Veneer	$1.50-2.00	Difficult	Very good	Poor	Fair

*Price includes materials for installation (adhesives, grout, etc.).

Ceilings

Except for application technique, ceilings can be treated much like a horizontal wall, since many of the same coverings used on walls are also used on ceilings. Paint and wallpaper are the two most common methods of covering a ceiling. There are, however, several alternative things you can do with them. You can put up acoustical tile, decorative ceiling beams, or install a skylight. All of them can be simply and easily done by the do-it-yourselfer.

Acoustical Tile

The noise levels in an average kitchen can sometimes be very high. Prolonged exposure to high noise levels can be extremely annoying, and can damage the hearing. Acoustical tiles can absorb about 50 to 75 percent of the sound waves striking them. This does not mean they will cut the noise level by that much, but they do help a lot. In addition, you get the advantage of a good looking ceiling that may cover up existing imperfections.

There are two main systems of suspension commonly used to put up acoustical tiles. They can be glued or stapled directly onto a solid, level and smooth ceiling in much the same way as laying floor tiles. If the ceiling is badly cracked or marked, furring strips should be installed first; they should be leveled, and then the tiles can be glued or stapled to the strips.

The second method is to suspend the tiles by one of the various systems; this method is especially good if the ceiling must be dropped to hide unsightly wires, ducts or other imperfections. The suspension system can be any form of metal grid hung from wires or attached to the ceiling by nails. The tiles, in turn, rest in metal troughs or tees once the grid is installed. Any of

Installing acoustical tile can significantly cut the noise levels in a kitchen.

these systems must be leveled properly, otherwise there will be observable dips or high spots.

No matter which of the two systems you choose, look for the following when purchasing ceiling tile:

1. All ceiling tile is not acoustical. It must be labeled with this information; otherwise you may get a nice looking decorative surface with none of the sound absorbing qualities.
2. Ceiling tiles are available in many decorator patterns, with each tile forming one pattern unit. However, when installing these tiles, the pattern must be balanced on all four sides of the ceiling; i.e., to get a professional look, you must make even cuts on all four sides. An easier alternative is to select acoustical tile with a continuous pattern so that the individual tiles are not detectable. This will eliminate any trimming during the installation.

Ceiling Beams

The addition of ceiling beams offers a nice change from the normal flat ceiling. They are available in either wood or plastic, unfinished or finished. The beams can be cut to fit the width of the ceiling to be covered, and instructions for installation will be included. Plastic beams are especially light and easy to handle, and can be bought with realistic carving. Some custom cabinet makers also make beams, and these can be finished to match the cabinet color.

Skylights

It is possible to buy a kit and cut a skylight in at any point in the roof over the kitchen where space permits. Skylights can offer a good solution to a general daytime lighting problem, without the energy wasting addition of a new light fixture. Here are some buying tips for a self-installed skylight:

1. Make sure you have the room to install a skylight before you purchase one. Check carefully in the attic or crawl space for clearance. While a light shaft from the roof through the attic and into the kitchen is not difficult to construct, it is simpler to install a skylight without one.
2. Buy a skylight made of clear, shatterproof plastic and not glass. This will prevent hail or other weather damage. Also look for one made with a built-in layer of dead air space for insulation purposes.

CEILING MATERIAL RECOMMENDATIONS

Acoustical Tile

Acoustical tile is made by a number of national manufacturers. Acceptable tiles and suspension systems can be had from Armstrong Cork, United States Gypsum, National Gypsum, Marlite, United Foam, and Certain-Teed Products. All these manufacturers produce their own variety of suspension system, but many can be stapled or glued directly onto the bare ceiling.

A suspension system is one method of installing acoustical tiles.

Ceiling Beams

Most manufacturers of simulated wood beams offer several styles and finishes. Manufacturers of plastic beams include Lite-Beams, Marlite, Modular Materials, Paeco, and Rex Plastics. Genuine wood beams are available from Barclay Industries, Bohemia, Mann and Parker Lumber, and Maher Forest Products.

Skylights

National manufacturers of skylights include Ventarama, Skymaster, and Solartron. All make a variety of skylight products, and some of the skylights have special features like wall mounts and the ability to be opened for ventilation.

Material	Price, per square foot covered	Do-it-yourself installation	Durability	Cleanability	Do-it-yourself repair
Acoustical tile					
Glued or stapled	$0.30-0.75	Easy	Good	Difficult	Fair
Suspended	$0.50-1.05	Fair	Good	Difficult	Easy
Ceiling beams					
Plastic	$1.50-2.50	Easy	Good	Fair	Easy
Wood	$2.30-4.00	Difficult	Good	Difficult	Difficult
Skylights, 2 feet square	$100.00-150.00	Difficult	Fair	Fair	Difficult

Plumbing

Sinks should be judged in a decorative and a functional sense. This buying guide will help you in your selection and point out some of the features you should look for in your sink.

There are basically four varieties of kitchen sinks on the market. In order of popularity, they are stainless steel, pressed steel, cast iron, and an integral bowl(s) molded into a Corian countertop. If your dealer has a large inventory, he may also have the cultured marble or the vitreous china types. Both are uncommon and because of maintenance problems are not recommended for use in the kitchen.

The stainless steel sink that you see in the showroom is not really 'stain'-less. All will show marks, and the durability of the finish depends upon the composition of the steel. Stainless steel sinks will have a percentage of chrome added to preserve the finish and a nickel content that helps to withstand corrosion. You will want to get the largest percentage of each you can find for a quality sink. Cheaper models of stainless steel sinks are constructed of 20-gauge stainless, while the more expensive ones are 18-gauge. The heavier ones will take more punishment and are less noisy during use.

Cast iron and pressed steel (which may be called enameled ware, enameled steel, or porcelain-on-steel) have a surface material that is baked on after the sink shape is made. Porcelain will chip, but you can get these sinks in a wide variety of colors. Cast iron and pressed steel sinks are easy to care for and will last a long time if you do not use an abrasive on them.

Corian sinks are molded directly into the countertop. This creates an effect of one unbroken sweep of countertop and bowl. The price for them is high and that is a reason why they have not been installed in many kitchens. They are available in either single or double bowl models. Corian will scratch and nick and while such marks can be sanded out, they do require more care than the other types.

You can purchase any of these sinks in a variety of shapes and sizes. Standard is 22 inches deep (front to rear), 33 inches wide (in a double bowl), and 7-1/2 inches in depth. Variations from these standard sizes are available, as are corner models to fit in the countertops used in L- or U-shaped kitchens.

On the back of all sinks is the deck or a mounting platform with three or four holes. These are for the faucet with its incoming hot and cold lines, a sprayer, and other appliances. If you choose to install one of the new instant-hot-water devices and there is no room, an extra hole can be cut into the deck. Integral drainboards are another optional feature with any of the sink varieties.

Some buying tips when going to purchase a kitchen sink are:

1. Be sure any sink you purchase is coated with a sound deadener, especially if you plan on installing a disposer. A sink can act as a sounding

20-gauge stainless steel sinks are lighter and less expensive than 18-gauge units.

18-gauge stainless steel sinks will take more punishment than 20-gauge models.

board and create many un-wanted echoes.

2. If you want stainless, buy the heaviest gauge sink you can afford. The literature should say 18-8 (the respective percentage of chrome and nickel) or series 302 or 304 (industry designations). A satin or brushed chrome finish is the easiest to care for.

3. Cast iron sinks are heavier and there is less noise from water splashing. These sinks can chip, and while they can be touched up, it will show. Check the length of the warranty period. In addition, the finish on porcelain is a coating that will wear well if it is not abraded—you should not use abrasives on porcelain sinks.

SINK BUYING RECOMMENDATIONS

With the exception of Corian sinks, most sink manufacturers make a separate line in each of the categories discussed. Those companies listed offer products of good to excellent quality (depending upon the price) and a warranty service in case something is defective.

Corian Sinks

Corian is a trade name of a Du-Pont product and is offered by many dealers from a catalog. The most expensive sinks available, these molded countertops with an integral bowl have an elegant simplicity.

Cast Iron Sinks

These are heavy, but wear well and are the quietest when water is running into them. There is a possibility of enamel flaking, so check on the warranty. Better manufacturers are Kohler and American Standard.

Pressed Steel Sinks

Pressed steel sinks are lighter than cast iron but alike in appearance and properties. Better brands are Kohler, Crane, Eljer, and American Standard.

Stainless Steel Sinks

Price categories in stainless vary according to gauge, number of bowls, and finish. Top brand names in stainless are Moen, Elkay, and Just.

FAUCETS

Modern faucets can do an amazing variety of things besides turning on the water supply. Some are engineered to eliminate washers, others have automatic restrictor devices to cut down on the water flow. Most have a single handle so that they can be worked with an elbow if your hands are full. No matter what additional features the faucet may have, it must be able to do one thing well: Regulate the flow of water. All the rest are add-ons, both to the basic function of the faucet and to the price.

Your kitchen dealer will also have available other devices that can be added to the sink deck. An instant-hot-water heater is a handy device, especially if there are cocoa or hot tea drinkers in the house. This instantly heats a single cup of hot water and eliminates a draw on the water heater.

FAUCET BUYING RECOMMENDATIONS

Almost any faucet you can buy will do the basic function and do it well. Washerless faucets are offered by Moen and Delta. All Moen faucets have a restrictor device to cut down on water consumption. One interesting faucet is offered by Ultraflo. This works by pushbuttons and can be hooked up to bypass the existing kitchen water system in a house with old piping. While expensive, it is much cheaper than installing a new set of pipes.

Instant-hot-water dispensers are offered by a number of companies. Leading brands are KitchenAid, In-Sink-Erator, and Manesco. All will give years of troublefree service, and can cut down on hot water consumption.

Sink type	Price, single bowl	Do-it-yourself installation	Durability	Cleanability	Do-it-yourself repair
Stainless steel, 18 gauge	$85.00-150.00	Fair	Excellent	Very good	Fair
Stainless steel, 20 gauge	$30.00-100.00	Fair	Good	Very good	Poor
Enameled steel	$36.00-80.00	Fair	Fair	Excellent	Fair
Cast iron	$86.00-100.00	Fair	Good	Excellent	Fair
Corian (integral with 10' countertop)	$800.00-1000.00	Difficult	Very good	Excellent	Excellent

Buyers Guide: Major Appliances

Ranges

It is no wonder that Americans are often hard to figure out. Take, for example, our cooking habits. At the same time as a massive trend toward fast-cooking products was developing, most notably with microwave ovens and small specialty electrics like hamburger cookers, a strong market for gourmet cooking was also emerging. The latter trend can be seen in the increasing popularity of food processors, crepe makers and gourmet cooking classes.

Thus, while there were some cooking enthusiasts predicting the dawn of a new type of kitchen—one filled with dozens of small specialty devices and no central appliances—what we actually have seen unfold is a more complete kitchen. The complete kitchen has central appliances, in the form of ever more sophisticated ranges and ovens, refrigerators, dishwashers and the like, plus the addition of special cooking appliances and food preparation products. The result: a kitchen that can serve up everything from the fanciest full-course meals, to the quickest, on-the-run snacks.

Front and center, or in some other prominent location, you find the range. But it isn't the same appliance your mother would have had in her kitchen. Today, it might be a combination range (one that combines both microwave and conventional cooking processes in one product) or a convection range (one that cooks with forced air heat for faster, moister results). It might have an oven that cleans itself, or one that does its best to look clean at all times. If it's gas, it might not have pilot lights. If it's electric, it may have a smoothtop surface—a product straight out of space-age advances in ceramics.

With all the choices, picking out a range for your kitchen can become a nightmare of an extended shopping trip.

Gas Or Electric

Because of energy situations in various parts of the country, there is some confusion about the availability of natural gas and electricity. While some natural gas restrictions still exist in certain parts of the country, it is beginning to look like the residential gas customer will get long-term, preferential treatment. New gas hookups are being allowed in some areas for the first time in as many as five years. That indicates that gas utility companies plan to keep residential customers, add residential customers wherever possible, and promote the use of gas appliances. Gas ranges, as well as other gas appliances, are far from dead, even though electric ranges now outsell them.

Both gas and electric ranges do a good job when it comes to cooking. Preference probably stems from familiarity more than anything else. Here are some generally accepted truths about gas and electric ranges: gas surface burners allow more precise control; electric ovens do not dry foods out as much as gas ovens; electric ranges are a little cheaper to buy; gas ranges generally are a little cheaper to operate.

The Range Of Ranges

Probably the most attractive and convenient way to put a range/oven into a kitchen is to build it into a wall or counter. The built-in range becomes an integral part of the kitchen, rather than simply an addition. Built-in models feature a separate wall oven and cooktop. The cooktop usually is set into a counter above cabinets. There also are drop-in and slide-in models that fit special custom-type kitchen designs. Drop-ins, for example, are designed to be installed into an island, sidewall, counter or peninsula. Slide-ins normally have frame sides and back, similar to drop-ins. They fit snugly between cabinets, with a top lip that overlaps the counter on both sides.

Modern Maid ET-350

Kelvinator REC305M

Tappan 77-4967

Jenn-Air 88370

Amana AO-24BT

Tappan Z14-3621

Of course, there are the ever-popular free-standing models. These units, available in several different widths, offer a complete range of features. The free-standing range has an oven below a cooking surface. It also has sides and a back and requires no special installation other than line cord plug in and/or gas line connection.

A popular free-standing style today is the over-and-under unit. It has two ovens, one above the other with a cooking surface in between. A range that is growing in popularity and will be tomorrow's sales star is the combination model. Combinations offer both conventional and microwave capabilities. There are two basic types. One type is the free-standing electric that has two ovens in one—a conventional electric oven and a microwave. Units of this type are available from Litton, and just recently, Caloric introduced such a model. With these units, you can cook with conventional heat, a combination of conventional electric heat and microwave energy, or microwave energy alone.

Also available are both gas and electric eye-level or over-and-under combination ranges. With these units, the lower oven usually is a conventional oven and the upper oven is a microwave. Units of this type are available from most manufacturers. See the section on Microwave Ovens for a discussion of countertop microwaves versus combination ovens.

The smoothtop range is a variation of the electric range. It has a smoothtop ceramic surface, usually one piece. The electric elements are hidden under marked areas of the surface. This type of range has been a hit because it appears easy to clean and has a certain modern look. The drawbacks are that smoothtops are slightly less energy-efficient than standard electric ranges, and there can be problems cleaning the ceramic top. Ceramic cooktops generally require careful daily cleaning with a special cleaner. The bottoms of your pots and pans have to be clean or they can mar the surface. The surface can discolor without proper care, and spills while cooking can be hard to

clean. For safety, you should wait until the top cools to wipe up a spill; because the cooktop cools slower than conventional electric elements, the spill can bake on the surface. Smoothtops come in a glossy ceramic and matte finish. The glossy finish is easier to clean. The heat-up is slower than a conventional cooktop and the lengthy cooling-off period can be a safety hazard.

Convection ranges also have gained popularity. A convection oven uses a fan to move heated air over and around food. In gas models, this accounts for faster cooking at lower temperatures, reducing the amount of energy required. While there may be some energy savings, in electrics the prime benefit is said to be moister oven-cooked foods. Gas models are available from Tappan; electric models are available from Jenn-Air and Tappan.

The Energy Picture And Ranges

Range manufacturers and the government have been working on a program to reduce energy

Jenn-Air 88353

Tappan 30-3457

consumption in both gas and electric ranges. To date, this program has been mostly voluntary insofar as the public is concerned. However, the National Energy Program that President Carter has pushed for more than a year seeks to set energy standards that will apply to ranges. In essence, the government probably will publish within the next two years a maximum amount of energy that any given range can consume. Ranges that consume more than this set amount will not be allowed.

Most range manufacturers have already done quite a bit to reduce energy consumption. Better insulation and oven door seals have been used. Electronic ignition systems have replaced standing pilots on many gas ranges.

In particular, we recommend gas ranges with pilotless (electronic) ignition systems over gas ranges with standing pilots. The added cost for the ignition system can be recovered in reduced natural gas costs.

As manufacturers improve their ranges to reduce energy consumption, prices are going to go up. Pilotless ignition can raise the price of a new gas range between $20 to $30. Other improvements on ranges, both gas and electric, could add $15 or more. Ranges that rely on new or different principles to reduce energy consumption, such as convection cooking, may cost $50 or $60 more than conventional units.

It is important to understand that unlike the simple addition of features, energy improvements should bring you lower costs over the lifetime of the unit. And since gas ranges last about 13-1/2 years and electrics about 12 years, your payback can go on for many years beyond the amount necessary to offset the higher purchase price.

Perhaps the most important aspect of buying any energy consuming product today is the life cycle cost of an appliance. The life cycle cost gives you a concrete picture of the real difference between various models. This cost includes purchase price, maintenance costs (expected) and anticipated energy bills over the entire life of the product.

Features On Ranges And Ovens

Item for item, ranges and ovens offer more features than most other appliances. Not only are there major styling differences from one model to another, but many convenience features as well. Remember that features are good investments only if they will be used.

Similarly, just because a range brand is popular does not automatically make it a best buy for you. Your likes and dislikes, habits and expectations are more important. For example, Jenn-Air offers some of the most exotic and versatile ranges available. They are extremely popular among professional kitchen designers and remodelers. And, the range is a fine product. However, for many consumers not into serious cooking, such a range might not be a good buy simply because they would not use it enough. Many of the optional features of the range, such as the grill, may require extensive cleanup that some consumers would be unwilling to do.

Caloric EJP395

General Electric JBP87G

Recommended Ranges

Manufacturer	Model	Style	Type	No. ovens	No. burners	Height x Width x Depth
Amana	A0-24BT	built-in	electric	2		49-¾ x 23-¾ x 23-½
Amana	AKF-1B	cooktop	electric/smoothtop		2-6-¼", 2-9"	4-⅜ x 34-¹¹/₁₆ x 21-⅜
Caloric	RSP366	free-standing	gas/pilotless	1	4	44-⅜ x 30 x 26-½
Caloric	EJP395	over/under	electric	2	2-6", 2-8"	71-¾ x 30 x 25-¼
Caloric	RTP307	cooktop	gas/pilotless		4	2-⅞ x 29-½ x 21
Frigidaire	Reg 38	free-standing	electric	1	2-6", 2-8"	50 x 30 x 29-¼
Frigidaire	Reg 38-C	free-standing	electric/smoothtop	1	2-6"; 2-8"	50 x 30 x 29-¼
Frigidaire	RE-94D	built-in	electric	1		31-¹/₁₆ x 23-⁹/₁₆ x 23-⅛
Frigidaire	RB-131	cooktop	electric		2-6", 2-8"	4-⁷/₁₆ x 32-¼ x 20-¼
General Electric	JKP26G	built-in	electric	2		49-⅝ x 24-¾ x 24
General Electric	JP661V	cooktop	electric		2-6", 2-8"	6 x 30-¾ x 21-⅜
General Electric	JBP87G	free-standing	electric/smoothtop	1	4	47-¾ x 29-⅞ x 25-⅛
General Electric	JBP-26W	free-standing	electric	1	2-6", 2-8"	26 x 29-⅞ x 26-½
Hardwick	CK-7224-800R	built-in	gas	1		44-²⁵/₃₂ x 25-⅝ x 23
Hardwick	C423	cooktop	gas/pilotless		4	2-⅞ x 30 x 21-¹³/₁₆
Hardwick	EK971-650AS	free-standing	electric/smoothtop	1	4	46-¹/₆ x 30 x 24-6
Hotpoint	RC548W	free-standing	electric	1	2-6", 2-8"	45-¾ x 30 x 27-½
Jenn-Air	88370	free-standing	electric	1	4 (convertible)	36 x 29-¹⁵/₁₆ x 25-¾
Jenn-Air	88353	cooktop	electric		6 (convertible)	46-¹¹/₁₆ x 21-⁹/₁₆
Jenn-Air	88890	cooktop	electric		4 (convertible)	29-⁷/ x 21-½
Kelvinator	REC305M	free-standing	electric	1	2-6", 2-8"	44-⅛ x 30 x 26-⅞
Kenmore	22 H 72981	free-standing	gas/pilotless	1	4	47-⅜ x 29-¹⁵/₁₆ x 28
Kenmore	22 H 78581	free-standing	gas/pilotless	2	4	65-⅝ x 29-¹⁵/₁₆ x 28
Kenmore	22 H 9288	free-standing	electric/smoothtop	1	2-6", 2-8"	47-⅜ x 29-⅞ x 28
Litton	621	combination	electric	1	2-6", 2-8"	47-¾ x 29-⅞ x 28-¼
Litton	631	combination	electric	1	2-6", 2-8"	47-¾ x 29-⅞ x 28-¼
Litton	970	combination	electric	2	2-6", 2-8"	66-¼ x 29-⅞ x 28-½
Litton	880	combination, built-in	electric	2		48-⅞ x 25 x 23-¾
Magic Chef	338W-6KLPX	free-standing	gas/pilotless	1	4	46 x 30 x 26-⅝
Magic Chef	228W-6BLX	over/under	gas	2	4	65-⅝ x 30 x 26-⅝
Magic Chef	267W-6CLXM4	combination	electric	2	2-6", 2-8"	65-⅝ x 30 x 26-⅝
Magic Chef	247W-6HKPXWM4	combination	gas/pilotless	2	4	65-⅝ x 30 x 26-⅝
Modern Maid	QCO-480	built-in	electric	2		45-¾ x 23-¾ x 23-½
Modern Maid	ET-350	cooktop	electric		4	3 x 28-½ x 21-⅜
Roper	1088	built-in	gas/pilotless	2		50-⁷/₁₆ x 23-¾ x 23-¾
Roper	1638	free-standing	gas	1	4	36 x 30 x 24
Roper	1178	cooktop	gas/pilotless		4	3 x 28-½ x 20-¾
Tappan	30-3457	free-standing	gas/pilotless	1	4	46-⅝ x 29-¹⁵/₁₆ x 25-¹/₃₂
Tappan	30-3847	free-standing	gas/pilotless	1	4	46-⅝ x 30-¹/₁₆ x 27-³/₃₂
Tappan	12-1267	built-in	gas/pilotless	1		42-⅜ x 23-¹⁷/₃₂ x 21
Tappan	Z14-3621	cooktop	gas		4	3-²⁵/₃₂ x 36 x 18-⅝
Tappan	77-4967	combination	electric	2	2-6", 2-8"	66-⁵/₆ x 30 x 25
Whirlpool	RFE 3300	free-standing	electric	1	2-6", 2-8"	46-⅛ x 29-⅞ x 27-⅛
Whirlpool	RFE-395P	free-standing	electric	1	2-6", 2-8"	55 x 29-⅞ x 27-⁵/₁₆
White-Westinghouse	KF332	free-standing	electric	1	2-6", 2-8"	45-⅞ x 30 x 25-¹³/₁₆
White-Westinghouse	KB451	built-in	electric	2		49-⁹/₁₆ x 26-½ x 23
White-Westinghouse	KP830	cooktop	electric/smoothtop		4	5-⅜ x 34-¹³/₃₂ x 21-⅜

Recommended Ranges

Cleaning	Programmed oven	Clock/ timer	Oven door window	Oven light	Warranty	Approximate retail price
self	yes	yes	yes	yes	1 year	$809.95
					1 year	$419.00
self	yes	yes	yes	yes	1 year	$679.95
continuous	yes	yes	yes	yes	1 year	$574.95
					1 year	$174.95-white, color $204.95-chrome
self	yes	yes	yes	yes	1 year	$629.95
self	yes	yes	yes	yes	1 year	$839.95
self	yes	yes	yes	yes	1 year	$719.95
					1 year	$159.95
self	yes	yes	yes	yes	1 year	$719.95
					1 year	$199.95
self	yes	yes	yes	yes	1 year	$829.95
self	yes	yes	yes	yes	1 year	$579.95
continuous	no	yes	yes	yes	1 year	$422.00
					1 year	$144.00
continuous	yes	yes	yes	yes	1 year	$542.00
manual	yes	yes	yes	yes	1 year	$380.00
self	yes	yes	yes	yes	1 year	$692.00
					1 year	$488.00
					1 year	$328.00
continuous	yes	yes	yes	yes	1 year	$349.00
continuous	yes	yes	yes	yes	1 year	$499.95
continuous	yes	yes	yes	yes	1 year	$699.95
continuous	yes	yes	yes	yes	1 year	$469.95
manual	yes	yes	yes	yes	1 year	$629.00
self	yes	yes	yes	yes	1 year	$879.00
self	yes	yes	yes	yes	1 year	$899.00
self	yes	yes	yes	yes	1 year	$1069.00
continuous	yes	yes	yes	yes	1 year	$460.00
continuous	no	yes	yes	yes	1 year	$599.00
continuous	yes	yes	yes	yes	1 year	$900.00
self	yes	yes	yes	yes	1 year	$1200.00
continuous	yes	yes	yes	yes	1 year	$500.00
					1 year	$149.00
continuous	yes	yes	yes	yes	1 year	$654.95
continuous	no	yes	yes	yes	1 year	$389.95
					1 year	$144.95
continuous	yes	yes	yes	yes	1 year	$519.95
self	yes	yes	yes	yes	1 year	$639.95
manual	no	yes	yes	yes	1 year	$369.95
					1 year	$159.95
self	yes	yes	yes	yes	1 year	$1120.00
continuous	no	yes	yes	yes	1 year	$339.95
self	yes	yes	yes	yes	1 year	$629.95
continuous	yes	yes	yes	yes	1 year	$389.95
continuous	yes	yes	yes	yes	1 year	$469.95
					1 year	$429.95

Features And Comments

• Most units have a broiler in the oven cavity or under the oven in a separate compartment. Waist-high broilers rate as a slight convenience advantage because they are at the top of the oven cavity or in their own compartment above the oven.

• Most electric ranges have two 6-inch elements and two 8-inch elements. Gas ranges usually have four surface burners of the same size. They may have standing pilots or pilotless ignition, either spark-type or glow-type. Some range models offer thermostatically controlled burners. By and large, these are a source of service trouble and not wholly worth the extra cost. Infinite heat controls are a plus, as are fast-heating elements.

• Removable pans or bowls under burners and elements help when it comes to cleanup. Lift up and lock tops are a plus.

• Two oven cleaning systems exist—self-cleaning and continuous-cleaning.

Self-cleaning ovens use a pyrolytic, or high heat, system to incinerate oven grime to a powdery ash. An expensive feature, both initially and in use, it actually does remove heavy oven soils. If you do not do a lot of roasting or baking, a self-cleaning feature probably will not be worth the extra cost.

Continuous-cleaning or catalytic systems are in fact a special porous finish on interior oven liners. The finish tends to absorb and spread oven soil in a way that promotes oxidation at normal oven temperatures. It will handle small splatters, but large spills should be wiped up.

• The best programmed oven is one that delays the start of cooking to a preset time, cooks for the set period, then drops to a keep-warm temperature until you terminate the cycle. Next best are cook-and-hold systems. Two other systems are available—delay-and-cook and start-and-stop. The cook-and-hold and delay-cook-and-hold features are the better of the systems, but if you won't use a feature like this, save your money by not buying it.

• An optional item, a range hood can help reduce grease and odors. Two types are available—vented and unvented. Unvented units trap and hold grease and odors; vented units actually remove them and are preferable.

• A lift-off oven door makes cleaning easier on standard ovens.

• Location and amount of storage differs from unit to unit. If you have special needs or desires, look to the wider units for more versatility.

• A warming shelf located above the cooktop is available on some models. It is nice, but not necessary.

• Many models come with oven door windows or black glass doors with windows. A window combined with an interior oven light is recommended because it allows you to check cooking progress without opening the oven door, which saves heat and energy.

• Clocks, timers, and control panel and cooktop lighting are nice features. You should base buying decision on what you like and what you'll use.

• Models come with a variety of decorator options, such as the black glass doors already mentioned. Kits are not normally available for ranges. However, Magic Chef and other manufacturers offer special decorative features in their ranges.

Frigidaire RE-94D controls

Roper 1088

Magic Chef 267W-6CLXM4

Refrigerators

If you have not shopped for refrigerators in a while, you will be surprised at the color selection and expanded features found on today's units. In addition to white, avocado, gold, and brown or coppertone, refrigerators are available in almond and terra cotta or with front panels that allow paneling or wallpapering for personalized decor. Among the new features are an unwrapped-food storage drawer from Frigidaire and a tilt-out ice bin from Whirlpool. But perhaps most important of all, the new refrigerator models are going to save you energy and lots of it.

The New Models And Energy

The federal government and refrigerator manufacturers have been working to reduce energy consumption, and changes in design already have been made. A major problem—sweating on doors—is being overcome with door heaters or post-condenser loops. The heaters are switch-controlled and can save up to 10 percent on energy consumption; with post-condenser loops, hot refrigerant gas is used to prevent sweating.

Increased insulation or a switch to polyurethane foam insulation instead of fiberglass has resulted in energy improvements. Foam insulation can save energy when combined with liners made of plastic, especially ABS. Manufacturers such as Amana have significantly increased the amount of insulation to produce major energy reductions.

Other areas of improvement include better evaporator heat exchangers, condenser heat exchangers, and door seals; improved cabinet designs and compressor motors; and demand defrost.

The Cost Of Saving Energy

Whatever the improvements on modern refrigerators, they all mean higher purchase prices. However, CONSUMER GUIDE Magazine recommends taking a life-cycle approach to figuring the cost of a new refrigerator. This involves considering the cost of the unit over its expected life (15 years is average), including an examination of the purchase price, expected maintenance costs, and energy costs, which undoubtedly will rise. You might find that a unit with a higher price tag actually is the cheaper buy over time.

Energy Recommendations

CONSUMER GUIDE Magazine recommends purchasing the most efficient refrigerator you can afford. Sales people will be talking about EEFs—Energy Efficiency Factors—when you shop. You should know that an EEF equals the unit's number of cubic feet divided by the number of kilowatt hours of electricity it will consume in one day. The higher the EEF, the more efficient the refrigerator. Eventually, refrigerators will bear energy labels that will detail consumption and provide a means of comparing a particular model and its efficiency with others of its size.

Refrigerator Trends

In spite of predictions that smaller capacity refrigerators would gain in popularity as family size declines, large capacity units still are more popular, possibly because women who work outside the home find them more convenient for storing foods purchased in large quantities at infrequent intervals.

For everyone, though, styling is still the number one concern, inside and out. Textured steel doors that hide fingerprints currently are walking away with the popularity contest prize, so expect to see more of them offered.

Inside, there are some wood-grained details, as well as multiple color combinations.

Refrigerators with bottom-mounted freezers are making a comeback. Whirlpool and White-Westinghouse recently introduced such models, and Amana has kept one in its line. Many people prefer bottom-mounted freezers because they mean better access to items in the refrigerator section.

Size Does Make A Difference

The kitchen space you can make available for a refrigerator might determine the size and style unit you can buy. Some refrigerators vent to the front and so don't require extra depth or an air space above the unit. Others need air circulation space at the sides and top, while some models can be built in, such as those from Sub-Zero. Remember to check if the door swing will be limited in any way; if the refrigerator will be next to a side wall, see if you will be able to remove drawers and shelves for cleaning with the door open at just a 90 degree angle.

As far as capacity is concerned, match it to the size of your family for minimum energy waste. Most guidelines suggest 8 to 10 cubic feet of fresh food space for two people; add 1 cubic foot for each additional family member. The freezer should be about 3 cubic feet for a family of two; add one cubic foot for each extra person. Of course, these suggested sizes should be altered as special needs demand.

Refrigerator Types And Features

Models with one door usually have a small freezer compartment inside with a small access door. Top-mounts, or units with two horizontal doors, have separate doors for the fresh food section and the freezer. As previously mentioned, bottom-

Whirlpool EET-171HK

Sub-Zero 3211 RFD

Recommended Refrigerators

Manufacturer	Model	Type	Capacity (cubic feet)	Defrosting type	Shelves	Door shelves	Freezer shelves
Admiral	NT-1595T	top-mount	14.6	automatic	3	2	0
Admiral	NT1896T	top-mount	18.4	automatic	4	3	1
Admiral	INS2299T	side-by-side	21.7	automatic	5	6	3
Amana	ESRF16B	top-mount	16.2	automatic	4	3	1
Amana	BC-20B	bottom-mount	17.74	automatic	4	4	1
Amana	TD-23B	top-mount	22.9	automatic	5	3	2
Amana	SR-25B	side-by-side	25.2	manual	5	6	5
Frigidaire	FPE-17TSB	top-mount	17	automatic	4	2	2
Frigidaire	FPC1 21TSB	top-mount	20.6	automatic	4	3	2
Frigidaire	FPE-20V3SB	side-by-side	20.3	automatic	4	3	4
General Electric	TBF-21DW	top-mount	20.8	automatic	4	2	2
General Electric	TFF 24RW	side-by-side	23.5	automatic	5	5	3
General Electric	TFF 22RW	side-by-side	21.6	automatic	5	5	4
Gibson	RT-17F6	top-mount	17.0	automatic	4	2	1
Hotpoint	CTF-14EW	top-mount	14.2	automatic	3	3	1
Hotpoint	CTF-18HW	top-mount	17.7	automatic	4	3	1
Kenmore	46 H 68771N	top-mount	17.0	automatic	3	3	1
Kenmore	46 H 68051N	side-by-side	19.1	automatic	4	5	4
Sub-Zero	3211 RFD	built-in	30.5	automatic	5	4	5
Sub-Zero	251 RFD	built-in	22	automatic	5	3	2
Whirlpool	EET-171HK	top-mount	17.2	automatic	3	2	2
Whirlpool	EET-221MT	top-mount	22.2	automatic	4	3	1
Whirlpool	EED-191PK	side-by-side	19.1	automatic	4	5	5
Whirlpool	EEB-191MK	bottom-mount	19.0	automatic	5	3	1
White-Westinghouse	RT-186A	top-mount	18.2	automatic	4	3	1
White-Westinghouse	RS-218A	side-by-side	21.0	automatic	5	4	4

Gibson RT-17F6

Amana SR-25B

Recommended Refrigerators

Freezer door shelves	Automatic ice maker	Height x Width x Depth	Temp. controls	Wheels	Warranty	Approximate retail price
1	optional	60 x 29 x 27-⅝	yes	yes	1 year	$539.95
0	optional	65-½ x 31 x 27-⅝	yes	yes	1 year	$619.95
5	yes	66-⅜ x 33 x 29-¼	yes	yes	1 year	$1099.95
1	optional	65-¾ x 28 x 31-⅜	yes	yes	1 year	$509.95
2	optional	67-⅝ x 32 x 29-¼	yes	yes	1 year	$819.95
2	optional	67-⅝ x 32 x 32-$^1/_{16}$	yes	yes	1 year	$739.95
5	optional	67-$^7/_{16}$ x 35-¾ x 31-⅞	yes	yes	1 year	$1029.95
2	optional	65-⅞ x 30 x 29-¾	yes	yes	1 year	$609.95
2	optional	65-⅞ x 33-¾ x 29-¾	yes	yes	1 year	$659.95
6	optional	65-⅞ x 33-¾ x 29-$^3/_{16}$	yes	yes	1 year	$839.95
2	optional	66 x 20-½ x 30-$^{15}/_{16}$	yes	yes	1 year	$599.95
4	yes	66-¼ x 35-¾ x 31	yes	yes	1 year	$1179.95
4	yes	66-¼ x 33 x 31	yes	yes	1 year	$1069.95
2	optional	62-$^{29}/_{32}$ x 31 x 29-$^1/_{16}$	yes	yes	1 year	$549.95
2	optional	61 x 28 x 29-$^3/_{16}$	yes	yes	1 year	$424.00
2	optional	66 x 30-½ x 30-$^9/_{16}$	yes	yes	1 year	$464.00
2	optional	65-⅞ x 32-¾ x 29	yes	yes	1 year	$519.95
6	yes	65-⅞ x 32-¾ x 28-⅞	yes	yes	1 year	$719.95
4	yes	83-¼ x 48 x 24	yes	no	1 year	$1900.00
1	yes	83-¼ x 36 x 24	yes	no	1 year	$1450.00
2	optional	65-⅞ x 32-¾ x 29	yes	yes	1 year	$529.95
2	yes	65-⅞ x 32-¾ x 32	yes	yes	1 year	$899.95
5	optional	65-⅞ x 32-¾ x 29-½	yes	yes	1 year	$669.95
2	optional	65-⅞ x 32-¾ x 29	yes	yes	1 year	$669.95
2	optional	64-¾ x 30 x 31-⅛	yes	yes	1 year	$539.95
4	optional	64-½ x 33 x 29-⅜	yes	yes	1 year	$669.95

mounted freezers are gaining popularity, and in these units, the freezer section is a slide-out drawer.

Two full-size vertical doors distinguish side-by-side models. The freezer usually occupies one-third to one-half of the capacity. This is a greater space than normally found in top-mounts and is one reason for the popularity of side-by-sides in recent years. A variation has two doors for the freezer section (for a total of three doors) so frequently used items can be reached without opening the entire freezer.

Refrigerator features abound, many of them geared for saving energy, others aimed at providing greater convenience. Those recommended by CONSUMER GUIDE Magazine include: automatic defrost, door heater switches, adjustable cantilever shelves, dual controls, removable bins and crispers, shelves in the freezer section, removable ice bins, and rollers.

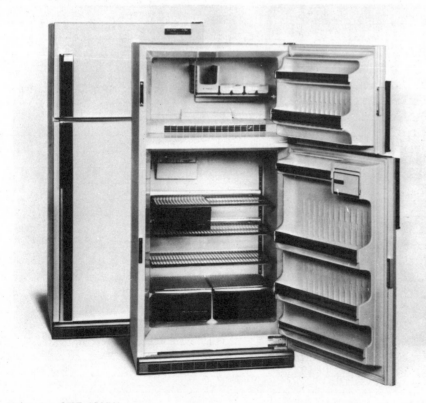

Hotpoint CTF-18HW

● Defrost—Manual defrost is the most economical, but it requires that the unit be defrosted periodically. Partial defrost, also called cycle defrost, requires freezer defrosting but the refrigerator section defrosts automatically. With automatic defrost (also called no-frost, frost-free, and other names), the freezer and fresh food section completely defrost periodically. The additional price and increased operating costs for automatic defrost do not deter most consumers.

● Power Savers—Door heater switches are recommended for consumers who live in air-conditioned homes or in low-humidity areas, while post-condenser models are best for use in non-air-conditioned homes or in high-humidity locales.

● Controls—A single control for both refrigerator and freezer sections is not as efficient as dual controls. Separate controls for meat keepers are available

● Refrigerator Shelves—Fully adjustable, cantilever shelves are the most functional, since fixed shelves or only partially adjustable shelves limit storage. Shelving materials vary from tempered glass (pretty and easy to clean, but they can break), to plastic (a good, all-around shelving material), to wire (easy to see through but these shelves allow spills to drip through).

● Liners—You will find liners of plastic or metal, though in the future the majority will be plastic as manufacturers turn to foam insulation in answer to energy challenges. A plastic liner, however, can be scratched or damaged with improper cleaning.

● Bins and crispers—Steel bins are more durable than plastic, though plastic ones are lightweight and easy to clean. Either should have stops that keep them from unintentionally being pulled all the way out.

● Refrigerator door shelves —Fixed plastic shelves with a butter compartment (and often a cheese compartment) and egg holder are the most common. A few models have cantilevered shelves in the door or adjustable pick-off bins.

● Freezer shelf—A wire shelf in the freezer helps you organize items more efficiently.

● Freezer door shelves— Side-by-sides have several shelves on the freezer section door, and most units also have a bin for bulk items. Top-mounts may have one or two door shelves; most have at least a shelf or rack for juice cans.

● Icemakers—An icemaker is a luxury whose cost may not be in proportion to its convenience. If you cannot afford one now but think you might want to have it in the future, look for a refrigerator that is prewired and plumbed for an add-on icemaker. Removable ice bins are worth having in any case.

● Rollers—Rollers are standard equipment on large refrigerators and are optional on others. They are worth having to facilitate moving the unit during cleaning.

Freezers

The planning stage of a kitchen remodeling is the ideal time to ask yourself whether you have a need for the freezing capacity of a full-size unit. If your family is large or you like to buy groceries in bulk quantities or prepare meals in advance, you will appreciate the convenience of such a freezer. Now is the time to consider the additional advantages of installing it in a kitchen location, rather than in the basement or other space.

Because of the rising cost of electricity, CONSUMER GUIDE Magazine has paid special attention to energy-efficient freezer models. Though freezers are purchased primarily for their convenience, we believe you should consider efficiency, too. An inefficient freezer, no matter how good it looks or useful it is, will drain dollars from your budget for years.

The Government, Industry, And Energy

The government, through the Department of Energy, is working with freezer manufacturers to improve the energy efficiency of the units. Improvements include anti-sweat door heater switches that turn off the heaters during dry periods, and new design methods for eliminating door sweating. Also being added are better compressors and motors, better and thicker insulation systems, and better door gaskets. The end result is a more efficient freezer that costs more money to buy; in the long run, however, the added original costs will be recovered in lower energy bills.

CONSUMER GUIDE Magazine recommends that you pay the increased up-front costs of high efficiency models since freezers last about 20 years and that is a long time to be paying for in-efficiency. Life-cycle cost analysis—looking at the total cost of a unit over its life, including purchase price, maintenance costs, and energy costs—dictates spending more now to save later.

CONSUMER GUIDE Magazine does not recommend automatic defrost on freezers. If you are a typical freezer user, you will not be opening yours very often and consequently will need to defrost the unit only two or three times a year. If you buy a manual defrost unit and defrost it when it needs it, you will be money ahead.

Chest Or Upright?

Your decision on the type of freezer—a chest or an upright model—will depend largely on its intended location. Uprights are generally preferred for kitchens since floor space there is at a premium and uprights make better use of vertical space. Chests become more practical for other areas of the home.

It is possible to build in a freezer. Check first with the dealer, however, since units require air space for proper operation.

Whirlpool EEV161F

Admiral F1676

Frigidaire F-203C

The Right Size Will Help

Since buying a too-small freezer defeats the purpose and a too-large freezer is both inefficient and costly to operate, try to tailor the size of your unit to intended usage. One guideline suggests 3 cubic feet per family member. Add 2 cubic feet for special purpose and an extra 2 to 3 cubic feet if you freeze garden products or meals prepared in advance.

Freezer Features

Many features are necessary inclusions, while others, such as the automatic defrost already discussed, merely offer additional convenience. Both uprights

Recommended Freezers

Manufacturer	Model	Type	Capacity (cubic feet)	Defrosting system	Defrosting drain	Shelves
Admiral	F1676	upright	15.8	manual	yes	4
Amana	ESU 13B	upright	13.1	manual	yes	4
Amana	ESU 17B	upright	17.1	manual	yes	4
Amana	ESU 15B	upright	15.1	manual	yes	4
Amana	C-15	chest	15	manual	yes	
Frigidaire	F-128U	upright	12.8	manual	yes	4
Frigidaire	F-203C	chest	20.3	manual	no	
General Electric	CA-12DW	upright	11.6	manual	no	3
General Electric	CA-21DW	upright	21.1	manual	yes	5
Gibson	FH10M4	chest	10.07	manual	no	
Kelvinator	UFS161MM	upright	16.1	manual	yes	3
Kenmore	47 H 38155N	upright	15.3	automatic	no	3
Kenmore	47 H 18092N	chest	9	manual	no	
Whirlpool	EEV161F	upright	15.9	manual	yes	3
Whirlpool	EEH182F	chest	18.2	manual	yes	
White-Westinghouse	FU189-T	upright	17.7	automatic	no	4

Frigidaire F-128U

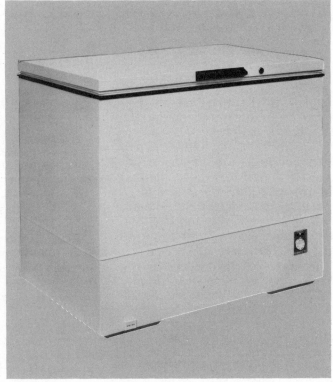
Amana C-15

and chests should have at least one bulk food basket, an indicator light to tell you the unit is functioning, a lock, and a drain to facilitate defrosting (some units even include a hose assembly to help in this chore). On up-rights, you will want deep door shelves.

Since few freezers are installed in the kitchen, styling choices are more limited than those of other major appliances. However, some manufacturers of upright freezers offer decorator kits similar to those available for refrigerators. These allow wallpaper or panels to be inserted on the door. For chests, choices are just a basic white or a simulated woodgrain, vinyl-clad steel top.

Recommended Freezers

Door shelves	Baskets	Height x Width x Depth	Indicator light	Lock	Warranty	Approximate retail price
4		66-½ x 30 x 29-¼	no	yes	1 year	$409.95
5	1	62-$^{27}/_{32}$ x 28 x 25	no	yes	1 year	$409.95
6	1	66-$^{27}/_{32}$ x 28 x 30-$^7/_{16}$	no	yes	1 year	$489.95
5	1	62-$^{27}/_{32}$ x 28 x 28-$^{13}/_{16}$	no	yes	1 year	$449.95
	1	36-⅝ x 41-½ x 30-⅝	yes	yes	1 year	$399.95
3		59-⅛ x 28 x 29-⅝	no	yes	1 year	$379.95
	1	35 x 57 x 29-½	yes	yes	1 year	$489.95
5	1	63-½ x 28 x 27-$^{13}/_{16}$	no	yes	1 year	$339.95
6	1	70-⅛ x 32 x 28-⅞	yes	yes	1 year	$529.95
	1	34-$^1/_{16}$ x 41 x 23-¾	no	yes	1 year	$309.95
5	1	61-⅞ x 32-$^3/_{16}$ x 29-½	no	yes	1 year	$369.95
5	1	65-⅞ x 29-¾ x 30-⅛	no	yes	1 year	$489.95
	1	37-⅛ x 35 x 27-¾	no	no	1 year	$249.95
4	1	65-½ x 29-¾ x 31-⅝	yes	yes	1 year	$389.95
	2	36-$^1/_{16}$ x 50-¼ x 28	yes	yes	1 year	$419.95
4	1	64-½ x 30 x 28-⅞	no	no	1 year	$499.95

Dishwashers

Dishwashers have become as necessary a kitchen item as the sink, refrigerator, and range; in fact, there is hardly a new or remodeled kitchen to be found without one. The main reason, of course, is that they cut cleanup time, but another plus is the fact that they store as well as clean dirty dishes, keeping the kitchen presentable even when there are dishes to be done.

Dishwashers, which range in price from about $200 to $500, are available as built-ins or portables. The latter include convertible models, sometimes called convertible/portables, that can be used first as portables and then later be built in under a counter. Because of consumer demand for built-in models, few true portables are made; most portables are the convertible type. CONSUMER GUIDE Magazine believes you will find a built-in more beneficial both functionally and decoratively.

If you should decide a portable would better suit your needs, expect to find units that can load from the front or the top. They will have power cords to plug in and hoses to attach to water faucets, and they will be on casters so you can roll them out of storage for use.

Convertibles look like portables, but their casters, hoses, and electrical cords can be removed when the unit is built in. On built-in dishwashers, such connections are made permanently when the unit is installed under the counter. Generally, convertible/portable models are slightly more expensive because of the extra materials (hoses, cords, and side panels) not found on built-ins.

Anyone remodeling or designing a new kitchen should be aware of several "special" dishwasher models that fit unique needs or design solutions. KitchenAid offers a combination sink/dishwasher; General Electric has a dishwasher to install under a sink in a space-shy kitchen; and Modern Maid makes a combination range/dishwasher, again, to be used for space-saving reasons.

Dishwashers Consume Energy But You Can Conserve It

The amount of energy you will consume or save with any model depends to a great extent on how you use it. You can count on the recommended models to do a good job of cleaning, so save water by scraping off large pieces of food and skipping the pre-rinse. You also will get more work for less energy if you run your unit only with full loads and use a short-wash cycle or similar feature for lightly soiled loads.

When you are shopping for a dishwasher, consider one that has an energy saver—a switch to eliminate the powered drying cycle. The dishes will air-dry instead, and you will save about 10 percent on energy usages.

The government and dishwasher manufacturers are working to further reduce the energy that dishwashers consume. Most attempts are centering on reducing the amount of hot water used and/or the temperature of the hot water, since those are the areas of greatest energy usage and because there is not too much that can be changed with the mechanical action of the machine. Eventually energy-conserving improvements might add $25 or more to the initial price of a unit.

Dishwasher Features

Soft food disposers and screens that keep scraps from jamming a dishwasher pump are standard equipment on most good dishwashers today. The number of cycles, however, varies widely,

Recommended Dishwashers

Manufacturer	Model	Type	Loading	No. cycles	Drying system	Wetting agent dispenser
Frigidaire	DWU-44B	built-in	front	6	convection	yes
General Electric	GSD500	built-in	front	5	convection	yes
General Electric	GSD1000	built-in	front	5	forced air	yes
Hotpoint	HDB-776	convertible	front	6	convection	yes
Kenmore	65-H-7985	convertible	front	3	forced-air	yes
Kenmore	65-H-7974	built-in	front	4	forced-air	yes
KitchenAid	KDC-18	built-in	front	3	forced-air	optional
KitchenAid	KDI-18	built-in	front	4	forced-air	yes
KitchenAid	KDC-58	convertible	front	3	forced-air	optional
Maytag	WU401	built-in	front	5	convection	optional
Whirlpool	SDU-5001	built-in	front	3	convection	yes
Whirlpool	SDF-3700	convertible	front	3	convection	no
White-Westinghouse	SU-450	built-in	front	6	forced-air	yes

KitchenAid KDI-18

Whirlpool SDF-3700

Maytag WU401

though most consumers' needs can be met by three—short wash, normal, and pots and pans. Select added cycles to suit your requirements. For example, a rinse-and-hold feature is handy if you have just a few dishes to wash on an infrequent basis. Sanitizer, plate warming, and china-crystal are among other settings to suit individual needs.

Dishes will be dried with either a forced-air or convection (radiant) system. The more common is convection, which utilizes a heating element at the bottom of the tub. Forced-air drying, available from General Electric, KitchenAid, Sears (Kenmore), and White-Westinghouse, uses a blower to force air over a heating element and then around the dishes. Though forced-air drying does a better job, this difference has been made less significant by the move to save energy by eliminating the drying cycle.

Units have spray action on one, two, or three levels. Most better dishwashers have two- or three-level spray action. The best results are achieved with spray arms at top and bottom, with a separate spray for the upper rack.

Other features CONSUMER GUIDE Magazine recommends include porcelain enamel on steel interiors, detergent/rinse dispensers, removable silverware baskets, and adjustable upper racks.

For a decorative exterior, virtually every manufacturer uses a panel pack that allows a choice of four colors—two door inserts with a color on each side. Optional kits make it possible to have a black-glass door look or a door customized with paneling or other treatment to match a decorative theme.

Recommended Dishwashers

Height x Width x Depth	Heating element wattage	Volts	Energy saver	Sound insulation	Warranty	Approximate retail price
34-1/2 x 24 x 24	900	115	yes	yes	1 year	$419.95
34-1/2 x 24 x 25-1/2	700	115	yes	yes	1 year	$319.95
34 x 24 x 25-1/2	700	115	yes	yes	1 year	$489.95
36-3/4 x 24-3/8 x 25	700	115	yes	yes	1 year	$280.00
34-1/4 x 24-1/8 x 26-7/8	750	120	yes	yes	1 year	$329.95
34-1/2 x 23-7/8 x 25-1/2	750	120	yes	yes	1 year	$339.95
34-1/2 x 24 x 24-9/16	800	115	yes	yes	1 year	$394.95
34-1/2 x 24 x 29-9/16	800	115	yes	yes	1 year	$434.95
34-1/2 x 24 x 26-3/16	800	115	yes	yes	1 year	$459.95-white $469.95-color
35-1/2 x 24 x 24-1/16	750	115	yes	yes	1 year	$469.00
34-5/32 x 23-7/8 x 25-15/16	800	120	yes	yes	1 year	$329.95
36-3/8 x 24-1/8 x 26-1/4	800	120	yes	yes	1 year	$289.95
34-1/2 x 24 x 25	760	120	yes	yes	1 year	$319.95

Disposers

A disposer sounds like a rather dull and mundane product, but it can be an important aid in kitchen cleanup. For a few cents a month, you can let an unseen food waste disposer get rid of wet garbage. And, an in-the-sink food waste disposer will help you keep your kitchen free of odors resulting from wet garbage.

Better units can handle virtually any type of waste—soft foods, stringy foods, rinds, and even corncobs. Disposers will range from an economy price of about $50 up to around $175 for a top-of-the-line model. Unlike many other products, better disposers are quite different from inexpensive bargain units. Better models feature heavy-duty motors, usually 1/2 horsepower or larger, and more components made from high-quality corrosion-resistant materials, such as stainless steel. These factors make such disposers the best values.

CONSUMER GUIDE® recommends middle and top-of-the-line disposers. From every standpoint—reliability, lifespan, performance—they are worth the extra initial cost. Inexpensive units may not stand up well to tough food wastes. Overloading and jamming can be the troublesome result of a unit not built to handle a tough job.

There is also the matter of safety. Heavy-duty models usually have an anti-jam system of some type. Such systems reverse the grinding direction or use some other mechanism to clear obstructions. These systems virtually eliminate the need to put something, like a hand, into the unit.

In general, any home with a standard kitchen sink will accommodate a disposer. However, if you have a septic system, check with a local expert before installing a unit. All homeowners should make sure that any installation work is done in accordance with local building codes.

Types Of Disposers

Disposers come in batch-feed and continuous-feed models. Both have advantages, as well as specific modes of operation.

Batch-feed units are a bit more expensive to purchase, because the "wiring" is already done on these models. They have the on-off switch control in the cover. Thus, they are slightly less expensive to have installed, per-haps about $35 total for installation. With a batch-feed unit, you load it, put in the cover, and turn it to the "on" position to activate the unit. You cannot add additional wastes without stopping the unit.

Continuous-feed units are wired through a wall switch. These units require an additional cost to install, perhaps about $60 total, because of the need for an electric line to the switch. However, the units are less expensive to buy. With continuous-feed models, you load them, put in a cover that prevents garbage from flying out yet allows water into the unit, and turn on the wall switch. Additional wastes can be added while the unit is running, although this is not a recommended procedure. With the safety cover removed, items can fly out or fall into an operating disposer. The units are safe, as long as you use them as intended.

For consumers replacing a disposer, you probably should stick to the existing type to keep installation simple, unless you have a dislike for its method of operation.

Most manufacturers offer one or more models with grounded power cords that simply plug into a below-the-sink outlet rather than requiring wiring. These

Recommended Disposers

Manufacturer	Model	Feed type	Dishwasher drain	Mounting	Motor, hp	Volts/Amps.
Frigidaire	FD-5	continuous	no	quick mount	1/2	115/5.9
General Electric	GFC810	continuous	no	3-stud keyhole	1/2	115/7
General Electric	GFB910	batch	no	3-stud keyhole	1/2	115/7
In-Sink-Erator	77	continuous	yes	quick lock	1/2	115/6.9
In-Sink-Erator	707	continuous	yes	quick lock	1/2	115/6.9
In-Sink-Erator	17	batch	yes	quick lock	1/2	115/6.9
KitchenAid	KWI-200	continuous	yes	quick click	1/2	115/7
KitchenAid	KWS-200	batch	yes	quick click	1/2	115/7
Maytag	FC20	continuous	yes	quick connect	1/2	115/7
Maytag	FB20	batch	yes	quick connect	1/2	115/7
National	660E	continuous	yes	easy mount	1/2	115/7
National	770E	batch	no	easy mount	1/2	115/7
Sinkmaster	900	continuous	yes	easy mount	3/4	115/8.2
Tappan	51-1086	continuous	yes	3 bolt quick mount	3/4	115/9.2
Waste King	SS 8000	continuous	yes	quick mount	1/2	120/5.9
Whirlpool	SYD-80	batch	yes	adjusting ring	1/2	120/7.5

In-Sink-Erator 17

Tappan 51-1086

Waste King SS 8000

models may carry different model numbers to distinguish this feature. They are usually identical to other models with this one exception.

Disposer Features

Many features on a disposer will help it do a more effective job of grinding and removing wastes. Other features, such as fancy housings and attractive styling, are to entice buyers. The unit will be hidden under a sink once installed, so do not judge by appearance.

Anti-jam systems or features that reverse the operation or apply power jolts to clear obstructions are worthwhile.

Better units have stainless steel grind/impeller assemblies, sink flanges and drain housings. Such units also have heavy-duty motors of 1/2 horsepower (3/4 horsepower is the largest motor on the market); less expensive units have 1/3-horsepower motors.

Many mounting methods exist. To keep installation costs down, or to make the job easy for you, look for a quick-mounting sys-

tem. Many manufacturers offer a system that allows the disposer to be installed easily and without special tools.

Sound insulation is another primary difference between inexpensive units and better disposers. The better models will have rubber, plastic foam or other sound insulation.

If you are remodeling and adding a dishwasher, take a look at disposers that have a drain inside of the body that can be connected to a dishwasher. That type of drain connection may simplify the plumbing work.

Recommended Disposers

Motor protection	Anti-jam system	Sound insulation	Warranty	Approximate retail price
no	no	yes	1 year	$104.95
yes	no	yes	1 year	$129.95
yes	no	yes	1 year	$149.95
yes	yes	yes	1 year	$100.75
yes	yes	yes	1 year	$121.75
yes	no	no	1 year	$120.00
yes	yes	yes	1 year/5 year parts	$154.95
yes	yes	yes	1 year/5 year parts	$164.95
yes	no	yes	1 year/5 year parts	$170.00
yes	no	yes	1 year/5 year parts	$180.00
yes	yes	yes	1 year/5 year parts	$149.95
no	yes	no	1 year/5 year parts	$159.95
yes	no	yes	1 year	$79 - $89.95
yes	no	yes	1 year	$118.95
yes	no	yes	1 year/5 year parts	$175.00
yes	yes	yes	1 year	$114.95

Compactors

Maybe nothing can make putting out the trash something that is truly fun to do, but most people would agree that having a trash compactor in the house would make it much less of a chore. Trash compactors reduce solid waste to about one-fourth of its original bulk, so for every four trips you now make to the garbage with a conventional load of refuse, you would make only one with a compacted bag. Of course, compacted trash weighs more per bag—typically between 25 and 30 pounds, and bags containing mostly bottles and cans can weigh as much as 40 pounds—but the refuse is neatly bundled so it is easier to handle than loose trash.

Built-ins Aid Kitchen Appearance

Since a major goal in remodeling or designing a new kitchen is to achieve a more attractive room, CONSUMER GUIDE Magazine has concentrated on built-in compactors. These are integrated in the total design of a kitchen, the room where most of the waste in a house is generated. However, there are

free-standing units (which consumers have found useful in basements, utility rooms, or garages, as well as kitchens) and convertible models that can be used free-standing or built in under a counter. Depending on the type you choose for your kitchen, you will have to leave room under a counter (for a built-in) or allow floor space (for a free-standing unit). Compactors typically are as wide as standard base cabinets (15 or 18 inches).

Design Differences

The major noticeable difference in compactors is the design of the waste bucket; it will be either round or rectangular. Many consumers find the round bucket more convenient because they think it is easier to pick up, but either shape can be lifted comfortably by handles. Some manufacturers recommend the use of their own liner bags, while other units can function with a common paper grocery bag. In any case, it is suggested that the bag be capable of holding wet garbage.

Hidden design dissimilarities include the compaction method, which will be one of two pressure systems. Since each does an effective job of developing the necessary force for compaction, there is little reason to favor one over the other.

Compactor Features

While the results of using a compactor vary little—they all will yield a neat package—there are some design differences that will appeal to individual tastes and budgets. One of the major ones to note is whether a unit has a deodorizing system. Nothing will truly "deodorize" a large amount of trash that has remained in the home for a few days, especially in warm weather or if "wet" garbage such as food scraps and other spoiling wastes are involved. (A food waste disposer in the sink will help avoid this situation.) Still, both automatic and manual deodorizing systems are aids. The automatic method pulse-sprays the garbage each time a cycle is initiated, while a manual system is operated whenever you decide it is necessary. Some units are freshened with a solid deodorant or charcoal air filter.

Locks are used mainly to limit or control operation of the compactor, a feature especially appreciated and required in a home where there are children who might play with the unit. Types include key locks and on/off knobs that can be removed. CONSUMER GUIDE Magazine finds the removable knob better, but keep in mind that both keys and knobs can be misplaced.

Access to the compactor con-

Recommended Compactors

Manufacturer	Model	Type	Height x Width x Depth	Volts/amps	Lock type
Amana	SMCD-2W	convertible	34 x 17-¾ x 21	120/10	removable key
Frigidaire	TCU-3B	built-in	36 x 15 x 18-¼	115/11	removable key
General Electric	GCG661	convertible	34 x 14-⅞ x 18	115/7.5	removable on/off knob
Hotpoint	HCH411	built-in	34 x 14-⅞ x 18	115./7.5	removable on/off knob
KitchenAid	KCS-100B	built-in	35 x 17-¾ x 23-½	115/9	removable key
Whirlpool	SFC-8000	built-in	34-¼ x 15 x 24	120/10	removable key
Whirlpool	SFC-4500	free-standing	34-¼ x 15 x 24	120/10	removable key

General Electric GCG661

KitchenAid KCS-100B

Frigidaire TCU-3B

tainer varies with the model's design. Among units on the market are those with automatic slide-out drawers, pull-out drawers, automatic swing-out buckets, side-opening doors, and doors that tilt from the top. The most convenient of these are the automatic slide-out drawer, which opens when a toe bar is depressed, and the automatic swing-out bucket. The automatic features does add extra cost to the unit, but many consumers have found worthwhile the convenience of being able to open the unit with hands full.

A color selection is available from most manufacturers and is keyed to the most popular colors for other major kitchen appliances. Built-in compactors normally come with two front panels, each with a different color on each side, for a choice of four colors. Many manufacturers also offer decorator kits that allow the consumer to customize the unit with paneling, wallpaper, or other special material.

Recommended Compactors

Motor, hp	Container shape	Access	Deodorizing system	Warranty	Approximate retail price
1/3	round	glide-out bin	no	1 year	$309.95
1/3	round	gliding drawer	aerosol deodorizer	1 year	$309.95
1/3	round	easy-open door	odor control spray	1 year	$289.00
1/3	round	easy-open door	manual spray	1 year	$289.95
1/2	rectangular	litterbin; gliding drawer	charcoal air filter	1 year	$389.95-white $399.95-color
1/3	rectangular	touch toe bar sliding drawer	solid deodorant	1 year	$269.95
1/3	rectangular	gliding drawer	no	1 year	$249.95

Microwave Ovens

If you are planning to buy a microwave oven for your new kitchen, you are not alone. Microwave ovens are expected to be added to the appliance lineup in more than two million households this year, and it is estimated that by 1985, one out of every two homes will have one. A microwave oven is a convenience appliance that is becoming as much a "necessity" as the dishwasher is thought to be.

The major attraction, of course, is the time savings over conventional cooking. Visions of a steamy baked potato in five minutes or a juicy standing rib roast company-ready in 20 minutes tantalize everyone from office-weary wives to busy homemakers and bachelor cooks. Add to the cooking speed the bonus of quick defrosting, and the microwave oven is clearly an appliance tailor-made for today's fast-paced society.

Oven Safety

There have been "scares" about microwave leakage, and some people even have questioned whether eating food cooked in a microwave oven is harmful. Manufacturers answer that microwaves are simply a source of heat energy, just like gas and electricity. All three produce cooking in the food, but nothing stays "in" to be eaten.

Standards for microwave ovens are set and monitored by three separate organizations — Underwriters' Laboratories, the Federal Communications Commission, and the Department of Health, Education, and Welfare. These standards, adhered to by manufacturers, limit the level of typical exposure in normal use to approximately 1/10,000 the level known to affect humans.

In addition, your oven will be equipped with several safety features and devices. There will be a door seal to prevent microwave leakage and interlocks to prevent the unit from operating with the door open. All microwave activity is stopped before the door opens.

Microwave ovens can leak after several years use due to wear on interlocks, a loosening of the door hinges, or deterioration of the seals. It is a good idea, therefore, to have the oven inspected periodically and especially if it is moved or damaged.

Use And Care

Carefully following the owner's manual will not only help you get the most convenience from your oven; it will help you do it safely as well. Pay particular attention to the things you should NOT do with your oven. Regardless of the brand you choose, you will be instructed never to operate the oven empty, which can result in damage to the unit or leakage; not to use food containers that are composed, even in part, of metal, again because of possible damage; and to keep the seal clean and to protect the door and hinges from damage, all to maintain a tight fit that will prevent excessive leakage. Also study the manual for special electrical connection information or clearance requirements for proper functioning.

Energy Savings

Used correctly, a microwave oven will save not only time, but electricity also. Several studies have demonstrated electrical savings of 60 to 75 percent over conventional cooking. A two-person family may save the most — up to 85 percent on cooking electrical energy annually. Next best are four-person families, saving about 60 percent annually. The approximate cost to operate a microwave oven is $7 to $10 per year, depending on electric rates.

Advantages Of Microwave Cooking

In most situations, microwave ovens are time-savers for the cook in a hurry. Although a few foods, such as noodles and other

Amana RR10

forms of pasta, take almost as much time to prepare as they do in conventional cooking, most foods require one-quarter to one-half the cooking time in a microwave oven. The fact that you don't have to preheat the oven also saves time and electricity.

Another key feature of microwave cooking is cleanup convenience. Most of the time, you will be cooking in the serving dish or directly on dinner plates or paper products, eliminating dirty pots and pans. The oven itself is easy to clean, too; the oven walls do not heat up and therefore allow spills and spatters to be wiped merely with a damp cloth. As a bonus, the kitchen stays cool, too.

Since foods reheat rapidly, and therefore don't dry out when warmed in a microwave oven, leftovers taste better and fresher. This means even meals prepared in advance can be expected to taste delicious. Coupled with quick-defrost capability, this feature is a major drawing card for busy people.

Microwave Cooking Has Some Disadvantages

One drawback to this cooking method has been termed the "multiplier effect." While one strip of bacon takes about 1 minute to prepare, for example, four strips require 4 minutes or more. The more food in the oven, the longer the cooking time, and large amounts of food often take almost as long to cook as they would in a conventional oven. In fact, sometimes a meal can be prepared more quickly if the different foods are cooked sequentially.

A microwave oven handles some cooking tasks better than it does others, too. It is best for single servings, snacks, reheating, and defrosting. Because the cooking process is on the "wet" side (microwaves excite the water molecules in foods and this friction produces heat), it is good for food that tends to dry out and for defrosting frozen snacks and meats. It probably will not meet expectations for anything requiring crispness. Home bakers, in particular, have disappointing results with a microwave oven. However, dough can be raised in a microwave oven successfully.

Unsatisfactory texture and browning problems also are mentioned by consumers. Unsatisfactory texture usually is the result of overcooking, a problem that can be overcome with experience with the oven. As for browning, meats cooked longer than 8 minutes should brown if there is sufficient fat covering. Smaller food items such as steaks, chops, and hamburgers might not cook long enough to develop a deep, dark color. To aid in browning these smaller pieces of food, some ovens have built-in browning elements or a browning tray accessory. Sauces, seasonings, and toppings also help.

One thing many consumers are not prepared for is the labor-intensive nature of a microwave oven. While a unit does save time, it also requires more attention during the cooking process, particularly if not equipped with a memory. Many foods will cook better when cooked for a period of time at one setting and finished at a different power setting. If the unit does not have a memory feature, which automatically switches to the second phase at the appropriate time, you will have to wait for the first phase to be completed and then return to the oven to set the second phase. Even with mere one-phase cooking, though, the time often is so short that it hardly pays to leave the unit.

Microwave Oven Features

Numerous special features are available, and each adds to the price of a unit. Consider how serious a microwave oven cook you will be before deciding if an option is worth the extra cost.

● Wattage and Power Settings—Although the power of models varies (from about 400 watts on up), most ovens designed for the home are in the 600 to 700 watt range. Wattage determines how fast the oven will cook. Low power units cook as well, just not as quickly. Cooking times need to be adjusted to the oven's output and the setting used, if the unit has multiple power levels. Inexpensive models commonly have only one, full-power setting. Better models add a defrost or partial-power setting, while still better units offer several power levels and so offer greater control over the cooking process, especially for delicate foods. CONSUMER GUIDE Magazine recommends models with at least two power settings—full and partial (defrost). Settings have various names and mean different things on different brands, so study the manuals individually.

● Controls—Microwave ovens are controlled by a variety of systems ranging from dials to push-buttons to electronic programming. Inexpensive units are the easiest to use because all you have to do is set the cooking time. Middle-range units have dial or lever settings. Sophisticated touch-control models allow a great deal of flexibility, and ovens with memory features permit two or more stages of cooking instructions to be entered and run automatically. Memory-equipped models, for example, allow you to defrost, cook, and keep foods warm, all without even being home.

● Timers—The timer is an important part of a microwave oven since cooking instructions are based more often on time than temperature. Inexpensive ovens have dial settings for minutes and seconds. The first three or four minutes at least should be divided into 15-second intervals so you can follow recipes accurately. You should be able to set the minute timer for about 30 minutes so you don't have to constantly reset it. Better units have solid-state time control and

Magic Chef MW217Z-6P

program touch surfaces. Typically, time can be set for longer periods—up to 90 minutes—on these units. Many models also have countdown displays that show the cooking time left; these can double as digital clocks when the oven is not in use. Since the timer is used every time the oven is operated, make sure it is easy to set and to read. Many

people prefer strip dials as easiest to read and use. Look for units that feature a separate start button for the timer. This will prevent the oven from restarting automatically if the timer has not run down and the door is shut. (Since ovens should not be operated when empty, this can damage the unit.)

● Oven Window—The window

is made of perforated metal covered by clear or "black" glass. Though you can see through the holes, they are too small for microwaves to pass through. Since the look of the food is one way of judging whether it is cooked, good visibility is important.

● Oven Size—Oven cavity size varies with brands and models. Smaller ovens are adequate for preparing one or two servings at a time, but a large family may need greater capacity. One rule of thumb suggests that an oven of a full cubic foot or larger is large enough for the average family.

● Oven Finish—There is some debate about the merits of acrylic and stainless steel finishes. Those who favor the acrylic coating say it allows more even heating and is easier to clean. The acrylic, however, can absorb odors; the stainless steel does not. Stainless steel advocates maintain that the material is less likely to scratch and is more durable over time. Both materials are acceptable.

● Shelves—The shelf at the bottom of the unit will be built-in or removable, depending on the model. CONSUMER GUIDE Magazine recommends glass if it can be removed. This is important because if a built-in glass shelf is broken, the entire oven must be returned to the manufacturer.

● Turntables — Microwave ovens typically cook unevenly, a fact most manufacturers don't mention. The problem is known, however, and many recipes call for food rotation to assure even cooking; manufacturers have added stirrer fans to their ovens to help distribute the microwaves. If you don't want to perform this chore manually, select a model that offers a turntable to automatically rotate food. Even turntables have drawbacks, though. They tend to have a cold spot in the center, limit the size of utensils you can use, and can be difficult to clean.

● Temperature Probes—Increasingly, microwave ovens are equipped with a temperature

Sharp R-9400

probe that works on the same principle as a meat thermometer. It is inserted into the food before cooking, and the oven then is set for a specific food temperature. In most ovens, when the predetermined temperature is reached on the probe, the oven shuts off automatically. The probe is useful on large cuts of meat and dense, solid foods. Standard oven thermometers cannot be used in a microwave oven because they are made of metal.

• Light—On some units, changing the light bulb requires the removal of an exterior cover and therefore the services of an electrician. Look for a model on which you can conveniently change the bulb yourself.

• Other Features—Outer appearance of the oven is a matter of personal preference. Units are available with simulated woodgrain, vinyl-laminated steel wrappers; embossed or textured steel; or chrome finishes. Oven doors open to the side or drop down. Most manufacturers offer an accessory kit for building a microwave oven into a wall. This kit usually contains a sleeve, into which the unit slides, and grills for air ventilation. If you are planning to build in a microwave, be sure the manufacturer will warrant the unit as a built-in; some will not.

MANUFACTURERS REVIEW

Amana: Amana's line includes the RR model series of five fully featured units, the ML series of economy lower power units (400 watts) and a 500-watt model MR-3 and 675-watt mode R-3 with variable cooking capability. The RR10 Touchmatic II now heads the line. It features 10 Cookmatic power levels and an advanced automatic temperature control (probe) system and four memory banks. The new RR8 is similar to the RR10, except it has dial controls and Amana's Cookmatic Power Shift feature of six power levels. The shift feature also is on RR9 and RR7. Another new model is RR7D. It has four power settings and conventional dials. All RR models can be built in with an optional accessory kit.

Frigidaire: Frigidaire's line con-

Amana RR8

sists of five models, including built-in model RWM-7. At the low end are RCM-1 and RCM-3. Both lack a defrost feature. The RCM-6 is a touch-control model with memory. All three top-end units have a Cook Selector for a variety of cooking speeds. The ovens come with a full one-year warranty and an additional four-year limited warranty on the magnetron. Frigidaire buys the units from Amana.

General Electric: GE has expanded its line to six countertop models. The top-of-the-line unit is the Jet 110, which includes touch controls, three-way cooking, cooking by time or tempera-ture, plus a simmer-and-cook cycle that simulates slow cooking. The Jet 110 has a temperature probe and comes with a crockery pot for the slow cooking cycle. Middle-price Jet 88 has three power settings, automatic cooking, a 60-minute timer, and a temperature probe. Jet 87 has two power levels and a 35-minute timer, while Jet 85 has two power settings and a 25-minute timer. At the bottom of the line is Jet 81, which does not have a defrost cycle. All units have a 1.3 cubic foot interior, black glass windows, and a one-year full warranty and an additional four-year limited warranty on the magnetron.

Hardwick: The line offers three units, from bottom-of-the-line model E222 to top-of-the-line E228. The top model features touch settings and variable power, while the least expensive model has a dial timer and a defrost setting. Units feature 1.3 cubic foot interior cavities and black glass oven doors.

Hotpoint: The Hotpoint Division of GE has added new models to the line, similar to the GE offerings. All five Hotpoints have 1.3 cubic foot interiors and defrost settings. Top model RE944V features touch control, three-way cooking, a temperature probe, and other features similar to GE's

Litton 540

Jet 110. Model RE928V has three power levels, a temperature probe, and a 60-minute timer. The lowest priced unit, RE925V, has two power settings and a 25-minute timer.

Litton: Litton's Meal-in-One models—540 and 520—can cook several dishes at once in the 1.5 cubic foot cavities. The ability to cook more than one dish at a time is a welcome improvement, and more advances are planned in this area. Litton continues its 400 series with four touch-control models featuring microprocessors and temperature probes. Variable cooking is on all but the lowest priced model in the line. Low-end units offer defrost settings.

Magic Chef: Magic Chef has concentrated on touch control and memory units. MW317Z-6P is a glass, touch-control model with three levels of memory. Model MW317Z-6BP has touch controls and two memory levels; both units have probes. Other countertop models include compact MW217Z-6P, which also has a two-level memory and a temperature probe. Even low-end space-saving models offer defrost settings.

Panasonic: Panasonic has four models in its line. At the top is NE-7900, its Feather-Touch programmable oven with up to 700 watts of variable cooking power and a probe. The NE-7800 also has a probe, variable power and 700 watts of power at maximum. The NE-7750 has variable power and 700 watts of full power, and the NE-5610 model offers an economic 500-watt unit that includes a defrost setting. Panasonic units come with a five-year limited warranty.

Roper: Roper has five units with large interiors, 1.38 cubic feet. Model 2957 has automatic temperature control with a probe, an automatic defrost cycle, 650 watts of power, and a 35-minute timer. It has variable power set-tings. The other models, 2927 and 2917, have a 35-minute timer, a defrost cycle, and 650 watts of cooking power. Model 2927 has variable power. Models 2906 and 2907 are economy models with 20-minute timers and 650 watts of power. Model 2907 has a defrost setting; 2906 does not.

Sanyo Electric: Sanyo Electric's line of seven units features a touch-control, solid-state model (EM-9005) at one price end and a 450-watt economy model

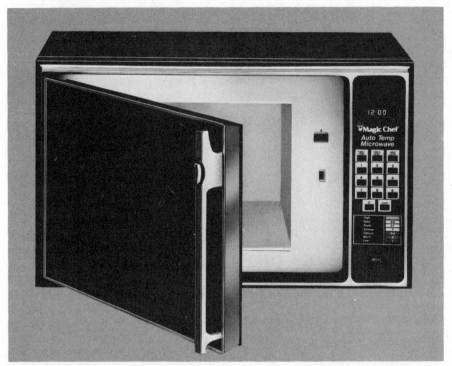

Magic Chef MW317Z-6BP

Panasonic NE-7800

Sanyo EM-9004C

(EM-8205B) at the other. Five of the units have 1.5 cubic feet in the cavity. Three of the units have temperature probes (EM-9005, EM-9004C and EM-9104), and one model offers a turntable (EM-9102T).

Sharp: The Sharp line offers eight units. All of the models except the two low-end models (R-6350 and R-5350) have the Carousel turntable that rotates food to eliminate the need to stir and turn foods. The turntable can complicate cleanup and also has a cold spot in the middle. One model includes a browning ele-

ment (R-8200). At the top of the line is R-9400, a touch-control, solid-state unit. A second touch-control unit is the 500-watt R-9200, a compact, solid-state model. Sharp units come with a seven-year limited warranty on the magnetrons and a two-year full warranty on other parts.

Sunbeam: Sunbeam's five-unit line is headed by model 39-35, which offers touch control, a browning element, and programming. Deluxe models have 1.7 cubic feet, while the economy models have interiors of 1.1 cubic feet. None of the units has a temperature probe. The units are purchased from Tappan.

Tappan: Tappan has seven countertop models. At the top is the Tap 'N Touch 56-4888 with memory, a temperature probe, and a browning element. Tappan also offers a "family size" unit, model 56-1408, with a large interior and a seven-setting selector control. The mid-priced model 56-4770 has a temperature probe and browning element. One of the low-end models, 65-1226, has a defrost cycle and a 28-minute timer.

Recommended Microwave Ovens

Manufacturer	Model	Power (wattage)	Controls	Memory	Variable power	Defrost	Timers
Amana	RR9	675	touch	no	yes	yes	yes
Amana	RR8	675	dial	no	yes	yes	yes
Amana	RR10	675	touch	yes	yes	yes	yes
General Electric	Jet 91	625	button, dial	yes	yes	yes	yes
Hardwick	E225	625	push button	yes	yes	yes	yes
Kenmore	22H 99591	625	sliding bar	no	yes	yes	yes
Litton	540	650	touch	yes	yes	yes	yes
Litton	445	650	dial	no	yes	yes	yes
Litton	120	600	dial	no	yes	yes	yes
Magic Chef	MW317Z-6BP	650	touch key	yes	yes	yes	yes
Magic Chef	MW217Z-6P	600	touch key	yes	yes	yes	yes
Panasonic	NE-7800	700	dial	no	yes	yes	yes
Roper	2957	650	dial	no	yes	yes	yes
Sanyo	EM 9004C	650	dial	no	yes	yes	yes
Sharp	R-9400	650	auto touch	yes	yes	yes	yes
Tappan	56-4888	650	touch	yes	yes	yes	yes
Whirlpool	REM-7600	650	sliding bar, dial	no	yes	yes	yes

Toshiba: Toshiba is one of the world's leading manufacturers of magnetron tubes. Five of the six units in the line have 1.5 cubic foot cavities. Power setting features range from two settings to infinitely variable power control. An automatic temperature probe is available on top-of-the-line models, including the flagship unit, touch-control ER797BT.

Whirlpool: Whirlpool offers five ovens, all with 1.14 cubic foot cavities that have a sealed-in cook shelf and smooth interior. Two low-end models do not have variable power settings. The low-end model REM7000 has a high power setting and a defrost cycle. Other models have infinite power settings from warm to high. Model REM7800 is a touch-control, programmable unit. The 7800 has an on-off switch in the oven to prevent the unit from being turned on accidentally. The top two models have temperature probes that cut down the power setting as food approaches the set temperature.

White-Westinghouse: This line has four units, including Touch 'n' Set top model KM650W and

Tappan 56-4888

low-end unit KM350W with 500 watts. All units have defrost capability. All models except the low-end unit have 1.25 cubic feet in the oven. The top-of-the-line and the two middle-of-the-line units have variable power control. The high-end model has a temperature probe.

Other Brands: Every week, it seems, brings new entries in the microwave oven field. Among other brands you will find are the mass merchandisers'—Sears, Wards, and Penney. Units also are available from Jenn-Air, Norelco, Hitachi, Quasar, Admiral, and Modern Maid.

Recommended Microwave Ovens

Height x Width x Depth	Oven window	Oven light	Temperature probe	Warranty	Approximate retail price
15 x 22-¾ x 17-¼	yes	yes	no	1 year	$476.00
15 x 23-¾ x 17-¼	yes	yes	yes	1 year	$545.00
15 x 23-¾ x 17-¼	yes	yes	yes	1 year	$595.00
15-½ x 22-½ x 20	yes	yes	yes	1 year	$529.95
15 x 25 x 17	yes	yes	no	1 year	$399.95
24 x 20-⅛ x 14-¾	yes	yes	yes	1 year	$409.95
15-¾ x 27 x 18-⅝	yes	yes	no	1 year	$629.00
15 x 24-¼ x 17	yes	yes	yes	1 year	$469.00
13 x 24 x 14-½	yes	yes	no	1 year	$329.00
15 x 25 x 16-⅛	yes	yes	yes	1 year	$569.00
13-¼ x 21-⅞ x 14	yes	yes	yes	1 year	$449.00
15 x 25-⅝ x 16-⅛	yes	yes	yes	5 years	$529.95 - $559.95
15-²⁷/₃₂ x 23-⁹/₁₆ x 16-⁹/₃₂	yes	yes	no	1 year	$449.95
15-⅞ x 24 x 21-¼	yes	yes	yes	1 year	$328.00
15-¾ x 24-⅝ x 17	yes	yes	yes	2 years	$599.95
15-½ x 25-⅜ x 16	yes	yes	yes	1 year	$669.95
15-½ x 25-½ x 18-¼	yes	yes	yes	1 year	$469.95

Directory of Manufacturers

A

Admiral Corp.
Rockwell International
1701 East Woodfield Rd.
Schaumburg, IL 60196

Agency Tile
499 Old Nyack Tpk.
Spring Valley, NY 10977

Allied Plywood Corp.
Box 56
Boston, MA 02129

Allmilmo Corp.
122 Clinton Rd.
Fairfield, NJ 07006

Amana Refrigeration, Inc.
Amana, IA 52204

American Institute of Kitchen Dealers
114 Main St.
Hackettstown, NJ 07840

American Olean Tile Co.
1000 Cannon Ave.
Lansdale, PA 19446

American Standard Inc.
P.O. Box 2003
New Brunswick, NJ 08903

Amsterdam Corp.
950 Third Ave.
New York, NY 10022

Amtico Flooring Div. American Biltrite Inc.
Amtico Square
Trenton, NJ 08607

Aristokraft
Aristokraft Square
P.O. Box 420
Jasper, IN 47546

Armstrong Cork Co.
Liberty & Charlotte
Lancaster, PA 17604

Asrock Floor Products Div. Uralde Rock Asphalt Co.
P.O. Box 531
San Antonio, TX 78292

B

Bally Block Co.
Bally, PA 19503

Barclay Industries, Inc.
65 Industrial Rd.
Lodi, NJ 07644

Beckermann Custom Kitchens, Ltd.
44 Otonabee Drive
Kitchener, N2C 1L6
Ontario, Canada

Bohemia, Inc.
2280 Oakmont Way
Eugene, OR 97401

Boise Cascade Corp.
Kitchen Cabinet Div.
P.O. Box 514
Berryville, VA 22611

Brammer Manufacturing Co.
1701 Rockingham Rd.
Davenport, IA 52802

Bruce Hardwood Industries
4255 LBJ Freeway
Dallas, TX 75234

C

Caloric Corp.
Topton, PA 19562

Cambridge Tile
P.O. Box 15071
Cincinnati, OH 45215

Certain-Teed Products
750 E. Swedesford Rd.
Valley Forge, PA 19482

Congoleum Industries, Inc.
195 Belgrove Drive
Kearny, NJ 07032

Connor Forest Industries
131 W. Thomas St.
P.O. Box 847
Wausau, WI 54401

Consoweld Corp.
700 DuraBeauty Lane
Wisconsin Rapids, WI 54494

Coppes, Inc.
401 E. Market St.
Nappanee, IN 46550

Crane Co.
300 Park Ave.
New York, NY 10022

D

Del-Mar, A Triangle Pacific Co.
15 Linkwood Rd. N.W.
Atlanta, GA 30311

Delta Faucet Co.
931 E. 82 St.
Box 40668
Indianapolis, IN 46240

E.I. DuPont De Nemours & Co., Inc.
Tatnall Bldg.
Wilmington, DE 19898

Dur-A-Flex, Inc.
100 Meadow St.
Hartford, CT 06114

E

Eljer Plumbingware Div. Wallace-Murray Corp.
3 Gateway Center
Pittsburgh, PA 15222

Elkay Manufacturing Co.
2700 S. 17th Ave.
Broadview, IL 60153

Environmental Graphics
Pandora Productions, Inc.
1117 Vicksburg Lane
Wayzata, MN 55391

Excel Wood Products Co., Inc.
P.O. Box 819
Lakewood, NJ 08701

F

Formica Corp.
120 E. Fourth St.
Cincinnati, OH 45202

Frigidaire Div. General Motors Corp.
300 Taylor St.
Dayton, OH 45442

G

GAF Corporation
Building Materials Group, Floor Products
140 W. 51 St.
New York, NY 10020

General Electric
Appliance Park
Louisville, KY 40225

Gibson Appliance Corp.
Gibson Appliance Center
Greenville, MI 48838

Goodyear Tire Co., Flooring Dept.
1210 Massillon Rd.
Akron, OH 44306

H

Hardwick Stove Co.
240 Edwards, S.E.
Cleveland, TN 37311

Hotpoint, General Electric Co.
Appliance Park
Louisville, KY 40225

I

Imperial Wallcoverings
23645 Mercantile Rd.
Cleveland, OH 44122

In-Sink-Erator Div. Emerson Electric Co.
4700 21st St.
Racine, WI 53406

IXL, Division of Westinghouse
Elizabeth City, NC 27909

J

Jenn-Air Corp.
3035 Shadeland
Indianapolis, IN 46226

H & R Johnson, Inc.
State Highway #35
Keyport, NJ 07735

Just Manufacturing Co.
9233 King St.
Franklin Park, IL 60131

K

Kelvinator Appliance Co.
4248 Kalamazoo S.E.
Grand Rapids, MI 49508

Kenmore, Sears, Roebuck and Co.
Chicago, IL 60607

Kentile Floors
58 Second Avenue
Brooklyn, NY 11215

KitchenAid Division Hobart Corp.
Troy, OH 45374

Kitchen Kompact, Inc.
KK Plaza
Jeffersonville, IN 47130

Kohler Co.
Kohler, WI 53044

L

Lite-Beams, Urethane Fabricators, Inc.
7th & Washington St.
P.O. Box 204
Red Hills, PA 18706

Litton Microwave Cooking
P.O. Box 9461
Minneapolis, MN 55440

Long-Bell Division International Paper Co.
Box 579
Longview, WA 98632

Lusterock International
4125 Richmond Ave.
Houston, TX 77027

M

Magic Chef, Inc.
740 King Edward Ave. S.E.
Cleveland, TN 37311

Maher Forest Products Ltd.
P.O. Box 387
Medina, WA 98036

Manesco, Inc.
157 Haven Ave.
Port Washington, NY 11050

Mann and Parker Lumber Co.
Box 18
Constitution Ave.
New Freedom, PA 17349

Mannington Mills, Inc.
Salem, NJ 08079

Marlite Division Masonite Corp.
Dover, OH 44622

Masonite Corporation
29 W. Wacker Drive
Chicago, IL 60606

Maytag Co.
Newton, IA 50208

Merillat Industries, Inc.
2075 W. Beecher Road
Adrian, MI 49221

Micarta, Decorative Div. of Westinghouse Electric
   Corp.
Hampton, SC 29924

Michigan Brick
Corunna, MI 48817

Michigan Maple Block Co.
P.O. Box 245
Petosky, MI 49770

Modern Maid, A McGraw-Edison Co.
Box 1111
Chattanooga, TN 37401

Modular Systems
Fruitport, MI 49415

Moen, a Division of Stanadyne
377 Woodland Ave.
Elyria, OH 44035

Mohawk Carpet
57 Lyon St.
Amsterdam, NY 12010

Mutschler Division Triangle Pacific Cabinet Corp.
302 S. Madison St.
Nappanee, IN 46550

N

National Disposer Division Hobart Corp.
Troy, OH 45374

Nevamar Carefree Kitchens
National Industries New Enterprises
Midway Industrial Park
Odenton, MD 21113

O

The Overton Co.
Box 848-K
Kenly, NC 27542

P

Paeco, Inc.
500 Market St.
Perth Amboy, NJ 08861

Panasonic Co.
One Panasonic Way
Secaucus, NJ 07094

Pavco Industries, Inc.
P.O. Box 612
Pascagoula, MS 39567

PermaGrain Products, General Electric Co.
1 River Rd.
Schenectady, NY 12345

Pionite, Pioneer Plastics Div. LOF Plastics, Inc.
Pionite Rd.
Auburn, ME 04210

Poggenpohl USA Corp.
222 Cedar Lane
Teaneck, NJ 07666

Poraflor
2300 Shames Dr.
Westbury, NY 11590

Q

Quaker Maid Kitchens, Div. of The Tappan Co.
Leesport, PA 19533

R

Rex Plastics, Inc.
P.O. Box 948
Thomasville, NC 27360

Rich-Maid Kitchens, Inc.
Box 38
Wernersville, PA 19565

Roper Sales Corp.
1905 W. Court St.
Kankakee, IL 60901

Rutt Custom Kitchens Div. of Leigh Products, Inc.
Route 23
Goodville, PA 17528

S

St. Charles Manufacturing Co.
1611 E. Main St.
St. Charles, IL 60174

Sanyo Electric, Inc., Appliance Div.
51 Joseph St.
Moonachie, NJ 07074

Scandecor, Inc.
1105 Industrial Highway
Southampton, PA 18966

H. J. Scheirich Co.
P.O. Box 21037
Louisville, KY 40221

Sensenich Corp.
P.O. Box 1168
Lancaster, PA 17604

Sharp Electronics Corp.
10 Keystone Place
Paramus, NY 07652

Sinkmaster
4240 E. La Palma Ave.
Anaheim, CA 92803

Skymaster Div. of Tub-Master Corp.
413 Virginia Dr.
Orlando, FL 32803

Solartron, General Electric Co.
1 River Rd.
Schenectady NY 12345

Sub-Zero Freezer Co., Inc.
Box 4130
Madison, WI 53711

Supergraphic, Inc.
P.O. Box 291
Bame, Ontario, Canada L4M 4T2

T

Tappan Appliance Division
Tappan Park
Mansfield, OH 44901

Textolite, General Electric Co., Laminated Products
  Dept.
1350 S. Second St.
Coshocton, OH 43812

Tibbals Flooring, Hartco
P.O. Drawer A
Oneida, TN 37841

Tielsa, Contemporary Systems, Inc.
132 New Boston Pk.
Woburn, MA 01801

Trayco, Inc.
693 S. Court St.
Lapeer, MI 48446

U

United Foam Corp.
2626 Vista Industrial
Compton, CA 90221

U.S. Ceramic Tile Co.
1375 Ruff Rd. S.W.
Canton, OH 44711

United States Gypsum Co.
101 S. Wacker Dr.
Chicago, IL 60606

V

Ventarama Skylight Corp.
75 Channel Drive
Port Washington, NY 11050

Viking Carpets, Inc.
10 W. 33rd St.
New York, NY 10001

W

Waste King Disposers, Thermador/Waste King, Div.
  Norris Industries
5119 District Blvd.
Los Angeles, CA 90040

Weyerhaeuser Co.
Box B
Tacoma, WA 98401

Whirlpool Corp.
Benton Harbor, MI 49022

White-Westinghouse Corp.
930 Ft. Duquesne Blvd.
Pittsburgh, PA 15222

Wilsonart, Ralph Wilson Plastics Co.
600 General Bruce Dr.
Temple, TX 76501

Wood-Mode Cabinetry
Kreamer
Snyder County, PA 17833

Index